The
Death Camps
of Croatia

The
Death Camps
of Croatia

Visions and Revisions, 1941–1945

RAPHAEL ISRAELI

Routledge
Taylor & Francis Group

LONDON AND NEW YORK

First published 2013 by Transaction Publishers

Published 2017 by Routledge
2 Park Square, Milton Park, Abingdon, Oxon OX14 4RN
711 Third Avenue, New York, NY 10017, USA

Routledge is an imprint of the Taylor & Francis Group, an informa business

Library of Congress Catalog Number: 2012021894

Library of Congress Cataloging-in-Publication Data

Israeli, Raphael.
The death camps of Croatia : visions and revisions, 1941-45 / Raphael Israeli.
   p. cm.
   1. World War, 1939-1945--Atrocities.   2. World War, 1939-1945--Concentration camps--Croatia.   3. World War, 1939-1945--Prisoners and prisons, Croatian.   4. World War, 1939-1945--Croatia.
   5. World War, 1939-1945--Collaborationists--Biography.   6. Serbs--Crimes against--Croatia--History--20th century.   7. Holocaust, Jewish (1939-1945)--Croatia.   8. Husayni, Amin, 1893-1974. I. Title.
D805.C84I86 2012
940.53'1854972--dc23

                                                            2012021894

ISBN 13: 978-1-4128-6408-4 (pbk)
ISBN 13: 978-1-4128-4975-3 (hbk)

To the Victims of the Ustasha Fascists:
Serbs, Jews, and Gypsies,
Whose Memory Had Been Suppressed,
But Has Now Seen the Light of Day

Contents

Foreword

How Was This Book Born?

Less than a decade ago, the very names of Jadovno and Jasenovac were foreign to me. I have visited Serbia a number of times, in the decade that followed the Dayton settlement that put an end to the Bosnia War of 1992–95, and participated in several conferences convened by the Serbian Academy of Science, which hammered out the security and political ramifications of those arrangements, especially the ensuing Kosovo War and the rising Islamic radicalism that was being fomented by foreign Wahhabi preachers and by jihadists who had come from as far as Iran, Chechnya, Afghanistan, and Dagestan, to stir up more trouble in the Balkans. During those conferences, the participants made field trips to Vojvodina and Kosovo, to learn and experience something of the uneasy coexistence between the Serb majority and its Croatian, Albanian/Muslim, Hungarian, and other minorities.

A follow-up conference, which was convened by the President of Republika Srpska—who also happened to be an academician—in his capital, Banja Luka, in 2005, to deal with Jewish communities in Yugoslavia in history, also comprised a field trip to "Jasenovac," where we spent half a day walking through the vast camp, on the banks of the Sava River. Large posters alerted the scarce visitors about the disturbing numbers of Serbs, Jews, and Gypsies who were purportedly systematically murdered during the four years of its operation that allegedly rendered it the third in size in Nazi-occupied Europe (after Auschwitz and Treblinka), in terms of its sinister "productivity" in human corpses.

No doubt, the advertised numbers seemed both well-founded and grossly inflated at the same time, but you cannot tell a Serb or a Jew or a Gypsy, whose family had been picked up by the Ustasha state, incarcerated in the camp, and never seen again, while scenes of floating corpses on the Sava had become familiar to anyone in the neighborhood who wished to know, that the reported numbers were exaggerated, or were abused in the propaganda war between Serbs and Croats, which persists to this day. That enmity has been kindling more flames in the ever-growing hatred between the two Slavic nationalities, which has certainly been at the base of the savagery that characterized the Bosnia war in the 1990s, and is still spectacularly deepening the divide between these two ethnic groups, who had shared the same state, nationality, identity, and language until the death of Tito, the Croat, who had ruled from Belgrade until 1980.

For the Serbs, the most vivid memories are those voiced by the Croat-Ustasha regime, which had announced its intention to render Croatia and its subordinate territories *Serben und Juden frei*. That meant persecution, oppression, expulsion, and outright extermination. That policy was relentlessly implemented during the four years of their ruthless rule, under the Nazi wings, no matter what the exact numbers of their victims were, mainly in the camps of Jadovno and Jasenovac, which had been built for that purpose and in reality served it, precisely like their many counterparts throughout Germany and Eastern Europe. For the Croats, while there is no denial of the horrors perpetrated by the Ustasha or of the slogan they had floated to the effect that the Serbs should be one-third expelled, one-third exterminated, and one-third converted (into Catholicism, which was coterminous with ethnic Croat nationalism), they blame the pro-Nazi regime. They claim it did not represent the Croats, exactly as the Austrians today claim that they were themselves Hitler's victims after the *Anschluss*, and they should not be treated today as his collaborators, or as the Norwegians, who have taken on the image of the most liberal regime in Europe after they had accepted with almost quietist equanimity their pro-Nazi Quisling regime during the war.

The unbridgeable hostility between Croats and Serbs, which is today detectable in all international fora, even those regarding the Shoah, which should be neutral grounds for all, has been anchored in those unforgettable events, even though their deeper roots can be sought in the earlier competition between the two groups since medieval times. Add to that the mutual hatred between, on the one hand, those two Slavic groups, who came to claim a specificity of their respective languages, literature, and culture (Serbian and Croatian) in a land that only three decades ago was boasting Serbo-Croat as their common national tongue, and on the other hand, the Bosnian Muslims who are despised by all the others, and you have a recipe for permanent friction, hostility, suspicion, competition, and Schadenfreude, between all three major components of modern Yugoslavia. Anyone who circulates freely between all three, has dear friends in all of them, and attempts to collect factual and objective data in all of them, will always be accused of having missed a "critical datum" here, or having been "swept away by emotional arguments" there, or having been handed "inaccurate data by a scheming party" here and there, or having interpreted in a "biased fashion" "facts and events which are otherwise known to all."

Any historian who has worked on primary sources has encountered the criticism of having been "selective," or having failed to tell the entire truth, or of having misinterpreted this or that fact. Worse, many "new historians" have substituted their "narratives" to the "historical truth," if there is one. Since the historian is not an inanimate object, but embarks on his history writing while carrying on his back his educational, cultural, ethnic, religious, national, and ideological luggage, it is probable that he or she cannot claim to be completely detached from his background. Thus, rather than pretending to be what he or she cannot be, swearing by the "objective truth" and the "strict fact," it would be much more honest and truthful to admit to one's biases, but at the same time to attempt to be fair in presenting facts and events on all sides, and judge them in a balanced and measured way, taking into consideration the context, the atmosphere, and the constraints in which decisions were taken and policy was implemented. One must recognize that one can clearly carry out the same evil policy with satanic zeal or with human clemency. Conversely, one can very well overstep the borders toward a human and liberal policy, to include within it people who are not strictly entitled to it or can disrupt or procrastinate on applying it to those for whom it was devised.

While hearing scholars, journalists, and politicians on all sides present their respective cases, listening to common people with whom I have conversed or whom I have interviewed, reading books and documents presented to me or that I sought and searched for, or on field visits where the sounds of dreary silence were more deafening and frightening than the cries of tortured victims, or on occasional conversations or exchanged emails, I came to the mixed conclusion that the horrors of Jadovno and Jasenovac have to be reported to the public in some nonpartisan way, beyond the partisan thousands of books and articles churned out by both parties in their propaganda wars, admittedly side by side with some fine scholarly production; but, at the same time, the only way to keep my sanity, my access to my sources, my close ties to my friends, and a reasonable timetable for completing this job, was to try to remain emotionally uninvolved to the extent possible. Since I have no axe to grind, except for my deep sympathy for all the victims of that insanity, my commitment to my profession, and my added sentimental closeness to the tens of thousands of Jews who perished there as part of the all-European Shoah, I trust that I can maintain this approach of impartiality all throughout this endeavor, save for my partiality and commitment to truth and fact.

Except for the survivors and the victims, there are no pure saints, and except for the evil perpetrators there are no complete villains in this story, for abuses as well as supreme acts of human decency always occur in wars, side by side with excesses beyond what necessity or war constraints would dictate. The question is always to distinguish between what individuals did and the preponderant mood that guided the public, in general, while those acts of horror or of generosity were being done. For example, if we learn that while the Ustasha ruled ruthlessly "greater Croatia," most of the population opposed it, then we might desist from linking automatically between Ustasha and Croat; conversely, if we have proof that some Serbs themselves collaborated with the Nazis and perpetrated horrific massacres against their opponents and Jews, then their attempts to project an image of innocent victims of the war might be blunted; or, if we can show that those who complain about being persecuted and wronged by others have themselves acted in kind with their rivals, then we might balance our views and stereotypes on the side of the "good guys" and on the other of the "bad guys." Since we know today that the most oppressive regimes, such as Communism, Libya, Syria, Yemen, Imperial Iran, and others could be brought to their end by public resistance and rebellion, we are then likely to be less tolerant to those who disagreed with their regimes but accepted in silence their rule. In any case, this volume is not about judging one side against the other or pronouncing a verdict condemning the one and acquitting the other. It is about the unquestioned evil they both caused, or were made to cause, to the Jewish minority in their midst, in particular, and to others, in general. It is a fact that Serbs, Muslims, and Croats continue to dominate the ex-Yugoslavian scene, which has been their arena of battle for the past centuries, while the flourishing Jewish minority culture in that area has all but come to a historical standstill and almost totally vanished.

When I thought I saw it all on the Serbian side, I experienced an awakening on the Croatian side, when I repeatedly visited the Jewish communities of Zagreb, where I discovered that there were two of them, and met with Croatian scholars (Jews and non-Jews), young and veterans of the War, officials and common people, and spent time in the two camps of Jadovno and Jasenovac, as I became aware that two of the latter existed. Two Jasenovacs also meant two different holocaust narratives. The rifts, suspicions, and hostility between Croats and Serbs, internal and external, are so deep as to dwarf the controversies about the numbers of victims, for much more fundamental and qualitative issues than numbers and quantities are at stake. I learned that what I had seen as the "Jasenovac Camp," was only that part across the Sava, in Bosnian territory today, which Serbs cultivate as "their" Jasenovac, where they can exhibit the horrors of the war as they see them, as opposed to the Jasenovac Memorial on the Croatian side where one learns about a different, more diminished narrative, and a varying intensity of the horrors perpetrated there. On the Jewish side, one community, the Zagreb Jewish Community, which claims to represent the majority of the Jews and has actual possession of the remaining Jewish assets, stands aside and seems to engage in a bitter organizational battle for its exclusivity in speaking for all Jews; while their rival community, though representing the minority of the members, seems to teem with Jewish, Zionist, and pro-Israeli activity of all sorts, to merge its activities with those of the Israel-Croatia Association and to toe the official national line.

As against the low profile adopted by the first group, to the extent that in all my previous visits I had only become aware of the other community, most of my contacts had developed over the years with the large variety of scholars, journalists, and former Israelis who congregate around the smaller community, though it has no formal offices of its own. The two communities, which total two thousand souls (compared to the prewar ten thousand) are not on speaking terms, are very stingy on compliments toward each other, and have developed a different way of thinking since they split in 2006. While the first is very critical of the new Croatia, of the Jasenovac Memorial which to their mind tries to minimize the *Shoah*, and almost hurl accusations of guilt against their rivals, the other shows more moderation with the numbers of victims and joins the harsh criticism of the Serbs who are blamed for inflating the numbers of the Jasenovac mass murder. Strange coalitions of bedfellows are emerging within the community: On the one hand, Jews who hate their fellow Jews and despise their Croat countrymen for attempting to whitewash the Shoah and make it more palatable and more forgettable; on the other hand, devoted

Jews and Zionists who are also patriotic Croats and who fight for their country's war narrative. The impression is that each side pursues vehemently its own "justice" and cares less about objective analyses and hard data. The second community usually upholds the figures of a hundred thousand victims in Jasenovac, Serbs, Jews and Gypsies all included, predicating its data on verified names that were painfully collected, identified, and registered, while the skeptics point out that the lack of evidence is not evidence of lack. Yes, countless thousands have left no traces in their mass tombs and deep pits, but that does not mean that they were not murdered.

The controversy of numbers which will persist for ever,[1] despite the sober numbers advanced by some historians,[2] as will the relative assessments on the two sides of the divide relating to the intensity and relentlessness of the horrors of the Ustasha on the one hand,[3] the contributing mythological motivation of the Serbs to annihilate the Croats on the other,[4] and the unexpectedly growing literature on the Croats who came to the rescue of the Jews in the Ustasha state in the midst of those dark days.[5] However one twists the data, it is evident that while the Ustasha did commit genocide (of Serbs, Jews, Gypsies, and others), even if we accept the minimal numbers admitted by the Croats and their Jasenovac Memorial, no such a blame could be hurled against the Serbs during World War II, either because they were themselves occupied by the Germans or because the project of genocide against Croats and Muslims had never been within their purview at that time. To project the savageries of the Bosnia War of the 1990s, in which all parties have participated, on the "national character" of the Serbs, is not a serious proposition, even when wrapped in scholarly dissertations and spelled out in fancy social science terminology. Serbs may or may not have been prone to genocide, just as the Hungarians, Lithuanians, Ukrainians, Poles, and others, but in World War II they did not commit one, though Nedic and his acolytes, in a different fashion than the Pavelic Ustasha followers, collaborated with the Nazis in carrying out their "final solution" for the Jews.

The adamant and unconscionable hurling of numbers, exaggerated upward or downward, has nevertheless produced over the years a process of leveling off, by force of erosion or under the hammer of perseverance by serious scholars on both sides. Serbs no longer buy that inflated number of eight hundred thousand murdered Serbs, which is still proclaimed in the Bosnian Jasenovac, nor do they buy the exceedingly low number of just over eighty thousand, including Jews and Gypsies, which has been advertised in a two-thousand-page directory of names of all victims to all visitors of the Croatian Jasenovac. Between these two extremes one finds various foundations, memorials, archives, and government and scholarly publications that under the impact of conferences, publications, and joint or separate research, have considerably narrowed the gap between the two, to the order of a few hundreds of thousands for the Serbs, and around one hundred thousand for the Croats. Both are a far cry from what politicians (like the Croat Tudjman, who declared that "only forty thousand Serbs" were killed) or descendants of the murdered (five hundred thousand or more victims) claim. At any rate, a genocide there was, not because of the numbers, but because it was perpetrated by the Ustasha as part of their ideology to annihilate the Serbs or parts thereof.

To try to penetrate the minds of the main actors in this sad narrative, and especially to overcome the language boundaries which have considerably limited my direct access to some of the sources, I had to rely on two dear friends on both sides of the divide: Nada Lubic, a scholar and public activist from Belgrade, and Boris Havel, a scholar and diplomat from Zagreb, who have devotedly spent endless hours to introduce me into the materials, to coach me into their archives, to facilitate my stay in their respective countries, and to translate for me otherwise inaccessible materials. Being loyal nationals of their respective parties, they tried undoubtedly to impact me with their biases and to emphasize their points of view, but I must also stress with admiration their scholarly commitment to the truth and their consistent and conscious efforts to remain neutral and open-minded to counterarguments all along. Both of them will certainly, and understandably, lament my "lack of comprehension," or my "selling off" to their rivals' ideas, or my "betrayal" of our long-lasting and deep-rooted friendship and whatnot. But as I shoulder alone the responsibility for any errors of fact, comprehension, and interpretation, and as I have no axe to grind, I know that I did the best I could to sort things out and fulfill my duty as a chronicler, and to interpret in order to share with the new generations that dark episode in the history of Yugoslavia, the Jewish people, Europe, and the world, which has for too long been obscured by political controversy.

Raphael Israeli,
Jerusalem, Winter 2011–2012

Introduction

Yugoslavia on the Eve of Nazi Occupation

The Ottoman state, which had reached Vienna at the pinnacle of its expansion in the sixteenth century, in its second quest to Islamize Europe, after the first attempt had ended in failure in the Iberian Peninsula around the same time, was multi-ethnic and multi-religious. Under its Muslim dominance, Christians, Jews, and others lived in a state of *dhimma* for many centuries, ostensibly as relatively free to exercise their respective faiths, but in fact they were often displaced, uprooted, lured, and at times forced to Islamize. For this coexistence was not born out of a modern concept of tolerance of the other on the basis of acceptance of differences and equality to all, and therefore a right of free choice, but on a sense of superiority which when it tolerated others, that was in spite of their inherent inferiority. Therefore, even though Muslim Turks may have temporarily constituted the minority of the population in some areas of the Empire, they reigned supreme by virtue of their Muslim master status, while the various Christian groups (and Jews for that matter) were relegated to the status of "protected people" (*dhimmis*). Christians and others who had integrated into the Ottoman system, by embracing Islam, speaking Turkish, and going into the government service, soon became part and parcel of the Ottoman culture, even when they kept their attachment to their ethnic origin and to their mother tongue. The Bosnians were a case in point; many of them felt privileged to go into the *devsirme* system of enrolling their boys to the prestigious Janissary Corps, and in the course of time, they were Islamized, though they preserved their Slavic roots and language.[6]

The Balkans were conquered by the Ottomans from the middle of the fifteenth century on. Serbia fell to the Muslim conquerors in 1459, and four years later Bosnia and Herzegovina succumbed. Caught between the economic interest of milking the tax-paying *dhimmis* by extracting from them the *jizya* poll tax, which necessitated maintaining the conquered population in place instead of expelling it or converting it by force, and the military and security needs that required the Muslim population be numerous enough to ensure the loyalty to the Empire, the Ottomans tended to implement the latter choice in the Balkans. They adopted the policy of deporting part of the native populations and settling their own people, or other conquered people in their stead, thus ensuring that no local minority should envisage any insurgency among a Muslim population. In Bosnia, the process of Islamization was reinforced by the turncoats who flocked to Islam and became the worst oppressors of their former coreligionists. So much so, that the Bosnians were notorious for their role in the Ottoman administration, the military, and especially the Janissaries. Much of the anti-Christian zeal, which burst in Bosnia in the twentieth century against Serbs and Croats alike, can be traced back to those early times. As late as 1875, way after the introduction of the modernizing *tanzimat* reforms into the Ottoman system, which were supposed to redress the situation of the non-Muslims throughout the Empire, the British Ambassador in Istanbul reported that the Ottoman authorities in Bosnia recognized the impossibility to administer justice in equality between the Muslims and the Christians, inasmuch as the ruling Muslim courts accepted no written or oral evidence from Christians. One 1876 report from Bosna-Serai (Sarajevo) by the British Consul in town, tells the whole story:

> About a month ago, an Austrian subject named Jean Udilak, was attacked and robbed between Sarajevo and Visoka by nine Bashi-Bazouks. The act was witnessed by a respectable Mussulman of this time named Nouri Aga Varinika, and he was called as a witness when the affair was brought before the Sarajevo Tribunal. His testimony was in favor of the Austrian, and the next day he was sent for by the Vice-President and one of the members of the Court and threatened with imprisonment for daring to testify against his coreligionists.[7]

As British Consul Majer tells us, Muslims, Christians, and Jews, for that matter, could keep to themselves in their own communities, with their lifestyles, rituals, and festivals running without hindrance, except in case of intermarriage. For here, the only allowed combination was Muslim men taking in Christian (or Jewish) wives, an act that consecrated their joint offspring as full-right Muslims. The result was that while non-Muslim culture merged into the predominant Islam, there was also an outside input into the Muslim civilization, with material culture (food, dress, habits, language) growing to become common to all. All this was acceptable to the Ottoman authorities who were reluctant to interfere, but as soon as the *dhimmis* became wealthy and were conspicuous in their dress and demeanor, it was considered a provocation to the Muslim population and dealt with accordingly. Christians who wanted to improve their lot in Bosnia and Albania could always do so through conversion to Islam or seeking the protection of their Muslim family members.[8]

Toward the end of the Ottoman rule, as economic problems arose and the state was no longer able to enforce law and order in the face of the nationalist awakening in the various provinces of the Empire, local rule grew more despotic in an attempt to hold on to the territories that were slipping out of the Porte's grip. The notions of equality coming from liberal Europe, which made the maintenance of legal and religious inequities untenable, were conjugated into national terms in the Balkans, and spelled out independence from the Ottoman yoke, since the idea of ruling an Empire held together by Islam was no longer operative. It was, ironically, the Ottoman attempts at modernity, opening up the system and addressing individuals instead of traditional communities, which brought to its downfall and opened the new vistas of nationalism and independence in the Balkans as elsewhere, a situation not unlike Eastern Europe after the Gorbachev Perestroika in the late 1980s and early 1990s. But in view of the Greek and Bulgarian plans for a Balkan Federation under their aegis, to take over from the Ottomans,[9] the gradual and parallel dreams to realize a Greater Serbia, a Greater Croatia, and a Greater Albania, and the tax repression imposed on all of them by the Bosnian Muslims on behalf of the dwindling imperial authorities, the Serbs rose up in arms (1875), and many of them ran into hiding, leaving behind, to the mercy of the Muslims, children, the old, and women, something reminiscent of the horrors of the Bosnian War and then the Kosovo War more than one century later. Preydor and Banja Luka were the most harmed by the insurgents when Serb churches and homes were burned.[10]

According to reports from the time of the rebellion, the Bosnian Muslims, descendants of converted Slavs who had become the landowners and acceded to the status of aristocracy by virtue of their conversion, now practiced their faith fanatically and ruthlessly toward their Orthodox compatriots, who would rather die in battle than submit to the tax exactions. What made things worse, again like in the recent events in Bosnia, was that the Catholics (later identified as Croats) allied to the Muslims against the Orthodox Serbs, as was to occur again during World War II when the greater combined state of Croatia and Bosnia was set up under the Ustasha. An eyewitness of the time reports:

> United under oppression, it was natural that the Serbs should respond by rebellion. But in the entire northern part of Bosnia and Turkish Croatia, . . . the antagonism between the two [Catholic and Orthodox] denominations is vast enough for us to have eye-witnessed Catholics marching on the heels of the Turks against Greek insurgents. . . . By an inexplicable aberration, the priests of the two denominations entertain hatred [toward each other] and we could say without exaggerating that, if given the choice the Catholics would rather be dominated by the Turks [Muslims] than by the Orthodox Serbs.[11]

That reporter had concluded that the Muslims of Bosnia maintained their loyalty to the Ottomans, and that there was no chance of a fusion between the populations, in view of the fact that those Serbs (or Croats) whose ancestors had embraced Islam as a political expediency, were now too imbued with it and too captured by the teachings of their Holy Book to relent from their intense hatred, which had germinated in their bodies and taken them over completely.[12] But this was to be only a foretaste of things to come, as henceforth the politics of Yugoslavia would be dominated by the alliance of two of its major religious groups, and later ethno-national communities, against the third. After the Berlin Congress (1878) and the occupation of Bosnia by the Austro-Hungarian Empire, the Serbs allied with the Muslims against the occupiers, who were supported by the Catholics (Croats) in the province. The Hungarian governor of the province tried valiantly to create a new Bosnian identity merging together its three principal communities, but he failed.[13]

The annexation of Bosnia by the occupiers in 1908 created a new alliance: the Serbs of Bosnia, who wished their merger with Serbia (not for the last time), were pitted against the Croat-Muslim coalition who would rather reconcile to their occupation than allow the Serbs to implement their dream. As a result, repression of the Serbs in Bosnia, coupled with the expulsion of Serbs from Kosovo, brought to a record level the bitterness of the occupied Serbs against their oppressors. Sukrija Kurtovic, a Bosnian Muslim, sought the differentiation between ethno-nationality and religion, and pleaded for the unity of the Bosnians with the Serbs in one single national group by reason of their common Serbian roots, arguing that Islam was a common religion of the Bosnians and the Turks, but that in itself did not make them share any national common ground.[14] The idea of Yugoslavism, a larger entity where all the ethnic and religious groups could find their common identity, came to the fore after the Balkan wars and precipitated World War I following the Sarajevo murder of the heir to the Austro-Hungarian throne in 1914. That war reinforced the Croat-Muslim alliance in Bosnia, which swore to expel the Serbs from Bosnia altogether, and acted upon its vow by perpetrating large-scale massacres of the Serbs, thus demonstrating the vanity of an all-Yugoslavian identity.[15]

A Yugoslavian state was created in 1918 nevertheless, which once again attempted to fuse its components in the ethnic and linguistic domains and leave, as befits a modern European state, the question of religion to the realm of each individual. However, while the Serbs and the Croats of Bosnia could look up to Belgrade and Zagreb, respectively, the Muslims were left to vacillate between their Muslim, Ottoman, local, and Slavic roots. At first they allied with the stronger Serbs and turned their eyes on Belgrade where they ensured for themselves some privileges; but wary of the competition between the Croats, who championed their particularistic nationalism, and the Serbs, who regarded themselves as the guardians and sponsors of Yugoslavian unity, they focused more and more on their local and religious identity in the form of a Muslim Party (JMO), while the Serbs and the Croats continued to claim that the Muslims of Bosnia were of their respective origins.[16]

The Yugoslavian kingdom, which was formed in 1918, integrated into a single state embracing the southern Slavic nations of Croatia, Slovenia, Serbia, Bosnia-Herzegovina, Montenegro, and Macedonia. Each one of these nations dwelling in the Balkans, and being the protégé of conflicting interests and competing religious denominations, triggered more than once wide-ranging confrontations all over Europe, notably in Sarajevo in 1914, which launched the conflagration of the Great War in 1914 that caused the death of twenty million persons; deprived Europe of an entire generation of young lives of workers, intellectuals, artists, creative minds, and who knows who else; and instead paved the way for the larger and more cruel and destructive World War II, when frustrated madmen like Adolf Hitler and his ilk, who could not accept their country's and personal humiliation, set the world on fire. But when the first Yugoslavian state was created in consequence of that war, *inter alia* on the ruins of the Austro-Hungarian and Ottoman sick and obsolete empires, it was the result of positive Western attitudes toward its component parts, which were to shift totally later on. A 1923 history of the Balkans, describes the situation thus:

> In 1922 the new King, to the great satisfaction of his subjects, married, and at his wedding with a Roumanian princess, the Duke of York represented the British Royal family. Never have the ties between Great Britain and the Serbs been so close as since the [Great] War, when they fought side by side. Many Serbs found a refuge in England, many were educated at Oxford, and to Englishmen Serbia is no longer an unknown land.[17]

If one studies the major policy shifts of Britain during World War II—from an all out support for the young Yugoslavian king, who fled German occupation to England; to sponsoring the resistance of the *Cetniks* led by General Mikhailovic, the pro-royalty fighter; to abandoning that group, in favor of Tito's Partisans, and eventually forcing the king to dismiss Mikhailovic—one is surprised by the British turn about, effected by Winston Churchill personally, who even committed his own son, Randolph, to be parachuted over Tito-controlled territory, and channeled considerable British aid through him to the Partisans, as recounted in Churchill's war memoirs.[18] Obviously, even though Tito was a Croat in origin, he perhaps thought that Serbs, who were rebellious and famously not distinguished for their docility to foreign invaders, since they had resisted Ottoman rule and repulsed on many occasions the Austro-Hungarian forces that had tried to quell them on the southern front of World War I, would be amenable to resist the Germans. At that time, the pro-Nazi Ustasha state was established over Croat and Bosnian territory, immediately after the German occupation in 1941, and became by definition hostile to Serbia and the Serbs. Indeed, it did not take long for that state to establish extermination camps in Croatia, Bosnia, and the island of Pag, where major centers of physical elimination of Serbs, Jews, and Gypsies were built, preceding the Nazi camps in Germany and Eastern Europe that were to provide the facilities for the final solution. The major camp complexes in Jadovno and Jasenovac were proof of Ustasha determination to carry out their widely circulated slogan: kill a third (of the Serbs in Ustasha territory), expel a third, and convert a third. We are talking here about more than a million Serbs who found themselves trapped within the Ustasha state, both within the boundaries of Croatia proper, and the northern part of Bosnia and Herzegovina, now the domain of the new pro-Nazi state.

Even taking into consideration the unpopularity of the Ustasha state among the Croats and the Bosnians who constituted it, it remains a fact that those who did serve the Pavelic regime (and there were at least tens of thousands of them), not only fought against the Serbian Cetniks and made themselves the strategic servants of the Nazis, but they also built the Jadovno and Jasenovac extermination camps, intended for Serbs, Jews, and Gypsies (and some Croatian dissidents too). Similarly, while the Serbs did not experience, let alone devise, the horror of erecting camps to assemble there and annihilate their opponents (Croats, Muslims, and other Serbs), the Nedic regime they established in Belgrade, to collaborate with the Germans under debatable circumstances, did assist the Germans in rounding up Jews, Gypsies, and other Yugoslavs and ultimately in exterminating them, and in so doing, they served the war purposes of the Nazis. In any case, under war conditions, in a country torn apart by ethno-religious controversies and covered by a deep residue of historical hatreds, no one group came out totally unscathed, and no group other than the Ustasha emerged as singled out for total condemnation and doom.

Notes

1. See e.g., Vladimir Zerjavic, *Population Losses in Yugoslavia 1941–1945*, Zagreb, 1997.
2. Ivo Goldstein, *Croatia: a History*, McGill Press, Montreal, 2001. See also other works by this author on his own or in conjunction with his father Slavko.
3. See the following testimonies relating to Jadovno and Jasenovac.
4. Branimir Anzulovic, *Heavenly Serbia: From Myth to Genocide*, Hurst and Co., London, 1999; see also Boze Covic (ed.) *Roots of Serbian Aggression*, Center for Foreign Languages, Zagreb, 1993.
5. Esther Gitman, *When Courage Prevailed: Rescue and Survival of Jews in the Independent State of Croatia, 1941–1945*, Paragon House, St. Paul, 2011.
6. Ibid., 63.
7. Cited by Bat Ye'or, *The Decline of Eastern Christianity under Islam: From Jihad to Dhimmitude*, Fairleigh Dickinson University Press, Madison and London, 1996, 177–178. For documents about the inequities in Bosnia against the Christian population, see also 421–427.
8. Majer, 67–68.
9. Vrban Todorov, "The Federalist Idea as a Means for Preserving the Integrity of the Ottoman Empire," in S. Terzic (ed.), *Islam, the Balkans and the Great powers XIV–XX Century*, 1997. Belgrade as an edition of the Historical Institute of Serbian Academy of Sciences and Arts.

10. *Revue des Deux Mondes*, Paris, 1876, Vol II, No 1, 237–254. Cited by Jean-Paul Bled," La Question de Bosnie-Hercegovine dans La Revue Des Deux Mondes"; ibid., 330.
11. Ibid., 331–332.
12. Ibid., 332.
13. Dusan Batakovic, "La Bosnie-Herzegovine: le System des Alliances," in Terzic, op. cit., 335–343.
14. Ibid., 343–344.
15. Ibid., 346.
16. Ibid.
17. William Miller, *The Balkans: Roumania, Bulgaria, Servia and Montenegro*, Fisher Unwin, London, 1923, 513.
18. Winston Churchill, *The Second World War: Closing the Ring, Volume V*, Houghton and Mifflin, Boston, 1951, 461–478.

1

The German Expansion into the Balkans[1]

We are now called upon to talk about the German occupation of the Balkans during the war and its repercussions, internal and external, upon the entire region in general and the Ustasha state in particular. The problem is relevant to the context of the extermination camps, Jadovno and Jasenovac, in a very strange and oblique way. And that is the reason why there is some justification to talk about this topic, apart from all the other controversial issues that one comes across when reading the vast literature on the German occupation per se. I was struck by the paucity of research on the Muslim issue, and by the many other open questions that require a lot of digging, and a lot of research, without which one cannot distill truth from narratives and accusations from facts. The situation resembles more and more the Middle East where there is no accepted universal history any longer, and there is no one truth—there are only rival narratives. And a biased narrative is not, and cannot be, history. Because everybody can dream a dream, everybody can invent stories that never were, and in this way no one will ever reach the truth. For example, in regard to the question of the numbers of victims, one hears of anywhere from eighty thousand to seven hundred thousand (almost ten times more) Serbs murdered during the war; they were exterminated in Jasenovac or in Jadovno, under all sorts of horrible tortures and particularly cruel executions. These are large gaps that one cannot dismiss as just little errors of calculation or occasional exaggerations here or there. That means that there is a rivalry of political statements and a competition of narratives behind each issue, event, or analysis one wishes to embrace, depending on the national or ethnic group one belongs to.

Perhaps, first of all, we have to define: "What is extermination?" or what is *Shoah* or Holocaust for this or that party, when one hurls against another claims of murder, genocide, or disaster of some sort. For me

1

there is a working definition that I have determined for myself. If a few people are killed in this or that operation—I mean innocent civilian people, not in battle—then you say that's murder. If a few dozens of people are killed, then one might say that's mass murder. If it is a few hundred people who are killed, I say it's a massacre. If more, if thousands of people are killed, it's extermination, and only if it's tens of thousands, then it becomes genocide. And if it's more than genocide, like hundreds of thousands, or millions, then perhaps it becomes a disaster, or *Shoah*, or Holocaust. There must also exist an ideological element of genocide in the worldview of the perpetrators, within which a mass murder of many people by the perpetrators may be considered a genocide unless, if we determine that Holocaust or *Shoah* are the specific names of the Jewish genocide of World War II. It is very important to demarcate these terms, because if we define the scope of killings then we keep terminology from depreciating, as when the Palestinians term every clash where a group of their people are killed by Israelis, as a "massacre," while what they kill is "resistance." Unless we hold one yardstick to measure these killings, so as to avoid venturing into exaggerations or other sorts of hyperbole that detach events from reality, we would be describing accusations, not facts. At any rate, even according to the Croat definition—which admits that at least eighty thousand Serbs were exterminated in Jasenovac and Jadovno, then it comes under all these definitions of murder, and therefore, call it as you wish—it remains within the most highly criminal act of mass extermination. Coupled with the accompanying ideology of murder, which was part of Ustasha ideology, you certainly have genocide there. And if we don't agree on these definitions, then everybody and anybody can continue to claim whatever they want to claim, and this will throw us into chaos once we lose a standard yardstick by which we all agree to measure the horror of these events. It is similar to the contemporary definition of terrorism, which for lack of an accepted terminology, turns Muslim murderers into "martyrs," who cannot by nature and definition perform terrorism, and the Americans and Israelis who defend themselves against those horrors as the "true terrorists."

Another issue that should torment us constantly, is the one that tends through easy comparisons to distort facts and to encourage one-upmanship between rival parties, either by bragging about the lesser amount of evil they caused compared to others, or by attempting to augment the amount of evil of their rivals compared with theirs. For example, one hears, "Well, the Serbs had their Nedic, who collaborated with the Germans, exactly like the Croats provided the Ustasha Pavelic on their side." But one might also argue that Pavelic was some kind of Quisling or Petain. He supported the Nazis ideologically; he had a political structure, a state which was a puppet of the Nazis, even when we recognize that it was a unique, unprecedented and aberrant event in Croatian history. By contrast, Nedic the Serb, who also collaborated in his own way, could be rather compared to the *Judenrat*, which the Germans set up in place in the occupied ghettos throughout Europe during the Jewish *Shoah*. Here it was somebody who took care of his kin, which was a great responsibility and also a great risk, and many of those unfortunate Jews who took the appointment did not themselves survive that trial, because they depended on the whims of the occupying Germans. To this day, the debates rage about whether the *Judenrat* were collaborators with the Nazis or their bitter rivals. They are viewed by different actors at different times and different places as either.

In the case of Nedic, it is said, he took care of the administration of his occupied Serbian countrymen, because if he did not do it, then the Germans would have done it directly, much to the detriment of his kin, and that would have been much worse. But on the other hand, as we see from certain research findings,[2] he had expressed some zeal in his collaboration and acted as the extension of other Fascist currents that were inherent in Serbian society since before the war. So, easy and superficial comparisons are not necessarily valid. It is the duty of the scholars in this field to deepen the research and dissipate the many contradictions and disagreements that handicap it. This is very essential. In the present situation, looking for the truth is like sending a blind man into a dark room to look for a black cat that is not there. And therefore one will never come to any truth of any sort if we persist only in the practice of accusations, narratives, and counter-narratives. Fact-finding is an essential prerequisite, and I believe that the first Jadovno Conference in June 2011, together with the field visits on the ground and the exchange of ideas between scholars, have greatly contributed to achieving that goal. However, having despaired of ever digging up the whole truth, I shall refrain from definitive overall judgment about this or that nation, but limit myself to the topic at hand, and try to reach as fair conclusions as humanly possible, about the Ustasha extermination machine of Jadovno and Jasenovac, which was primarily devised to commit genocide against Serbs, Jews, and Gypsies.

We shall now discuss the extraordinary convergence of several top-ics, several people, and several areas that I think is unique to World War II, during the period of Nazi occupation of the Balkans and other parts of the world. The convergence is between the Nazi occupation of the Balkans—which is the topic of this chapter—including the occupied Yugoslavian state, the phenomenon of the competition between the embattled and single-handed British at the earlier stages of the war, and the Germans as a whole. And we shall see, that part of the competition between those two bitter rivals will be reflected in what was happening both in the Balkans and the Middle East. This might seem quite surprising, for you might say: what does the Middle East have to do with that? But it has a lot to do with that. Add to that another two major elements: one, the rise of the Muslim Brotherhood in Egypt, which then spread to the entire world, and is again in the world news due to the "Arab Spring" in 2011–2012, and you will see that their very doctrine will seep into the Balkans via their ideological and strategic collaboration with the Nazis. And lastly, you will see that a certain prominent personality, Haj Amin al-Husseini, the great mufti of Jerusalem who was influenced by the Muslim Brothers, will be the man, the key man, who will connect between the Middle East and the Balkans, and specifically bring Middle eastern Islam to the Muslims of Bosnia; he will help recruit them to that special unit of the *Waffen-SS* division thirteen, and after some time a second division will be born, the twenty-first, which will help the Nazis, not only fight against the Partisans and the *Cetniks*, but it will also have the opportunity to implement the joint anti-Jewish extermination ideology of the Nazis and the Muslim Brothers, as they ended up weaving their common hatred toward the Jewish people into an operational idea and plan of action, which they started to implement in the Ustasha camps of extermination. These are the issues that we should be made aware of, if we are to comprehend this convergence of events.

Before we delve into details in the coming chapters, let us discuss the clash of the British with the Nazis, and we shall see how their interests, how their worldviews were in competition in the Balkans, specifically in Bosnia, and how that connects with the situation in the Middle East. Europe, prior to the outbreak of the war in 1939, was partly conditioned by Italy, the ally of Hitler, which was assigned the task of taking care of the Balkans as their zone of influence and security. That was their area of responsibility, in addition to North Africa, so as to free the German army to its operations in West and

East Europe and secure its southern flank. And indeed, the Italians seemed at first to be able to spread their prominence to those areas. In 1939 they invaded Albania and from there they intended to attack Greece in order to expand the Mussolini regime, or at least its supervision of that area of the world, down to the Aegean Sea. That was their idea, but the problem was that the Greeks proved to be stronger than what the Italians thought, and the Italians proved to be weaker than what the Nazis, their allies, were hoping for. So, as the Greeks resisted the Italian effort to take them over, the Nazis had no choice but to come to the rescue of their ally in the Balkans, and to interfere themselves with very precious elite divisions that they needed for their plan to open their second front with the Soviet Union.

That was the situation, and Hitler was caught by a pressure of time, because here we were in the beginning of 1941 while he had issued his order to invade the Soviet Union back on December 28, 1940, and to launch that war on May 15, 1941, ironically the very date when the Jewish people, whom he sought to wipe out, would set up their state of Israel exactly seven years later. The situation in the beginning of April was that the Italians were failing, and the Germans had to come to their rescue, in order to secure their flank when they prepared for the invasion of the Soviet Union. At the time, the Nazis were doing very well in North Africa, as their glorious general, Irwin Rommel, was advancing against the British, and Hitler thought that on that front he was pretty much assured. All he had to do now was to link overland between Central Europe and the Aegean Sea, in order to secure continuity from the Baltic through Western Europe, which was all under his occupation, and down to the Mediterranean, which was to become a German lake. And then, if he could control the entire Mediterranean together with its southern shore—that is the North African coast, held by Rommel and by his allies the Italians—then of course he could proceed without any fear, or without taking too much risk, into his attack against Russia.

That was the big plan, but fortunately for the world and for the rest of us, it did not work quite that way because of the deviation from the plan; for instead of launching the attack on May 15, it was postponed by 4.5 weeks, to June 22. That was the time that it took to control the Balkans and to invade Greece, due to Hitler's over confidence that the Italians would be able to control the Balkans expeditiously, which proved exaggerated. Hitler regarded himself a military genius, not for the first or last time, and that proved part of his undoing. Doing the job himself, against the advice of his generals, meant that he didn't make it to Moscow by the beginning of the winter, and that exactly was his burial place. To the world's good fortune, and to the German and Ustasha and their allies' misfortune, due to that grave mistake of Hitler and to his obstinacy on securing the Balkans before the invasion on the Russian front, he was bogged down in Stalingrad, and after Stalingrad all the way down until the Nazis' failure and the end of their fortunes in the war. That was the German side of the story.

As to the British side, we ought to be reminded that 1941 was the height of the German rival's success in Europe in the war, because North Africa and the entirety of continental Europe—except for the Balkans, where they were still in the process of fighting—were under German control. Even the Mediterranean waters were under Nazi domination, after the Germans sent paratroopers to Crete following the British retreat from Greece and some of the Balkans. The British were now in their worst situation of the war, after the damages done to British cities under the *blitz*, and the very costly Battle of Britain, which was draining their national and economic energies and constantly hammering at their valiant Royal Air Force. They were supplicating America to enter the war or at least to send weapons, because much of their weaponry had been lost in Dunkirk, when they withdrew from France in 1940, and the rest was being eroded in the fronts of Britain, the Middle East, North Africa, the Far East, and the universal maritime war. Against the big success of the Nazis on their side, here we have the major failure of the British in North Africa, where Rommel was advancing rapidly, and therefore they implored America to land in Morocco, something they would do only in 1942, after they were dragged into war by Pearl Harbor, thereby signaling the beginning of the reversal of the tide of the war in Europe and the Mediterranean for the Germans, and in the Pacific for the Japanese. The British had also other concerns in the Mediterranean, let alone their string of defeats in the Pacific at the hands of the ever victorious Imperial Japanese Army, in China, Singapore, Hong Kong, Indochina, the Philippines, and Burma, which came dangerously close to the Indian pearl of the shrinking British Empire.

The British still dominated the Suez Canal, however, which was a key strategic position in the communication link to India and the Far East; they also ruled Egypt and Iraq, and in both there were native movements directed against British dominion and tending to support the Nazis. In Iraq, in 1941 a pro-Nazi *coup d'état* brought to power a government headed by Rashid Ali, and that rebellion took a great deal of British troops to quell, which were very meager at the time in the Middle East. The Germans, on their part, sent some support to the rebels in Iraq. In Egypt, where the Suez Canal ran, making it a vital asset to defend, many officers of the Egyptian army, who resented the British occupation, linked with the Nazis in order to elicit their help against the British colonialists. Therefore, for the Nazis it was a very big occasion to ally with the local population in the Middle East against the British, who had been the main power and power broker there. They were hoping that by winning the approaching al-Alamein battle in the Western Desert, which was to take place eventually in 1942, they would take hold of the Suez Canal and choke the British link to the Far East, and they would then advance into Palestine and, of course, thereby get the entire Mediterranean shore under their control and complete their takeover of the Mediterranean. So the British deployed the utmost effort in order to keep the Arabs and Muslims of the Mediterranean coast on their side, knowing that the Nazis were doing exactly the reverse effort to get to ally them to the Nazi cause. At that point, the Nazis seemed to be winning, and the tide seemed to turn in their favor, both in Egypt and in Iraq.

Add to that the emergence at the same time of the power of the Muslim Brothers in Egypt, on the one hand, and of the mufti of Jerusalem, Haj Amin al-Husseini, who was connected to the Muslim Brothers and militated for their cause, on the other, and you have the complete picture that the Nazis schemed to accomplish as their war aim, while the British sought to resist valiantly against all odds. The Muslim Brothers, founded in Isma'iliyah, Egypt, in 1928 turned themselves into the most formidable opponent of the British colonizers along the Suez Canal, and it was natural that London should try almost desperately to lure several westernizing and modernizing elements in Egypt, as well as some other Islamizing and nationalist trends, into its fold in order to blunt their particularistic demands. But the Nazis were equally skillful in demonstrating to those Egyptian social and political trends that the success and the future were theirs, since their victory seemed assured, at least until they ventured into the Russia misadventure, which ruined their chances. In mandatory Palestine of those days, the Germans were also energetically at work to convince the leader of the Palestinian nationalists, Haj Amin, that his double-edged strategy of liberating his people from British rule and of undoing the Zionist plans of settling Palestine and absorbing the Jews who were persecuted, chased, and exterminated in Europe, was best served by them, since they also aimed at routing the British and exterminating the Jews. These two themes will be elaborated in more detail in the coming chapters.

We have seen from the very sketchy explanation presented here that all those seemingly unconnected issues and areas of the world, pertaining to World War II, were in the final analysis very much interconnected. The British, on their part, switched their support from the *Cetniks* to the Partisans, at some point in 1944, and that is best documented in the six volumes of Winston Churchill's history of World War II, especially volume V, which was written like a diary. Churchill indeed explained day by day all his correspondence with Tito, and how he sent his own son, Randolph Churchill, by parachute—together with other people, including Ambassador Maclean—in a delegation to assist the Partisan movement, which he saw as more promising to the war effort of the allies than the hesitating and unreliable *Cetniks*. It is clear from those documents that Churchill switched sides half-heartedly, due to the loyalty he felt to the young king of Yugoslavia, who was in exile in London. Some people would say: "Oh, he cheated, or he betrayed the *Cetniks*, he just threw them away," and so on. It is not so, because if you judge from his correspondence, he exerted tremendous efforts to convince Tito not to reject the king, since he had assured the young deposed monarch that after the war he would try to return to him his crown. But he also realized that the *Cetniks* were not operating exactly according to the British liking, when they concluded local understandings with the Nazi occupiers, while Tito was gathering power and also committed to fight the occupiers to the end, though he did not hide his ambitions to submit reconstituted postwar Yugoslavia to his Communist rule. Churchill then decided to transfer all the support, especially in arms, in food, in equipment and money, from the royalist *Cetniks* to their Partisan rivals.

The *Cetniks* pursued a policy of aggrandizing Greater Serbia and cleansing it ethnically during the war, in an atmosphere that arguably accepted a harsh treatment of the non-Serbs as a legitimate way to achieve that goal. Stefan Moljevic published a memorandum on June 30, 1941, stating the aim of the Serbs as building an ethnically homogeneous Serbia that should encompass all areas inhabited by the Serbs, and other territories that would enable them the development of their economic, political, and cultural entity. Except for the absence of an ideology of systematically annihilating their perceived enemies, this was an approximate mirror-image vision of what the Ustasha Croats devised for the Jews and Serbs in their territory, and both were a mini-replica of the Nazi dreams about *lebensraum* in the conquered east. The *Cetniks* viewed all territories where a Serbian population lived, even those where they were a mere minority, as appropriate for the development of that national space, hence their contempt for non-Serbs, once again mirroring the way the Nazis saw non-Aryan people whom they wished to either transfer out of Germany or to otherwise eliminate from their purview. In precise terms, the Belgrade *Cetnik* leadership decided in summer 1941 that in order to purify Serbia, some 2,675,000 people would have to be expelled (but not exterminated), including one million Croats and half a million Germans, in return for the 1,310,000 Serbs who would be brought in and included in Greater Serbia. Muslims were defined in that memorandum as a "serious problem," while the Jews, who were an insignificant minority, were hardly mentioned.

Unlike the German plan of extermination and conquest of territory, which was at least partly implemented, and the Croatian blueprint that was at least partly realized under the Ustasha state, the *Cetnik* vision was never put to the test because they never achieved power. In any case, even had they had their way, they spoke of expulsion of the unwanted elements, not of elimination, of transfer of populations not of their total eradication. Both ways are horrible, but one allows survival of the victims at least, while the other leaves no hope at all. In Jewish history, the heartless and fanatic expulsion of the more than two hundred thousand Jews of Spain and Portugal in 1492, who did no wrong, were partners in the flourishing of the Iberian Peninsula and loyal to the state, unless they agreed to convert to Catholicism, is considered clearly preferable to the massacre of the six million Jews by Germans during the war. The former did settle elsewhere, and reproduced and flourished again, and created and procreated, by the indulgence of North African and Ottoman lands, while the latter exist only in memory, and one-third of the Jewish people were irretrievably annihilated. For this reason, one cannot include the *Cetniks* among the most virulent Serbian anti-Semites, even though they were not particularly philosemites.

Greater Serbia in this vision would be made of Serbia, Macedonia, Montenegro, Bosnia-Herzegovina, and Vojvodina, but all cleansed from all non-Serbs, and the cleansing of the Sandjak from Muslims, and Croats and Muslims from Bosnia and Herzegovina. Incidentally,

9

most of the hundred thousand Muslims killed in Yugoslavia during the war were the victims of *Cetnik* violence, particularly on the part of those of the Montenegro branch thereof under Pavle Durisic. Some *Cetniks* also collaborated with the Ustasha and the Germans against the Partisans, at other times with the Partisans against the Nazis. They were opportunistic and accommodating despite their stiff doctrine, maybe because they aspired to seize power after the war and the prospective German defeat. They wished to restore the king to his throne and establish military rule under the justification that they were all along the true resistance to the Nazis. They also cooperated at times with the Italians against the Ustasha, thus avoiding the foreclosing of any option after the war and the victory of the Allies. But victorious Tito undid their plans, crushed their dreams, and even took vengeance after the war on some of their leaders and many of their rank and file.

When Churchill acted against the alliance with the *Cetniks*, whom he had previously supported, when he realized that they were unreliable, he was also tormented by what was happening in the Middle East, North Africa, and the Far East—hence his apparent zigzags and halfhearted decisions. To sum up, it is fortunate for the world that Hitler was mad, and that due to his madness, he took the fateful decision to postpone the attack on the Soviet Union by five weeks, which caused his disaster there. Perhaps all humanity was saved as a result—certainly the Jews, the Middle East, and Israel were. Those Middle Eastern considerations, which went into the German venture in Yugoslavia during the war, will be discussed in more detail in the coming chapters. It is sobering in the meantime to realize how the fate of nations and countries was decided by the great players of the war, some of whom were deranged people moved by megalomaniac delusions. At that point, Hitler and Churchill, on behalf of Germany and Britain, respectively, were the main actors in the scene, and they evinced how auxiliary considerations in the calculations of great power strategies could determine questions of life and death of small nations, who played the role of minor cogs in the war machine of either side. On the one hand, the extermination of European Jewry by the Nazis may have expedited the rise of the modern Israeli state; but on the other hand, the foundation of Israel has so far scuttled the efforts to bring to bear Palestinian nationalism. Had Germany won the war, and that could have happened had Hitler conducted himself more rationally, it would be the Palestinians who would have established their state at the expense of Jews, on the entire expanse of Palestine once their Zionist opponents would have been eliminated.

Before we delve into the Ustasha system, which created the extermination camps in Croatia and Bosnia, it is important to note that in the Serbian part of Yugoslavia, which was under direct German occupation, things were not much better for the Jews. For Serbia was not just occupied and did not passively undergo the torments of the war, but it also partly collaborated with the occupiers who enforced their anti-Jewish policy of discrimination, exclusion, incarceration, and annihilation. The Nedic government, which actively participated in carrying out this policy, was not perhaps like the Pavelic Ustasha regime, which willingly and enthusiastically embarked on Jewish extermination out of its own volition, but a softer version thereof, maybe more comparable to the Vichy government of Southern France as contrasted with the Nazi-devoted Ustasha, or the Lithuanians and Latvians of the Baltics, or the Ukrainians and Hungarians and Slovaks of Central and Eastern Europe, who were virulent anti-Semites of their own right. The difference between the two can be exemplified by Jews or Muslims who are compelled by hunger to eat pork for survival, and they do reluctantly, versus those who eat and then lick their fingers for pleasure. There is no doubt that the commonality of fate between the Serbs and Jews, who were both the victims of the Ustasha regime's program of extermination, helped forge a latent alliance between the two, which was projected into the postwar Serbian historiography of occupied Yugoslavia as if it were a planned endeavor.

That difference in the degree of enforcement of the occupation rules on different territories throughout Europe, was obvious from the outset in the gap that existed between the two styles of Fascism in rigid, doctrinaire, "religiously" fanatic, and pitiless Nazi Germany, on the one hand, and in the much softer, flexible, and sometimes even compassionate and human-faced Italian Fascism, on the other. From Italian areas of occupation, like Grenoble in Southern France, which a survivor dubbed a "Jewish Paradise"[3] until it was taken over by the Germans; or in the reverse direction, when the Italians arrived to take over the Jadovno complex from the Ustasha in August 1941, as recounted in detail in the Jadovno chapter below. That stunning difference between two occupying powers, which were both Fascist and also allies, was very salient. That meant that the mode of conduct of clients and collaborators of the Nazis did not always have to please their bosses, and the latter could not always control all the details of the occupation. Thus, the Danish king was able in occupied Denmark to wear the yellow patch in sympathy with his Jews, and his citizens understood his good intentions and smuggled all their Jews across the straits into neutral Sweden under considerable risks, while neighboring Norway did not hesitate to erect a fully collaborative puppet state under pro-Nazi Quisling. Many officials and citizens in occupied Holland collaborated with the Nazis and denounced their Jewish neighbors, knowing that they were sent to their death, while many others hid Anne Frank and her likes, under the risk of death if caught.

So was the situation in occupied Serbia, which was directly under Nazi control, and the controversial Nedic trying to mediate the best he could between his citizens and the master power. His attitude and conduct toward the Jews remain at the very least ambivalent, judging from the fact that most Serbian Jews were rounded up and sent to their death, even though his regime was far from the ideological anti-Semitic stringencies of his Ustasha neighbors, and from the active persecution of Jews that the Nazis and their collaborators in Northern and Central Europe evinced. David Riesman, an American sociologist, who wrote a foreword to Philip Cohen's seminal book,[4] *Serbia's Secret War: Propaganda and the Deceit of History*, said in effect that the ethnic cleansing of Yugoslavia was carried out by mountainous Serbs, not the cosmopolitans of Belgrade or Sarajevo. He claims that following the Bosnia war of the 1990s, the Serbs, in an attempt to exonerate themselves, made themselves the victims of the Nazis, just like the Jews, in order not to admit that there was collaboration with the Nazis during the German occupation after 1941, though it is clear to him that Serbian nationalism was subservient to the Nazi National Socialism. What the Serbs helped the Nazis do to the Jews cannot make them saints compared with the villain Croats, all right, but what the Croats did to Serbs and to Jews does not justify for them to monopolize by themselves in our eyes the entire burden of horrors perpetrated during the war. In fact, only British intervention prior to the war reduced and brought under control the level of anti-Semitism among the ignorant Serbian farmers, though there were also periods of generosity and fair conduct toward the Jews in the kingdom. The Croat population during that period was not particularly philosemitic either, one has to stress. Therefore, at a time when the Ustasha collaboration with the Nazis has been well documented and recognized, though no one claims that all Croats were Ustasha, the Serbs have opted to seek to gain the moral high ground just like the Jews. This is the alleged "distortion" that Philip Cohen set out to redress.

Riesman further claims that, unlike the situation in Serbia, where illiterate individuals made it to the top of the hierarchy, hence their primitive conduct with the Jews, in more educated Croatia and Slovenia, anti-Semitism was less likely. But these arguments seem to lose their weight when one reckons that it was precisely the "educated" Croats who planned and carried out the elimination of Serbs, Jews, and others, and that the British positive attitude toward Serbs when the Yugoslavian kingdom was constituted after World War I emanated precisely from the growing numbers of Serbs who were getting their advanced education in the top British universities. It is also claimed that the Orthodox Church, which took part in and supported ethnic cleansing in Serbia, was reputedly leading the pan-Serbian movement that was inherently so nationalistic as to become implicitly anti-Semitic and anti-others, something that was also reflected in the *Cetniks'* manifesto of December 20, 1941, which purported to cleanse Yugoslavia from all the non-Serbian national minorities. The book discusses the rise of the ZBOR Youth Movement, and its student faction, the *White Eagles*, who on October 23, 1940, threatened with pistols faculty and students at the Belgrade University, and stabbed some of them, all the while hailing Hitler and Mussolini as their heroes and screaming: "Down with the Jews!" The author claims that long before the German occupation, Fascist Serbs were enchanted by the rise of National Socialism, which they found corresponding to their ideas of Greater Serbia.

It becomes problematic then, as one seeks to completely detach Milan Nedic from the Nazi enterprise in general and the extermination of Jews in particular, when we know that at least part of the intellectual, clerical, and political leadership of Serbia under him was connected with the Fascist ZBOR, the Serbian Gestapo, and with several *Cetnik* groups under Draza Mikhailovic, who were not great Jews lovers, and in some cases evinced their proclivity to dispose with them, even though historians like Ivo Goldstein insist that they were not, in the main, anti-Semites. "The Yugoslav National Movement (Serbian: *Jugoslovenski narodni pokret 'Zbor'*), commonly known simply as ZBOR,[5] was a Yugoslav Fascist and conservative nationalist movement formed in 1935 by Dimitrije Ljotic." ZBOR's ideology, according to Wikipedia, "was a blend of Italian Fascism, Nazism, and Serbian Orthodox Christian fundamentalism. ZBOR under Ljotic's leadership promoted integral Yugoslavism, authoritarianism, corporatism, monarchism, anti-communism, anti-freemasonry, anti-democratic views, Serbian orthodox religious ethics, Serbian peasant paternalism, and anti-Semitism. The ZBOR party tried to create an alliance with Germany before the start of World War II. . . . It was eventually banned in Yugoslavia during the Cvetković government in 1940. This ban was short-lived. After the defeat of the Kingdom of Yugoslavia in 1941, the party placed itself in complete service to the German occupation forces, and soon created its own military arm Serbian Volunteer Corps (*Srpski dobrovoljački korpus*), which was the kernel of the Serbian military force"[6] in Nedic's Serbia. Ljotic also had a close relationship with the Orthodox church, as he served as a member of the Patriarchal Council in Belgrade, and entertained a close cooperation with Bishop Velimirovic. Ljotic also wrote profusely in support of the Nazis, dubbing the object of his admiration, Adolf Hitler, as the "Savior of Europe."

After Hitler met Prince Pavle, the Yugoslavian Regent, on March 4, 1941, dragging Yugoslavia into the Tripartite Pact, the Regent convened the Regency Council in Belgrade on March 6, where even the minister of defense, Pesic, supported collaboration with Germany, for the simple reason that he thought Yugoslavia was unable to defend herself against German power, after much greater powers, like France, had capitulated. The very same logic had compelled Czechoslovakia to yield to the Munich Treaty in 1938, and Petain's Vichy government to submit to Nazi tutorship in 1940. They reasoned that instead of seeing their peoples crushed and their country destroyed and enslaved, it would be better to collaborate with the mighty enemy until the storm abated. But the fact that those who collaborated in France and Yugoslavia were later tried as "traitors," means that those arguments were not universally accepted by their respective populations. The problem that concerns us here is the degree of collaboration beyond what the occupying power demanded, or the situation warranted, and what the occupied populations did to satisfy and cater favor with the Germans, beyond what was strictly required of them. In other words, to what extent did they attempt to soften and mollify the pains, and to lessen and alleviate the burden of the occupation in order to conform to the milder Italian (as an occupier) and Danish (as occupied) models; or on the contrary, were they more zealous than the Germans to implement Nazi policy, like Lithuanians, Latvians, Hungarians, or Ukrainians.

In any case, when the announcement of the Pavle agreement was made public, Serbian officers mounted a coup against the regent and put in his stead the young Petar, seventeen years old, as the new king. General Dusan Simovic was appointed as the new prime minister, and his government was immediately recognized by the British, who regarded this as a daring démarche on the part of the Serbs. Naturally, all those who hail that act today as the ultimate proof of Serbian anti-Nazi, anti-Tripartite Pact alliance, and of independent nationalist attitudes, would tend to conceal the fact that Foreign Minister Nincic promised the Germans, who were infuriated by this reversal, that his government would honor the Tripartite obligations that his country had undertaken. Eventually, the prominent Croatian statesman, Macek, president of the dominant Peasant Party, joined Simovic as deputy prime minister, and the united government accepted to appease the Germans. Ljotic and his ilk, who had been imprisoned under the previous government, were released, and there was even talk that he might join the government. Whether the coup had been mounted as a pro-British or anti-Pavle measure, or was concocted, as some claim, against Croatian autonomy, remains beyond the scope of this volume. Here we will only deal with the operation of the Nedic government and the extent to which it collaborated with the Germans in pursuing the Jews and others, and eliminating them.

The coup, which surprised Hitler and infuriated him, also forced him to reverse his plans and to invade Yugoslavia, which he had thought was secure under the pact, and to postpone in consequence the invasion of the Soviet Union that he had ordered for May 15, until the recalcitrant Serbs came into line. On April 6, Germany and the Axis Powers invaded Yugoslavia, parts of which had been promised in reward to the partners: Italy immediately annexed the Croatian coastline; Hungary, the province of Vojvodina where a sizeable Hungarian minority dwelt; and Bulgaria took over Macedonia, eastern Serbia, and parts of Kosovo. The invading forces were surprised by the near-passivity they encountered on the front lines. Little they knew that most Yugoslavian generals, like the generals of the defeated French army on the western front of the war, elected not to fight, arguably to avoid destruction of their country, and asked for a cease-fire. Thus, on April 12, merely six days after the invasion, and despite the rugged terrain in which the Partisans would later make German occupation impossible, Belgrade, like Paris, capitulated. The Germans had their way: like in France, Belgium, and Norway, they rejected a cease-fire and insisted on unconditional capitulation.

The new king went into exile, first to Greece and then to London. Simovic decided that he would not commit the disgrace of capitulating, even as the military did, and he joined the king in exile. He certainly was of the same mind as the king, and they preferred to continue to struggle from the outside rather than to surrender. To exemplify the scope of the Yugoslavian "resistance" to the invaders, one has to bear in mind the 345,000 Yugoslavian military who were taken prisoners, an army which if it had mobilized a fraction of the rebelliousness and the renowned fighting spirit of the Serbs, could have resisted for weeks or months, at a price of course, and perhaps changed the entire nature and outcome of the war, had it been able to delay the Nazi Russian invasion even longer. The same could be said of the million-strong French army, and the hundreds of thousands of the trained military composed of the Dutch, Danish, Norwegian, Belgian, and Czech forces, who did not evince the same fighting spirit as the Russians did. In contrast, the Nazis lost only a derisively low amount of 151 troops and suffered 322 wounded in their Yugoslavian operation. The proportions are ridiculously disproportionate, which can only prove how little or no resistance they offered, just like their other European counterparts who were so stunned by the rapidity and striking power of their adversaries that they stood hypnotized and paralyzed by the German *blitzkrieg*, and they were idly watching their enemy overtaking their respective countries, thus lending to the ideals of bravery, valor, sacrifice, and patriotism new meanings.

The German assault against the Soviet Union on June 22 compelled them to transfer to the eastern front most of their elite forces from Yugoslavia, leaving there only three reduced divisions (with two regiments instead of three in each), whose personnel were older, poorly trained, and less equipped than those who left. Conversely, as the power and the daring of the Partisans increased, the Germans and their allies had a hard time maintaining order and security. Hence the doubts that are raised today on the nature of collaboration of both Nedic and Mikhailovic, who could very well have resisted better, more resolutely, and more efficiently, as Tito did (at a price to be sure). Instead they slipped into the comfort and convenience of collaborating with the party, which seemed to gain the upper hand in the war at that point, and of engaging on the German side in the bitter and relentless war against the Partisans. They could have instead formed a united resistance front in spite of the ideological differences that divided them. In fact, on August 13, 1941, 545 Serbian opinion-makers, who included the elites of all walks of life, led by Velibor Jonic, published an appeal to their folks to collaborate with the Nazis, and condemned the Partisans for their determined and costly resistance. Passivity in combat and activity in submitting to the Nazis, what else needs to be brought up as evidence to the similarity of the Nedic administration to Petain's in Vichy?

Conversely, despite their partial collaboration, at times, with the Nazis, the *Cetniks*, who were nationalist Serbs, and more so the Partisans, whose Serbian membership was considerable, played a role in aiding the Allied war effort and reconstituting Yugoslavia after the war, albeit under Communism this time. One may wonder at this sharp zigzagging of the Serbian elites: intellectual, political, military, scientific and clerical, from democratic liberalism after World War I, to Fascism between the two World Wars, to collaboration with the Nazis during the war, to Communism after World War II, and back to outbursts of racism and genocide in the wake of the dismemberment of the federal state in the 1990s. It is therefore very difficult to discern much of a spine of consistency and idealistic commitment lying at the base of the various ethnicities which constituted Yugoslavia, save for the consistent mutual hatred that pits them against one another. Little wonder then, that when one watches the twists and reversals that the component ethnic groups of Yugoslavia underwent during the war, one detects more proclivity on the part of Yugoslavs of all brands to appeasement, accommodation, collaboration, opportunism, and other ways of avoiding conflict with the stronger occupying powers, than a tendency to argue about doctrines and ideals, to debate moral commitment or honorable obligations to fulfill. Apparently, all ethnic groups in Yugoslavia spent so much energy and so many resources and manpower in their internal struggles and domestic rivalries that they had none left to face foreign occupiers.

Another gathering of seventy-five influential Serbs convened in Belgrade at the end of August 1941 and decided that General Nedic should form a new government of national salvation, to replace the administration that was appointed by the Nazis. Thus, unlike Pavelic, who was naturally handpicked by the Germans to head the Ustasha puppet state, after Macek had declined that post, Nedic was designated by popular "consensus," due to his record as a hero in World War I, who had recently been removed from his position as defense minister in 1940, ironically since he sided with the Tripartite Pact and was allegedly even in favor of ceding Yugoslavian territory to the Axis.

He was appointed on August 29 and formed a cabinet of forty-one ministers, eleven of whom were generals, and four members of the former Acimovic government, another indication of how consensual the idea of collaborating with the German occupation was (those who opposed the idea, like the king and his prime minister, had gone into exile or joined the Partisans or the *Cetniks*). To meet his Nazi assignment to quell the Partisans, he took for himself the command of the *Gendarmerie*, the Volunteer Corps, which was the military arm of the ZBOR, and of some of the *Cetniks*, who moved to his side, such as the *Kosta Pecanac* group that split from Mikhailovic. But since he could not manage to overcome the Partisans, he asked for German help, more evidence of his zeal to please his masters, instead of taking advantage of German difficulties in general, after the opening of the eastern front, and weakness in place (the Germans had to bring in a division from their garrison in France to fill the gap in Yugoslavia), and dragging his feet and avoiding bloodshed against his own people, if he indeed wished to resist as some of his supporters now claim. All in all, Nedic ended up commanding a force of eighteen thousand, equipped by the Germans, which they would not have cultivated and armed had they questioned for a moment Nedic's loyalty to them.

Like the *Cetniks*, Nedic also put at the center of his platform Greater Serbia, and he profusely spoke about it in his speeches and acted toward it in his programs. He also talked about Bosnia-Herzegovina and the Dalmatian coast, eastern Slavonia, Macedonia, Montenegro, and even Albania. One of his ambitions was to meet Hitler personally, and from 1942 he indicated his intention to establish a National-Socialist Serbia based on its farmers, they being the "pure Serbian race," modeling himself on the German regime. He stressed the comparison of the Serbs to the "anarchistic and materialistic Jewish mentality," and their affinity to the "rest of the Aryans," who place the nation and the family at the top of their ladder of values. Never mind that in the Nazi racial theory, Slavs were not placed on the same plane as the Aryan Germans. Nedic's plea was rejected by the Germans, arguably due to his desire to get more authority from them, but they assured him that after the war, assuming that they would win it, they would look into the matter again. Only in 1943 did Hitler receive Nedic in audience, and hear about his client's blueprint of Greater Serbia. Nedic also pleaded to regain direct commandment of all his armed forces, something that may indicate his quest for autonomy. Of course, the fact that he met Hitler does not make him necessarily a sworn Fascist. Others like the

Palestinian mufti, also met him, but no one suspects him of ideological Fascism per se as a result of that meeting and of the joint interests of the two against the Jews.

In his longer talk with Von Ribbentrop, the Nazi Foreign Minister, Nedic was more explicit, once again on the Nazi model, when he requested more *living space* for the Serbs and asked to annex to Serbia also Montenegro, the Sandjak, east Bosnia, and Kosovo. But the Germans refused to discuss the expansion of boundaries until after the war, though they pledged to return the command of the armed forces to Nedic and to open a university in Belgrade. These demands of Nedic can also be interpreted as indications on his part of his patriotism and dedication to the interest of the Serbian people, demands that even the *Cetniks* could easily adhere to. In fact, when the situation of the Germans began to deteriorate in 1944, as the Allies were closing on them on all sides, the German command in Yugoslavia devised a plan to unite all national forces of Serbia, including Nedic, Ljotic, and Mikhailovic to counter the Communist Partisans, sensing that those were the forces likely to sustain their hold on that front, but due to Hitler's furious rejection of the "danger of Greater Serbia," that plan was shelved. However, Nedic did convene those leaders in 1944, when the British shifted their assistance from the *Cetniks* to the Partisans, and suggested that the former be armed by Germany by means of moneys that he was prepared to budget to them. That plan was partly carried out with Mikhailovic commanding in addition to his troops also the Serbian Volunteer Corps until its demise.

The main indication of Nedic's convictions when he collaborated with the Nazis transpired when the retreating Nazis left Serbia and he was left with the options of either evacuating to Germany, getting Tito's pardon if he joined the Partisans with his forces, or continuing to pretend, as many Serbs do today, that he had never collaborated. The Serbs who were too deeply implicated with the collaboration indeed withdrew with the Nazis. On August 28, 1944, Nedic appointed his minister of education, Velibor Jonic, to manage the evacuation of the entire government, after its majority, including Nedic, voted to move to the Reich. In the plan were included five thousand intellectuals who supported the collaboration with the Nazis, whom Jonic wanted either to hide in the monasteries of the Orthodox Church, which had also approved of the collaboration, or to transfer to Germany. The Nedic government stopped operating in October, when the Soviets entered Belgrade and submitted the rule to Tito. The escapees, including Nedic, took with them many state funds, and when he left on the night of October 3, he declared that he was moving to Germany to take care of the three hundred thousand Serbs who were already there. There was fear that the Partisans and the Croats who supported Tito would massacre all the intellectuals and the elites who had collaborated, therefore they had to move out. Today we can judge that patriots who wish to serve their people do not behave like that and do not flee their country in times of duress.

It remains to test Nedic's practical conduct with the Jews under his rule, which could counter the thoroughly ingrained narrative that links the Serbs in "eternal friendship" with the Jews, which has been propagated since the end of the war, in order to exonerate the Serbs from any wrongdoing during the war, and gain them a new legitimacy in the eyes of the world, both in their alleged collaboration with the Germans, and in their much demonized culpability for the massacres they are lately accused of in the Bosnia war. The history of the Jews in Serbia and Yugoslavia has been covered in depth since the Jewish immigration, when they were expelled from Spain in the fifteenth century and found refuge in what was then the Ottoman Empire territory of the Balkans. At that time, Jews dwelt in towns, and the Serbs were peasants; thus the two populations came into little contact. But when the Ottoman rule receded and the Serbian dominance began to emerge, the Jewish existence began to encounter difficulties. Jews were expelled by rebelling Serbs in the nineteenth century from several towns where they had dwelt before, and when the insurgents captured Belgrade in 1806, Jewish homes, stores, and the synagogue were attacked and destroyed. Then, the Jews were only confined to Belgrade and prohibited from settling in the interior or owning real estate there. By 1869 only 210 Jewish families remained in Serbia.

At the end of the nineteenth century concern was voiced at the British Parliament about the persecution of Jews in Serbia, at a time when the latter was seeking to take its place in the "civilized communities of Europe," and the point was made that anti-Semitism was popular among the populace, although not necessarily in government circles. Even when the Berlin Congress (1878) granted independence to Serbia, and made it conditional on an equal treatment to Jews, Serbian common sentiment refused to let Jews participate in Serbian national life. However, in Croatia Jews were accorded full civil rights in 1873, and by the turn of the nineteenth century, there were twenty thousand Jews there, compared to only 6,500 in the much larger and more populated Serbia. When the Yugoslavian state was created, the former Ottoman and Habsburg Jews were merged into one community, but their relative prosperity and well-being of the 1920s was replaced in the 1930s by the apprehensions of the Jewish communities, due to the rise of Fascism locally and the general positive atmosphere toward Fascism throughout Europe. In 1936, the Federation of Jewish Communities submitted a libel charge against the ZBOR's German language newspaper, *Die Erwache*, which, following their Nazi Germany model, called for war against the Jews. But the suit was dismissed by the Belgrade court. The Federation had sued also in 1934, demanding a ban on the publication of the infamous *Protocols of the Elders of Zion* in Belgrade, but it again failed, opening the way for the republication of that anti-Semitic tract in 1939.

The anti-Jewish ambience in Yugoslavia worsened as the war approached, led by the patriarch of the Orthodox church, Petar Rosic. The Yugoslav minister of the interior, Anton Korosec, declared in 1938 that "there was no Jewish problem" in his country, adding in the same breath that Jewish refugees from Nazi Germany were not welcome in Yugoslavia, a position that was pretty common to most European countries and to North America by then, which prevented the rescue of millions of Jews who perished in the camps as a result. At the end of 1938, the sole Jewish representative in the Yugoslav Senate, Rabbi Isaac Alcalay, was ousted at the demand of Prime Minister Stojadinovic, and the vacancy was filled by a non-Jew, a measure that did not evince much sympathy for the brewing plight the Jews would be thrown into in the following months, especially after the German invasion in 1941. Indeed, already in 1940, prior to the German invasion, so it cannot be claimed today that it was dictated by the Nazis, the Royal government issued two anti-Jewish decrees, banning the Jews from producing food, and imposing a *numerus clausus* on Jewish registration to high schools and universities. It is as if France had imposed the same limitations on its Jews in 1939, prior to the German takeover of the country in June 1940, when the Nuremberg laws were enforced on French Jewry. Incidentally, in Croatia these measures were not enforced until the Ustasha takeover.

As Philip Cohen copiously documented,[7] the German occupation of Yugoslavia, which was not particularly resisted save by the Partisans and at times by the *Cetniks*, also prompted a profusion of anti-Semitic press, which facilitated the mistreatment of the Jews, the raffles that rounded them up, their concentration in camps within Yugoslavia, and then their extermination either in place, in camps like Jadovno and Jasenovac, or were dispatched to their tragic end in the death camps of Eastern Europe. One of those papers, the *Obnova*, proclaimed the Jews as the "ancient enemies of the Serbs, and that the Serbs would not wait to the Germans to begin the extermination of Jews." Other Serbian writers followed suit in what could be seen as the sealed fate of Yugoslavian Jewry. Thus, no one can claim today that it was only an extremist fanatic fringe that hated the Jews and wished to dispose of them, for the long dissertations a priori justifying the elimination of Jews, based on their historical undermining of Serbian nationhood, were omnipresent and vocally supported by government, populace, intelligentsia, church, military, and the common man in the street. It was the margin, according to the available documentation, which may have dissented from this ill-disposition toward the Jews, but its voice was either silent or silenced. This virulent anti-Semitism was served by false "citations" from the Talmud, which, betraying the lack of scholarly and intellectual decency and rigor, was proof and symptom of the backwardness of science in those confines until post-Communist Yugoslavia opened up to the world and balanced the system once again.

Most of the Jews of Serbia were eliminated during the first seventeen months of German occupation, as part of the German blueprint for the final solution. When Belgrade was conquered, one of the first acts of state was the registration of all Jews, their compulsory wearing of armbands for identification, the confiscation of their property, and economic limitations similar to measures imposed in Germany, Poland, and the ghettoes of Eastern Europe. The final solution also necessitated the concentration of Jews to facilitate their deportation. That is what the meaning of a concentration camp was: not a concentration of effort or intellect, just a herding together of those destined to die by the claws of the death machine and devoured in the entrails of its crematoria. So, already in August 1941, the Jews of Banat were transferred to Belgrade. By the end of 1941, most of the Jews aged over fourteen were incarcerated in the Topovske Supe camp in Belgrade, the Nazi "excuse" being that they led the Partisan movement, which launched its anti-German operations in July. When the Germans announced that for each killed German soldier they would eliminate fifty to one hundred Communists, to be shot by the *Wehrmacht*, Jews and Gypsies filled that quota almost daily. So by the end of 1941 most Jewish men aged fourteen to seventy were executed. In December, 1941, the Germans built the Sajmiste (Semlin) Camp across the Sava, to concentrate there the Jewish women and children. When the camp stood erect in December, five thousand Jews were stuffed there, and they perished by hunger, cold, filth, and illnesses. February 1942 saw more Jewish women and children from other cities like Nis, crowded into the camp, which then reached its top capacity of 6,300 inmates, including 10 percent Gypsies.

But it was not all direct Nazi deeds, which were helplessly watched by the infuriated Serbs who could not bear the sight but could do nothing, as many Vichy officials later claimed when they were tried as traitors for their collaboration with the Germans; many Serbs helped the Nazis in pursuing the final solution, beyond what they were forced to do. Primary among them were the Serbian Volunteer Corps, originally the military arm of the ZBOR, which was sent as a labor brigade, under Ljotic, from Smederevo to Belgrade as an auxiliary to the Gestapo. They searched private apartments, guarded arrested Communists and Jews, and fought the Partisans. On July 27, 1,200 Belgrade Jews surrendered to the occupation power, and the Ljotic people were in charge of sorting them out professionally, sending most of them to forced labor, and keeping 120 of them as hostages, who were executed two days later in retaliation for a Partisan strike. Members of Ljotic's Corps continued to hunt for hiding elderly Jews to send them to forced labor. The local press praised the Volunteer Corps for capturing seven Belgrade Jews who tried to hide under Serbian names in Nis. Incidentally, when the *Cetniks* also began collaborating, they also scoured the countryside in search for hiding Jews, often murdered them by slitting their throats and mutilating them, or handed them over to the Gestapo. Jews complained about their relentless persecution by the *Cetniks* under Mikhailovic, who then slaughtered them "in a bestial way." This, of course, caused Jewish resistance fighters to abandon the *Cetniks* and join the Partisans. Conversely, part of the *Cetnik* plans to destroy the Partisans in Bosnia was predicated on the assumption that they were "composed of Ustasha, Jews, Bulgarians, etc. . . ."[8] On another occasion, the *Cetniks* did not give any useful information to the Germans about the Partisan leaders, except for mentioning a Jew named Lindenmaier.[9]

Mikhailovic counted the Jews among the worst enemies of the Serbian people, and so did Nedic when he accused the Partisans of being a "criminal-Jewish gang." These bewildering anti-Jewish attitudes, toward an element of society that was loyal, productive, and ready to fight in the resistance to the Germans, came to their apex in the Grand

Anti-Masonic Exhibition that opened in Belgrade in October 1941, under German occupation, which focused on the Jewish-Masonic-Communist conspiracy for world dominion and included vitriolic anti-Semitic propaganda. Nazi Germany had occupied most of Yugoslavia by April 1941, but after a Serbian uprising of July 1941, the Nazi General Hermann Bohme was given emergency powers to govern the country. Under him, SS *Gruppenfuhrer* Harold Turner and SS *Untersturmfuhrer* Fritz Stracke handled the administration of Serbia. Milan Nedic was the nominal local ruler, comparable to the collaborationist regime of Quisling in Norway. "Under the Nedic regime, the heavily anti-Semitic Grand Anti-Masonic Exhibition opened in occupied Belgrade on October 22, 1941, and ended on January 19, 1942. It was funded apparently by the German occupiers and supported by Nedic to intensify hatred against the Jews, although the title of the exhibit suggested that the target was the Masons (Masonic Orders had been closed in Germany."[10] But contrary to Nedic, who was a supporter of the German plan of extermination of the Jews, Serbian Partisan groups often tried to save Jews from their lot, often by incorporating them into their ranks. The history of this period is complex, filled with mutual accusations regarding the role of perpetrators and rescuers, so it is difficult to sort out the one from the other.[11]

Many Serbs, amounting to an impressive eighty thousand people—sadly and symbolically equivalent to the total number of Jews who perished in Yugoslavia and its vicinity—including an approving Nedic, and some of his ministers, attended the exhibition, which attests to the degree of consent and willing collaboration of the general populace with those vicious trends. The central theme was an alleged Jewish-Communist-Masonic plot for world domination, similar to propaganda once put out by the czarist secret police before the Russian revolution in the well-known forgeries *The Protocols of the Elders of Zion*. Besides the exhibits at the exhibition, an enormous amount of propaganda material was prepared: over 200,000 various brochures, 60,000 posters, 100,000 flyers, 108,000 samples of nine different types of envelopes, 176 propaganda movie clips, four different postage stamps, etc. Organizers advertised that "This concept of exhibition will be unique not only in Serbia and the Balkans, not only in southeastern Europe and Europe, but in the world."[12] The images on the posters shown in the exhibition were hardly new and had been seen before in Germany during "The Eternal Jew" exhibitions in Munich and Vienna during 1937–1939. Serbian newspapers such as *Obnova* (Renewal) and *Nasa Borba* (Our

Struggle) praised this exhibit, proclaiming that Jews were the ancient enemies of the Serbian people and that Serbs should not wait for the Germans to begin the extermination of the Jews.

The twenty posters shown there gave a sense of the vile flavor of the exhibition and the theme of Jewish domination. "In January 1942 the Serbian authorities issued a stamp commemorating the exhibition, and if anyone still had any doubts about its intention, Jewish symbols, which were printed on the stamps, portrayed Judaism as the source of world evil and advocated the humiliation and violent subjugation of the Jews by the Serbs, if any were left by then."[13] Some Serbian writers accused the Jews of bringing upon Serbia the March 27 coup, and in consequence the April 6 German invasion; therefore they taught that there should be little compassion for Jewish suffering.

The groups that ensured public order under Nedic also desecrated Jewish synagogues and cemeteries throughout Serbia, assisted in manhunts against Jews, and were responsible for delivering food to the inmates of the camps. But they delivered less than specified by the Germans to keep the prisoners alive, hence the massive amount of death from hunger and illnesses. A mobile gassing van then arrived from Germany to Sajmiste, and between March and May, it was loaded many times a day with women, the elderly, and children, mostly Jews. The exhaust fumes were then directed to the sealed vehicle, until all were choked, and the van directed to the burial site of Avala. In this fashion, seven thousand Jews were exterminated, and the dying cries and poundings of the victims became known in all Belgrade while the sealed vehicle was making its way to the cemetery. The clothes of the victims were sold to Serbian businessmen who had contracted with the Gestapo. Nedic and others in the Orthodox church, as Cohen definitively demonstrates,[14] were aware and supportive of the German extermination plan and execution, and they were not loath to lend a hand to the effort when asked.

A letter to the editor, which arrived at the offices of the *Independent* in London, on October 24, 1991, signed by Lea Bauman, who claimed to be a member of the Jewish leadership of Zagreb, wrote that "60,000 Jews from all parts of Serbia were transported to three concentration camps in Serbia, where they were destroyed.... The killing was carried out by Serbs." But this information was contradicted by the Jewish community in Belgrade, who established, citing the *Encyclopaedia of the Holocaust* and the findings of Christopher Browning,[15] that the entire Jewish population of Serbia on the eve of World War II was sixteen thousand, fourteen thousand of whom perished during the Holocaust at the hands of the *Wehrmacht* and the SS. Maybe the difference in numbers can be explained in terms of the similarity in pronounciation that make the two figures sound close to each other when spoken, and in any case, the Serbian version seems closer to reality than the Croatian, if there ever was an official figure backed by official Zagreb. Similarly, a Croatian source, Anto Knezevic, wrote in the *Time Literary Supplement*, on May 31, 1993 that in the Semlin Camp in Belgrade, it was Serbian soldiers who pushed the Jewish victims into the gas van, while the Jewish community of Belgrade rejected that allegation, insisting that it was the Nazis themselves. The controversy here is about technical detail and a matter of throwing off the yoke of culpability and placing it on the shoulders of the other. For the Jewish victims it made no difference who pushed them, they perished all the same. The numbers will remain a matter of conflict for years to come.

In 1993, an Austrian historian, Walter Manoschek, published his *Serbien ist Judenfrei: Militarische Besatzungspolitik und Judenvernichtung in Serbien, 1941–42.*[16] This was originally a doctoral dissertation presented at the University of Vienna, which won the London Wiener Library's Fraenkel Prize and raised a storm even before it was published as a book. A prepublication excerpt in the German weekly, *Die Zeit*, stirred a lot of comment about the *Wehrmacht's* doings during the war. In fact, Manosheck's book pursued the pioneer work of Christopher Brown, cited above, regarding the involvement of the German army in the massacre of Serbian Jews, based on three assumptions:

1. He supports Brown's contention that mass killings of civilians, especially Jews, began in Serbia before 1942. As a result, he too criticizes Arno Maye, who claimed that the radicalization of the Nazi anti-Jewish program only came after the military reverses on the Soviet front;
2. Manoschek proves conclusively that the German army, which ran the German occupation, cooperated with the SS and carried out, often on its own, brutal reprisal policies against civilians and Jews;
3. As an Austrian student, who chose his topic during the Waldheim controversy,[17] Manoschek underlined the strong presence of Austrians among the Nazi administration and occupation troops.[18]

Another sort of analysis is offered to us by Milan Ristovic,[19] who described the poignant reunion of the impoverished remnants of the Jewish community, who had survived the Nazi rampages by hiding in the surrounding villages, in the sole synagogue of Belgrade, which the occupying Germans soldiers had used as a brothel. That image alone is strong enough to encompass what Yugoslavian Jewry had undergone during the war. The general numbers are agreed: that some 80 percent of Yugoslavian Jews, who had counted some eighty-two thousand in numbers, including several European Jews who found refuge in Yugoslavia, were exterminated in camps—either in Yugoslavia or deported to Poland and Germany—while others were murdered by firing squads or when they succumbed to hunger and illness by the deprivations of the war or the persecutions by the Nazis and their collaborators. The fifteen thousand who survived that genocide did so by hiding, changing identity, or fleeing from the occupied zones to the Partisans (almost a third, or over 4,500, of them). Some of them had even spent time in POW camps as officers and enlisted men in the Yugoslav armed forces. Thus, among the almost twelve thousand members of the Belgrade Jewish community, only about 1,100, or 16 percent, survived. In other areas of the interior, many Jewish communities were eliminated in their totality. While these numbers are little disputed, it remains a matter of controversy to identify who exactly did the killing, especially in Serbia (the other areas under the Ustasha are dealt with separately under the headings of Jadovno and Jasenovac), under what circumstances, and whether Serbia deserved the self-assigned title of the "Righteous among Nations" or has undeservedly usurped it.

Forty percent of the Jews of Yugoslavia, about thirty thousand of the total, lived in Serbia prior to the war, the Ashkenazi part in the Vojvodina area, mainly in Novisad, which was related to the much larger Hungarian Jewry, while the Sephardic component dwelt south of the Sava and the Danube and emanated from old Ottoman subjects and Spanish exiles. There is also no denying that, since the rise of Nazism in Germany and the beginning of Nazi expansion in Europe, anti-Semitic politics became more widespread, which converged toward the final solution that the Germans and their allies started to implement even prior to the Wannsee Conference in 1942. Since Jewish refugees were flowing in from all over Europe, in search for a secure land to accept them, the Yugoslavian government, like others in Europe, imposed laws to restrict their immigration and absorption within Yugoslavian boundaries, although the Jewish community exerted tremendous efforts and took enormous risks to assist them, where and when it could. Several refugee camps were set in Serbia, notably in Niska Banja (160 people), Kursumlijska Banja (380 people), and the Sabac camp on the River Sava, where the 1,200 people, stranded travelers of the

27

"Kladovo transport," originating from Germany and Central Europe, who were headed for Palestine, but were barred by the British (after the White Paper of 1939) from setting foot there, or from getting further down the river, by the Romanians who were coming closer to the Axis when the war broke out.

In those early days, the killing of Jews and others was done by the *Wehrmacht* occupying units and not yet by the specifically designed SS or *Einsatzgruppen* units. The regular military forces turned to the active extermination of "unwanted groups," including Jews, right after they completed their occupation and set up a military government over the newly acquired territories. By the summer of 1941, upon completing the occupation of Serbia, most of the adult Jewish population of Belgrade, Banat, and Central Serbia were rounded up and decimated, totaling over five thousand victims, and since May 1942, the list of the murdered also included women and children who had been interred in the Jewish Camp Zemun (Sajmiste), in especially equipped gas-chamber vehicles. Many were executed in reprisal for *Cetnik* or Partisan attacks against the occupying Nazis, although most of them had nothing to do with those activities, and the only reason for their decimation was that they were to be annihilated in any case as part of the final solution. The mass execution of the bulk of Serbian Jews began in the fall of 1941, also prior to the adoption of the final solution in early 1942. Unlike other parts of Europe, where Jews were collected and then dispatched to the death camps eastward, most of the Serbian Jews were exterminated near their homes, and some, like those of Novi Sad, within their homes. We are talking strictly about the remaining Serbian territory directly ruled by the Nazis, after several parts were annexed either by the NDH (Ustasha State) or the other Axis allies, such as Italy, Hungary, and Bulgaria. The extermination of Jews (and Serbs) in those areas was conditioned, for better (in the case of the Italian-controlled territory) or for worse (especially under the Ustasha regime), by the nature of local authorities, without much interference by the Reich. Thus, this latter category had much less of a chance to escape certain captivity and death, while the former, under the more lenient Italians and Bulgarians, could slip between the narrow cracks of the murderers and escape, hide, fight, and survive.

In Belgrade, immediately upon the occupation, the Germans established a Jewish Police inside the city administration, supervised by the Gestapo, which initiated the registration of the Jews and marked them with yellow bands, with the help of the domestic collaborators.

This is the critical issue that can either exonerate or condemn Serbian anti-Semites for active participation in the Holocaust. Thus, 8,500 Jews registered in Belgrade in those three days, meaning that people who knew the Jewish community intimately enough to account for each of its individuals, had been hard at work to reveal its secrets, organization, and whereabouts, instead of hiding them, warn them of the coming arrest and calamity, and help them evade incarceration and death. By the end of June, the list had increased by six hundred more, indicating that after the first massive census, a search for more victims continued unabated. When similar procedures, under similar circumstances, were started in Copenhagen, to give a counterexample for the sake of comparison, the local citizenry, which was more humane and less collaborative with the occupiers, shipped at night, in volunteer fishermen's boats, all their thousands of Jews across the straits to Sweden to rescue them. No similar attempt, or even gesture toward it, was recorded in Belgrade, though the mountainous countryside and the forests around the capital were there to offer some hiding. The proof being that *Cetniks* and Partisans did hide there and did threaten German forces. Partisans did take in Jews, who fought with them, less so the *Cetniks*, whose arguable anti-Semitic propensities, born out of their fanatic nationalism, did not let them lift a finger in their regard. Ironically, and shamefully, not only did the Belgrade citizenry not do much to check and reduce the impact of German arrests of Jews, but by helping the Germans to find them, and then leaving them at the mercy of the occupiers, their numbers were rapidly decreased when they were taken hostage and executed in the retaliatory acts of the Nazis, until the daily hundred executions quota rapidly depleted their ranks.

It is one thing for the Serbs, with some remarkable exceptions, to feign helplessness in the face of the cruel German occupiers, and to invoke the constraint that the occupation imposed on them when they refrained from initiating any major move to rescue hundreds or thousands of their Jewry; it is quite another, not only to collaborate with the occupiers, at times enthusiastically so, in searching for the Jews and arresting them, but also to wash their hands clean of the whole episode and even advance the almost preposterous proposition that they were "righteous." Only three thousand, that is 25 percent of Belgrade Jews, never responded to the German orders to register; they went into hiding, either in the city or in the environing countryside. That a quarter of the Jewish population could be rescued proves, first of all, that it was possible, despite the domestic police that was under

29

German command, to evade the German finest nets, for those who dared and tried; and secondly that there were some decent and good-hearted Serbian people, who in the midst of the moral impotence and human indolence that had overtaken most European societies under the Nazi sway, several enclaves of human decency did survive, which saved the honor of human kind for the historical record and for generations to come. It is to those individuals and groups who made that high-risk human effort that this inquisitive and pessimistic chapter is dedicated.

It may well be that the local Serbs, like other occupied nations, could do little to alleviate the plight of the Jews given the enforcement of racial laws or in the expropriation of Jewish property or in banning Jews from public employment and from entering public places—even more so when surviving Jews, men and women, were obliged to forced labor. But here too a little ingenuity, like hiding Jews in monasteries, had the Orthodox church been amenable, or sabotaging the implementation of those harsh rules, if there were enough humane bureaucrats whose decency surpassed their hatred and prejudices, could have done wonders in soft-pedaling Jewish suffering. Quite the contrary, it seemed that the May 31 regulations, which codified all the anti-Jewish measures into one comprehensive system geared toward "legalizing" the ongoing horrors against the Jews and engraving in stone that Jews were an inferior race, whose persecution is unpunishable, went quite well with the Serbian well-entrenched anti-Semitic sentiment prevalent in such groups as the ZBOR, the *Cetniks* to an extent, and Nedic's administration, as shown above. In fact the Jews of Banat, some 4,200 of them, suffered the same fate and were degraded, humiliated, boycotted, and dispossessed, under the same regulations as their Belgrade coreligionists, mainly by their neighbors, the so-called *Volksdeutsche* collaborators with the Germans. Many of those Jews were arrested and executed by the *Wehrmacht* and its local collaborators, while others were transferred to Belgrade, where the extermination of Jews had accumulated some field experience and "efficiency." There, men were incarcerated in the former artillery barracks (*Topovske supe*), together with fellow Belgrade Jews, while women and children were taken to the Jewish camp at Sajmiste, described above.

On July 25, 1941, a seventeen-year-old Jew, Elijas Almosino, attacked a German truck, resulting in the shooting of 122 Jews, who would have died in any case, for the Nazis needed no pretext or justification. But the Germans explained that their mass executions had a double purpose: on the one hand, as retaliation for the resistance attacks against them, and on the other hand, for speeding up the elimination of Jews and passing on the responsibility for genocide to the resistance victims. The inclusion of many Jews in the quota of one hundred executed for every German killed in the attacks of the resistance was explained thus: that the Jews were also Serbs and in addition had to be eliminated as Jews. In this way, some five thousand Serbian Jews over the age of fourteen were executed, so many that at the beginning of November 1941, well prior to Wannsee, there were no more living male Jews (or Gypsies for that matter) to be used as temporary hostages until their inescapable execution. In December, Jewish women and children were rounded up and incarcerated in Semlin, and between March and May 1942, all were put to death in the mobile gas chamber, especially designed for them there, so that the regional German commander could report that Serbia was the only country where the Jewish (and the Gypsy) problem was "completely resolved," and that the only remaining Jews were those married to other nationals. The whole genocidal operation in central Serbia and Banat, resulted in 11,000 and 3,800 murdered Jews, respectively.[20]

These data, which indicate in no uncertain terms the German leading and determining role in the Jewish annihilation, leave nevertheless some open questions regarding the tenacity, enthusiasm, and eagerness of Serbian collaboration in this project, or conversely, the degree of Serbian reluctance, and their attempts to resist and to rescue the Jews from their sealed fate. The Milan Nedic government, which was installed in August 1941, under full control of the occupation forces, quickly became an instrument of brutal oppression. But even before that, as early as June, the Ministry of Interior, which comprised a Special Division for the State Protection, responsible for Jews and Gypsies, issued an order to all city and county councils of Serbia, to serve notice to all their Jewish and Gypsy employees of the coming discriminatory policies against them. Milan Nedic asked the German military commander to take measures against Jewish Yugoslav army officers for spreading infamous Communist propaganda. When extermination of the Jews began, the Germans assigned the role of auxiliary instruments to domestic civilian and military collaborationist authorities, which were made responsible for registration of the Jews, their arrest and imprisonment, search of fugitives, and for help in running the concentration camp Banjica in Belgrade. That camp was jointly administered by the German occupiers and their Yugoslav aids. Though the Germans took the leading and guiding role toward the final solution in Serbia, with the Gestapo supervising the operation, and they monopolized the killing of Jews, Gypsies, and dissident Serbs, they were actively aided in that role by Serbian collaborators.

According to Ristovic's account, the collaborationist Serbian police had three operational divisions: one dealing with foreigners, one to suppress Communist actions, and one for Jews and Gypsies, which operated from April 1941, when occupation began, until the spring of 1943, when the extermination was nearly completed and the German defenses started to crumble. Milan Acimovic held the post of chief of the Home Affairs Commissariat. The police force comprised 850 constables, who obediently suppressed all "subversive activity" and actively pursued the "enemies of the occupation." Milan Nedic, in a document that is cited by Ristovic,[21] did not seem to regret, much less to oppose, the persecutions of Jews, when remarking that "owing to the occupier, we have freed ourselves of Jews, and that is now up to us to rid ourselves of other immoral elements standing in the way of Serbia's spiritual and national unity." Taken at face value, that does not sound like a philo-semitic stance to take in the face of the German exterminationist policies. Thus, the collaborationist organizations, such as the Serbian State Guard, the Serbian Volunteer Corps, the domestic police, and the National Salvation Government of Nedic, did play a role in raids, arrests, and delivery to the Germans of the local Jews. No valiant attempt of note was recorded, in the operations of these Serbian bodies, to sabotage, slow down, or otherwise disturb the smooth and sinister operation of these tools of German extermination plans, of which all its operatives were aware. If anything, it seems that outbursts of overzealous diligence, in carrying out those horrible orders, marked those activities more than otherwise, which brought them close in nature and gravity, though not quite similar, to what the Ustashas did.

Serbs did not only collaborate with Germans in the implementation of their obvious anti-Jewish policies, but they were also aware of the incarceration and death camps that were erected on Serbian territory, without making much of any effort to hamper those plans, to attack the camps in order to free the inmates, or to show kindness toward the inmates so as to alleviate their suffering as long as they lived. In the area of Belgrade alone, three camps were set up:

Banjica (alias known as the *Anhalteleger Dedinje*), opened in July 1941. The extant camp registers contained some 23,000 names, 688 of whom were Jewish, including children and even babies. Among them were Jews of Belgrade, Banat, and the Serbian interior, and Jews of foreign nationality, originating from various European countries but caught up by the war. At least 382 Jews were murdered in the camp and another 186 were transferred to the "Jewish" camp Zemun (Sajmiste). Another 103 victims were taken from the camp by the Gestapo, and a small number of those who survived were sent to forced labor, were transferred elsewhere, or were not accounted for. In this camp, the Gestapo played the main role of executioners, but they were aided by the camp's administration and other camp employees under the authority of the Special Police, which was made up of Serbs.

Topovske Supe did not yield the same detailed information as **Banjica.** It was opened in August 1941, in the former artillery barracks outside Belgrade, and intended to intern the Jews of Banat, but Jewish interns from Belgrade also joined. Though it was operated by the Gestapo, it was guarded by the local gendarmerie. Its inmates served as a pool of hostages who were killed as part of the retaliation policy of the Nazis for any act of violence against them. Executions were carried out by firing squads in such locations as Jajinci and Jabuka, where mass graves were dug to bury the murdered victims. By October, 1941 those squads had executed two hundred Jews and two hundred Gypsies in those locations. By that time, very few of the initial interns were still alive, and the camp facilities were filled with the latest arrivals of the last roundups of the Jews of Serbia. In October and November 1941, some 2,200 people of each of the two ethnic groups (4,400 in total) were executed—so many that Belgrade became the "leading pit of the Holocaust," apparently a well-earned epithet, though of a sinister value.

The **Belgrade Fair (Sajmiste)** Camp was opened in October 1941; it absorbed some of the inmates of the older **Banjica** Camp and was dubbed the "Jewish" camp Zemun (Sajmiste, or *Judenlager* Semlin). The Jewish women and children were taken for execution and mass burial from there to Jajinci. The facilities of the Belgrade Fair, which had been destroyed in the April bombardment of the city, were refurbished and converted into accommodation space for prisoners and personnel. It was located on the left side of the Sava and commanded by a Gestapo officer. No complete registers of the inmates are extant, but in January 1942 there were some 6,500 prisoners there, and in February they went down to 5,500, including 332 men, 3,933 women, and 1,238 children. By April, by reason of the pace of extermination, there remained only 1,884 inmates.

Later, the camp was renamed the Concentration Camp Zemun (*Ahhalte Lager*) and served to accommodate the last groups of Jews who were arrested upon the capitulation of Italy in 1943, captured Partisan and *Cetnik* fighters, sympathizers of the Greek and Albanian Resistance, and Serbian peasants from villages in Srem or the mountain area of Kozara and other Serbian territories under Ustasha rule, who were transferred there from Jasenovac.

Apart from those three major camps in the Belgrade area, which were erected in and around the capital to facilitate supervision over them by the Nazi administration and its local collaborators, other lesser incarceration facilities were spread all over the country. Camp Sabac earned a particularly bloody reputation in the short time of its operation. It was opened in fall 1941, and it interned the inhabitants of the neighboring villages and the small, local Jewish community, as well as Jewish refugees from central Europe, known as the "Kladovo transport"—a sad story unto itself, which intermeshed with the tragedy of Yugoslavian Jews. As early as 1933, and especially after the Austrian *Anschluss* in 1938, the expulsion and then the annihilation of Jewish citizens became one of the main goals of the National Socialist regime. Moreover, first waves of deportations from Vienna to German-occupied Poland also started in October 1939. While pursuing its anti-Semitic policy, the Nazi government increasingly forced Jews to emigrate from the Third Reich until 1940. (Emigration was not officially prohibited until the fall of 1941.) In view of this situation, the so-called Free World more and more rigorously barred its doors to the refugee flow. Especially after the outbreak of World War II, Jews were only able to flee to certain countries overseas or join "illegal transports" to Palestine. These transports became a mass salvation program from mid-1938 onward. In spite of British immigration restrictions, refugees continued to be smuggled into Palestine from then on. These clandestine transports became all the more important in 1939 because the British authorities froze legal immigration into Palestine in May by way of the White Paper proclamation. After the outbreak of the war, Jews from the Third Reich were strictly forbidden to directly immigrate into Palestine as Jews born in Germany were considered by the British to be "enemy aliens." Only refugees who had already reached a neutral country were able to obtain an immigration certificate and even then only under certain conditions.

In view of the increasingly drastic persecution in Austria, now called *Ostmark*, and out of fear of new SS deportations, Georg Über-all (later Ehud Avriel), the secretary general of the Jewish *He-Haluts* (The Pioneer) movement and representative of Mossad in Vienna, made a grave decision in late 1939: He wanted all remaining members of his movement in Ostmark to leave the country, even though no deep-sea vessels were ready to transport them to Palestine from the Danube delta. For the first time, a group of 120 *Youth Aliya* (the official immigration movement of Jewish youth of the Zionist organization) members also joined an illegal transport. Several hundred persons, who were first brought to Bratislava, including 822 people from Vienna, 130 from Berlin, and 50 from Gdansk (then Danzig), initially joined the transport. In Bratislava another hundred refugees from Prague and Bratislava were added to the group. In the winter of 1939, the Danube was going to freeze over, and the Slovak authorities intended to send the group back to the German border. Georg Überall and Moshe Agami, the Mossad officials in Vienna and Geneva, respectively, urged the refugees to continue their trip, even though no ship was ready for them at the mouth of the Danube. After a ten-day sojourn, the refugees departed from Bratislava on the "Uranus," an excursion boat owned by the Danube Steam Boat Company and decorated with the swastika flag. No sooner had the boat reached the Hungarian border than it was unexpectedly stopped and turned back to its initial point of departure. On December 13 the trip started anew, but a few days later the passengers were transferred mid-river to three Yugoslav excursion boats—the "Car Nikola," the "Car Dušan," and the "Kraljica Marija." Sime Spitzer, the secretary general of the Association of Jewish Communities in Yugoslavia, had chartered these boats from the Yugoslav national shipping company on Mossad's instructions. The reason for this unexpected turn was because the Danube Boat Company refused to continue the trip on the "Uranus" as long as the transshipment at the mouth of the Danube remained uncertain.

The voyage on the Yugoslav ships also ended abruptly, however, this time in the tri-state area between Yugoslavia, Romania, and Bulgaria. The Romanian authorities prohibited the passage for the same reason. It soon became clear that the weather conditions made a continuation of the trip impossible in the foreseeable future. On December 31, 1939, the ships were directed to the winter harbor in the Yugoslav town of Kladovo near the Iron Gate. In this little town, fifty-four kilometers from the nearest railway station and practically cut off from the outside world in winter, the refugees waited for the ice to melt. Spitzer had to promise the Yugoslav government that he would be responsible for the group's upkeep. At that time, thousands of refugees from Germany and Austria were also living in Yugoslavia alongside the country's Jewish community of 71,200. Several assembly camps were set up for refugees from the Third Reich. Cramped conditions, dirt, and a biting frost made life on the boats unbearable. It would be weeks before the refugees were allowed to spend even a limited amount of time on shore. Finally, the shipping company urged the group to vacate the three steamboats. The refugees subsequently moved on land—some to the village, others to barracks and tents on shore. A malaria epidemic soon broke out in the tents and barracks, which were close to big swamps. Malnutrition, filth, and insect infestations also contributed to outbreaks of scabies and furunculosis. There were also isolated cases of polio and typhus.

In September 1940 the group was finally able to leave Kladovo. Their trip, however, did not lead them toward the Danube delta, but a few hundred kilometers upriver, to the Serbian town of Šabac on the Sava River. The rerouting of the group was caused by a large-scale resettlement of ethnic Germans from Romania overseen by the SS. These re-settlers were transported upstream, also on the Danube Boat Company steamboats, and temporarily put up in reception camps in the Serbian villages of Kladovo and Prahovo. On September 22, 1940, the refugees reached the small town of Šabac. There, older people and couples were put up in private rooms, while the majority of young people were quartered in an abandoned grain mill that had been adapted for these purposes. Although they had to observe some restrictions, the refugees were allowed to move freely about town. After the refugees arrived in Šabac, their living conditions improved. The transport participants enjoyed greater freedom of movement and a more stable way of life. The various Zionist youth groups gained in importance. They tried to give their members encouragement through a tight social structure, strict discipline, and extremely organized daily routines. Even though it was officially prohibited, many members sought to earn some pocket money through employment opportunities in Šabac. In spite of this relief, the refugees were still living on standby; many times their departure was announced, and they had to pack their bags and be ready.

In the final months before the German attack on Yugoslavia, in early 1941, the threat of war became more and more palpable in Šabac. Refugees from the Third Reich were still streaming over the borders, and the refugee community in Šabac increased to an estimated 1,400 people. Just prior to the German attack on Yugoslavia, a small number of the Kladovo refugees were able to escape to Palestine with certificates. Estimates, of those who survived, range from 200 to 280 people. Most of the transport participants saved were members of *Youth Aliya* (i.e., fifteen to seventeen year olds). Some adult attendants, a number of older girls with WIZO (Women Zionist Organization) certificates, and a small number of older people for whom relatives in Palestine had vouched, were also able to flee. When the German army marched into Yugoslavia, more than 1,100 Jewish Kladovo refugees remained in the Serbian town of Šabac. After the attack on the Soviet Union on June 22, 1941, the German regime started a systematic extermination of Jews in the East. The Kladovo Group thus did not stand a chance of leaving Serbia in the summer of 1941. Out of all the Kladovo refugees remaining in Serbia at the time of the German attack on Yugoslavia in April 1941, only a handful managed to escape from the Nazis and survive the war.

When twenty-one German soldiers were killed by Partisans in early October 1941, General Böhme, the German military governor of Serbia, ordered the execution of 2,100 people in retaliation—one hundred people for every German killed—and 805 Jews and Gypsies from the Šabac camp, which included all the men from the Kladovo Transport, fell victim to this reprisal. In January 1942 the women and children of the Kladovo Transport were sent to the Sajmište concentration camp near Belgrade, where Jewish women and children from Serbia were already interned. These former fairgrounds were ill-adapted to serve as a camp. More than seven thousand women—among them the very old, children, and newborns—languished in barracks in the biting cold. Many froze or starved to death, the remaining survivors were gassed inside transport trucks. It was not until the end of the war that some details became known of the tragic fate of the Kladovo Transport members left behind in Serbia. To this day, some family members do not know exactly how their relatives perished in Serbia. Be that as it may, though these Jewish refugees were not part of Yugoslavian Jewry, they were not rejected or ejected by the authorities prior to German invasion, and they were even given shelter that was refused in other European countries, a testament to Serbian generosity toward Jews in the country in that time, in spite of the anti-Semitic movements that we have described above. Only when the Nedic government was installed, which collaborated with the German occupiers, were the borders tightly sealed, and there was no escape for all trapped Jews. The fate of Jewish refugees in Serbia, like that of Serbian and other Yugoslavian Jews, was irrevocably sealed.

At the peak of October 1941, there were twenty thousand inmates at Sabac captured during the mopping up operations of the Nazis against resistance forces. Since facilities were rudimentary, some prisoners lived in open space, but the persistent overcrowding led the authorities by the end of the month to free 25 percent of the inmates, who were border cases in the eyes of the authorities, while the extreme 5 percent were executed by firing squads. Thus, the population was reduced by six thousand in that month, while the total of murdered prisoners amounted to 2,685 between September and November, including the Jews of the Kladovo transport. There was also the camp of the "Red Cross" in Nis, which was planned originally as a transitory facility (*Durchgangslager*), but it turned into a concentration camp in September 1941, where Jews were separated from other inmates. In 1941–42, five hundred Jewish prisoners were incarcerated there, originating not only from Nis but also from Leskovac, Zajecar, and Valjevo. After February 12, 1942, when 105 Serbian inmates escaped, half of whom perished or were recaptured, Germans initiated, in retaliation, mass executions of Jewish male prisoners, while women and children were transferred to Sajmiste near Belgrade and murdered there.

Jews were not spared in the Serbian zones that were annexed by Italy, Hungary, Bulgaria, and Albania either. On January 12, 1943, the Bulgar authorities rounded up the Jews of Pirot and transported them by cattle train to the Danube port of Lom in Bulgaria, where they were shipped to Vienna, together with Jews from Thrace and Vardar Macedonia, and then to Treblinka, where they all perished. The only Jewish survivors of Pirot were those taken as POWs by the Germans as servicemen of the Yugoslav army. Kosovo Jews, who came to be included under the more lenient Italian authorities, were interned in a camp in Pristina at the beginning of 1942. In March 1942, some of them were handed over to the Germans and transported to the Belgrade Sajmiste camp, where they were murdered. Others, together with Serbs, were transferred to the Berat Camp in Albania, where they remained until Italy's capitulation. Then, as the rule over Kosovo was taken over by local Albanian Fascists, who were backed by the Nazis, they arrested the rest of Kosovo Jews in Pristina and also transported them to Belgrade's Sajmiste camp. Altogether, some four hundred Jews, together with others arrested in Montenegro, were transported to their death in Bergen-Belsen, save for about a hundred of them who survived. In March 1942, the Gestapo arrested most of the three hundred Jews of Novi Pazar and dispatched them to Sajmiste where they were gassed to death.

In the Hungarian-occupied part of Serbia, Jews were exposed to plundering of property, maltreatment, forced labor, financial extortion, and internment in camps. Jews who had not been domiciled in that Backa region before 1918 were banished to Serbia Proper or to

Croatia or were handed over to the German occupiers in Belgrade. The Hungarians were particularly strict on "verification of status" for the Jews, as a means of more extortion and blackmail. Using as a further pretext the *Cetnik* and other Serbian "rebellions," and the need of their troops to maintain order, the Hungarians could avoid yielding to German demands to send stronger contingents to fight on the Russian front. In January 1942, they arrested more than eight hundred Jews in Novi Sad and then threw them in the ice-cold waters of the Danube, either drowning them alive or disposing of them after they were murdered by mallets and knives. Serbs also were victimized by the Hungarian occupiers, but in proportion to their minority numbers, the amount of the Jews was higher. For example, out of the 215 victims in Stari-Becej, 110 were Jews. In Curug, out of a thousand victims, one hundred were Jews. In Zabalj, all twenty-nine Jews were eliminated. All in all, some four thousand victims fell in the Backa area, which became practically *Judenrein*.[22] These raids, where Serbs and Jews were lumped together in the genocidal process launched by the Germans and their aids, have been one of the major reasons for the claims later advanced by Serbs of their joint lot with the Jews as victims of the Nazis, thinking that this in itself would suffice to remove the indelible anti-Semitic blots of Nedic, Ljotic, some *Cetniks*, and many ignorant commoners and bigoted intellectuals and professionals.

The fall of Horty and the direct occupation of Hungary by the Nazis, in spring 1944, also impacted the Backa region. The remaining Jews of Novi Sad and the other towns of the region were rounded up and sent to their death in Auschwitz, and a concentration camp for four thousand people was erected at Subotica. Eight thousand Jews of Vojvodina were incarcerated in the Hungarian town of Baya. A total of fifteen thousand inmates, including women, children, the old, and ailing, were sent for physical elimination in Auschwitz. Seven hundred were sent to Austria for slave labor. Earlier, some 1,500 Jews had been sent to the Ukraine as forced laborers and killed, and another 2,500 Jews from Backa had been mobilized to "work units" in Hungary, most of whom also perished. The Bor copper mines, in which mostly Hungarian Jews were forced to work, were abandoned during the German and Hungarian retreat from Serbia, and the Jewish laborers were marched in two columns of 3,600 and 2,500 prisoners respectively; most of them perished, except for a small number that arrived in Baya alive. In summary, out of the more than thirteen thousand Jews who lived in the Backa area of Serbia prior to the Hungarian invasion, more than ten thousand were murdered, mostly by Germans in their most infamous camp: Auschwitz.[23]

Once again, the mutual perpetual recriminations between Serbs and Croats as to who killed more Jews, and did so more readily in collaboration with the Nazis than the other, in which many Western writers have taken sides, will remain outside the frame of this volume, because that is not its main focus, and it is not my desire, or within my capacity, to add anything useful to this old, raging, and undecided debate. I have seen wide-ranging evidence on both sides, and it would require a separate inquest into that controversy to attempt to resolve it. Therefore, our focal interest will remain centered on what happened in the concentration camps: German, Ustasha, or otherwise. Views will be brought forward on the claims and counterclaims of both parties. What is clear is that both sides try to demonize each other, trying thereby to cleanse themselves, not by proving that they were clear of any sin or wrong doing, but by incriminating the other side and proving that it was worse. An old Talmudic saying taught that: "If you wish to aggrandize yourself, build a mound for yourself, do not dig a pit for others." The rivaling Serbs and Croats have a long way to go in comprehending and implementing these noble and lofty words of wisdom.

But a fair conclusion may suggest that most Serbian Jews were exterminated by the *Wehrmacht* and the SS, with some help from the many anti-Semitic and pro-Nazi groups like the ZBOR, who were native to Serbia well before the war, but most Croatian Jews (and Serbs executed by the Ustasha in Jadovno and Jasenovac for that matter) were eliminated by Ustasha cadres, with some help from the Nazis, who supervised and controlled the operations, and on occasion reproached them for their unwarranted excessive cruelty; conversely, those acts were often mollified by the Latin dictatorship and occupation, compared to the Germanic one. Both parties, Croats and Serbs, would be angered by this informal and inconclusive verdict, but since there is no absolute justice, one has to live with a relative one. One is reminded of the lawyer who represented his client in court and cabled the verdict to his client with the words: "justice has won," upon which he promptly received the answer: "appeal immediately."

The question persists nonetheless as to the acts of generosity, humanism, and courage, undertaken by individuals in Yugoslavia, as in other parts of occupied Europe, who took tremendous risks to hide and save the lives of other human beings who happened to be Jewish. In recognition of these extraordinary people, the *Yad Vashem* Memorial in Israel has established a distinct category of "Righteous Gentiles," which by now comprises several thousand people, famous among whom are Oskar Schindler, the German (whose name was immortalized in the *Schindler's List* movie), Vallenberg the Swede, and many others. It appears that more Serbs, despite the constraints of the brutal occupying German rule, earned the distinction of being included in this category (129 of them earned the title of "righteous among Nations" by 2010), than Croats, who were admittedly ruled by the no less brutal Ustashas native to the place. Arguments in favor of the one or the other can be voiced, and we leave it to the reader to judge. On the one hand, one can argue that, free from the German occupation that dictated adherence to its final solution for the Jews, the Croats could and should have shown more compassion toward the Jews and helped them into safety. But on the other hand, we understand that the Ustashas had embraced a no less anti-Semitic and annihilationist program than the Germans, which bound them to its principles. Conversely, the argument is advanced that the Serbs under German, Hungarian, Italian or Bulgarian occupation, had to be real heroes to do anything contradicting the rule of the occupier, and that when they did they indeed put their lives on the line, hence the higher degree of their commitment to humanism and human lives—all the more so in the hostile anti-Semitic ambience created in prewar Serbia by such organizations as the ZBOR, the Orthodox church, the *Cetniks*, and the Nedic government.

The manifestations of human conduct by the Serbs toward the Jews included providing shelter in their homes, assisting in procuring false identity papers for safe passage, and accepting and protecting parentless Jewish children inside families for the duration of the war. It is difficult to evaluate how many Jewish souls were thereby saved, and the holocaust of the majority who perished remains, unfortunately, the yardstick by which to gauge the fate of the annihilated Yugoslavian Jewry. And the annihilation of the majority of Yugoslavian Jewry, just like its counterparts in other parts of Europe, was made possible because most of the host population just looked on as it unfolded, some with indifference, some with satisfaction, while some actively aided in its destruction. And the precious few saved the honor of their nation by endangering their lives and acting as humans, where and when the official policy was inhuman. Indeed, from May 1941, a ban on aiding Jews was enforced by the Germans, sanctioned by a threat to punish violators who helped Jewish fugitives by making them share their fate, either in camps or facing firing squads, in addition to the general acts of vengeance that the Serbian population was exposed to by the Nazi occupier. Many Jews escaped by wandering southward to the zones occupied by Italy and Bulgaria, who were supposedly more lenient. [24]

Notes

1. Raphael Israeli, Presentation at Jadovno Conference, Banja Luka, June 2011.
2. Philip Cohen, *Serbia's Secret War: Propaganda and the Deceit of History*, Texas University Press, 1996.
3. Paul Giniewski, *Une Resistance Juive: Grenoble 1943–1945*, Cheminements. Paris, 2009, 100.
4. Philip Cohen, *Serbia's Secret War: Propaganda and the Deceit of History*, Texas University Press, 1996. Much of the following passage is based on this book.
5. This passage is based on the ZBOR entry in Wikipedia.
6. Ibid. See also an excellent discussion of the topic throughout Cohen, Philip, *Serbia's Secret War: Propaganda and the Deceit of History*, Texas University Press, 1996.
7. Ibid., 71 ff.
8. Jozo Tomasevich, *The Chetniks—War and Revolution in Yugoslavia, 1941–1945*, Stanford University Press, 1975, 194.
9. Ibid., 150.
10. www14.brinkster.com/philayu/SR/serbia3.htm.
11. This passage is largely based on http://www14.brinkster.com/philayu/SR/serbia3.htm.
12. Ibid.
13. Ibid.
14. Ibid., 80–84.
15. "The Final Solution in Serbia," in *Yad Vashem Studies*, Jerusalem, 1983.
16. Walter Manoschek, *Serbien ist Judenfrei: Militarische Besatzungspolitik und Judenvernichtung in Serbien, 1941–1942*, Munchen, R. Oldenburg Verlag, 1993.
17. Kurt Waldheim was an Austrian diplomat. He was the fourth secretary-general of the United Nations, from 1972 to 1981, and then the ninth president of Austria, from 1986 to 1992. While running for President in Austria in 1985, his service as an intelligence officer in the Wehrmacht during World War II raised international controversy.
18. Robert Keyserlingk, in his review article in the *Canadian Journal of History*, April, 1995.
19. Milan Ristovic, "Jews in Serbia during World War Two: Between the Final Solution to the Jewish Question, and the Righteous Among Nations," in Milan Vogel-Milan Ristovic-Milan Koljanin, *Serbia, Righteous Among Nations*, JOZ, Belgrade, 2010. The following passage is based on this analysis.
20. Ibid., 13–14.
21. Ibid., 16–17.
22. Ibid., 20–23.
23. Ibid., 24.
24. Esther Gitman, *When Courage Prevailed: Rescue and Survival of Jews in the Independent State of Croatia, 1941–45*, Paragon House, St. Paul, 2011.

2

The Roots of the Ustasha Regime

To implement his grand designs, Hitler needed local collaborators who could be trusted and committed enough to his cause to be left in charge of the groundwork, while he achieved his great goals elsewhere. Mad, unbalanced, and megalomaniacal as he may have been, Hitler was a great planner and did not lack in ambition, contingency plans, imagination, and drive to attain them. In fact, the first two years of the war were a stunning success, as long as he did not venture against the Soviet Union and as long as he could keep the Americans at bay, for without those two major powers, it was in his ability to handle the rest of the Western world, while his Japanese allies ably took care of Asia, as long as they did not venture into Pearl Harbor. As Hitler was carefully and rationally taking Central Europe step-by-step, he enlisted to his side not only willing allies—the likes of the "successful" Quisling experience in occupied Norway and the Vichy government of Petain in southern France—but he was probably pleasantly surprised to encounter zealous executioners in the Croatian Ustasha, like the Lithuanians, the Latvians, the Hungarians, and the Ukrainians in Eastern Europe, who seemed to delight in the extreme in the mass killing of Jews that those anti-Semites were assigned by their Nazi mentors. In occupied Yugoslavia, the main purpose of the Axis powers was to cleanse the Ustasha state from its Serbian, Jewish, and Gypsy populations. Annihilating the Jews, being also an imposed task by the Nazis, which their Ustasha clients did not seem to resent or to resist, served both partners equally well.

The Ustasha and their Muslim allies indeed embarked on an orgy of killing that many eyewitnesses describe as surpassing the Nazis' in cruelty, with one major difference. While after the Wannsee Conference the extermination of the Jews of Europe was at the top of the Nazi agenda, with the industrialized process of gassing the masses of

Jews and then burning their corpses in crematoria to eliminate traces of the crime, the Ustasha directed their main attention to their major historically hated competitors, the Serbs, of whom they wiped out countless hundreds of thousands, while the Jews and Gypsies were a secondary target, and "only" tens of thousands of them perished in that fashion under the Ustasha subcontractors of the Nazis. The industry and mechanization-minded Germans quickly invented their industrial mode of genocide, when they realized that shooting every individual Jew or Gypsy was too slow, too expensive, and too risky. The Ustasha killers were less developed and knew no sophisticated way to eliminate their enemies beyond using the primitive tools that they were familiar with: hammers, ropes, knives, sickles, and strangulating by hand, or dumping their victims live into territorial pits or maritime killing-by-drowning fields; they jubilantly resorted to what they knew and were overjoyed to carry out freely, without restriction and without fear from any authority, the orgy of murder that had brewed in their minds against their Serbian sworn historical enemies and they millennially despised Jewish "killers of Jesus," and the Roma people as a bonus.

Immediately after the German invasion of Yugoslavia in April 1941, Croatia declared its independence, under the instigation of Croatian nationalists called the Ustasha. Following Nazi policy, with which they willingly collaborated, they declared the Serbs, along with the inferior Jews and the Gypsies, as "enemies of the Croatian people." In that land, which was dubbed by Yugoslav Nobel Prize in Literature winner, Ivo Andric, as "the land where they love to hate," massive persecutions of all three peoples were launched where hundreds of thousands of people were eliminated, with the active participation of Croat Catholic and Bosnian Muslims, at least those among them who supported the Ustasha regime. The Partisans, mostly Communists and Jews, and some royalist *Cetniks*, but by no means all Serbs or most of them, reacted rapidly and started the resistance to both the occupier and its local collaborators. So tangled were the relations between the competing factions, that eventually even the *Cetniks* and the Partisans, both initially dedicated to the anti-German resistance and united in that endeavor, would eventually split and set out against each other. When Belgrade was liberated by the Red Army in September 1944, with the collapse of the main Nazi fronts in Normandy and Eastern Europe, Josip Broz Tito seized power and proclaimed the establishment of the People's Republic of Yugoslavia, divided, as in the past, into the six republics corresponding to the six Slavic peoples living in the country. Well prepared toward the end of the war, Tito already formulated in 1943 the federal constitution of the future Communist Yugoslavia (meaning, literally, the southern Slavic country, save Bulgaria), to differentiate it from the northern Slavs dwelling in northern Europe (i.e., Russia and Poland) and the Central Slavs in Czechoslovakia. His slogan, *"Vidimo se u Beogradu"* (Rendezvous in Belgrade), already indicated the focus of his rule, which would unite under his charismatic leadership the Partisans from various ethnic groups, to the exclusion of the Royalists, and act with determination for the liberation and postwar rebuilding of Yugoslavia.

The Axis invasion of Yugoslavia, which was launched on April 6, 1941, and completed eleven days later, created a new situation in the Balkans. The Independent State of Croatia (NDH) was headed by Colonel Edmund Veesenmayer, in the name of Ustasha leader, Ante Pavelic, as *Poglavnik (Fuhrer)*. Hitler had previously supported a united Yugoslavia that was to join him in the Tripartite Pact, but the coup mounted that month by a group of Serbian army officers, against the German-Yugoslav Alliance, prompted Hitler to lend his support to the Ustasha, a Fascist militant grouping in Croatia, which until then did not enjoy much local popular support, and it is doubtful whether it ever gathered a large constituency. This Nazi move would be equivalent to placing the Ku Klux Klan in power in the United States.[1] At the Vienna Conference of April 21–22, 1941, as Bosnia-Herzegovina was placed entirely within the NDH, a border was established marking its confines. On May 18, the Rome agreement was signed between Italy and the Ustasha state, which left the Adriatic islands of Brac and Hvar in the hands of the occupiers. The total population of Greater Croatia at that time was determined at 6,285,000, of whom 3,300,000 were Croats, 1,925,000 were Serbs, and 700,000 were Slovenes, meaning that Croats constituted just over half the total population, and that the Croats also included Bosnians who were considered Croats of the Muslim faith. On April 30, the Jews were already deprived from the right of movement, and from May 23 on, they were all forced to wear the yellow patch for identification. But their mass arrest for alleged "anti-state activities," in Sarajevo and elsewhere, and deportation to the death camps, started only a few days after the new discriminatory laws were in force in Croatia.

During the months of August–November, the rounding up of the Jews was completed from small towns, so that by early 1942, out of the Sarajevo prewar Jewish population of ten thousand, only a few hundred remained. Of the exterminated Jews, mainly by the Nazis and Ustashas, small groups were also eliminated by *Cetniks*, Muslim SS troops, and Italian forces; however, most were executed at the concentration camps within NDH, so that the fourth largest ethnic group in Bosnia, after the Muslims, Serbs, and Croats, was effectively removed from the Bosnian scene. Conversely, Jews became one of the staunchest groups that supported the Partisans, as 4,572 Jews fought in their ranks. By contrast, the Gypsy population of Bosnia, which counted some thirty thousand, was almost totally wiped out by the Nazis and the Ustashas.

Ante Pavelic, whose name has been irrevocably linked with the Ustasha state and the horrors it committed, was not the Nazis' first choice to head their puppet state in Croatia-Bosnia. Before the March 27 coup, and after Prince Pavel pledged his loyalty to Hitler, the Nazis had no interest in dismantling Yugoslavia, in spite of the Italian ambition to annex the entire Croatian coast. Therefore, Mussolini rather encouraged Croatian separatism, and the Serbian Coup gave him the pretext to facilitate it, since Hitler's orders allowed the invading powers (Germany, Italy, Hungary, and Bulgaria) to annex to themselves parts of their occupied territories though there remained two main zones of influence: German and Italian. Thus, the *Wehrmacht* entered Zagreb on April 10, and the next day, it invited Pavelic to announce an "independent" Croatia. Pavelic had not made a name for himself as yet, so the Germans first turned to the much more famous president of the Peasants Party, Vladko Macek, to make of him a sort of French Marshal Petain, but he declined and remained throughout persistent in his refusal to collaborate in any way with the occupiers. Pavelic was the next choice by default.

Already at the end of World War I, Croats had supported the idea of a southern-Slavic state (Yugo-Slavia), though they feared Serbian predominance in the federation, because they hoped that Serbian strength would guarantee their protection, especially from Italian ambitions on their coastline, and ensure their freedom from Austrian and Hungarian dominion. They thought that, together with Serbs and Slovenians, they could build a new state and society where all three ethnicities would be equal, thus they accepted being ruled from Belgrade by a Serbian king. Ante Pavelic was, at that time, the president of the Bar Association of Croatia and a member of the federal parliament in Belgrade, when he witnessed *in camera* the murder of Stjepan Radic, then leader of the

Peasants Party, before his eyes, which triggered a Croat rebellion and caused the royal governor to suspend the constitution, to disband the Parliament, to outlaw all political parties, to abolish the freedom of speech and assembly, and to launch censorship in the press and mass arrests, culminating in the dictatorship of King Aleksandar in 1929.[2]

Pavelic had run to Hungary under these circumstances, determined to struggle for Croatian independence, even by means of arms and terror, and he founded, together with his associate, Gustav Percec, the Ustasha–Croatian Revolutionary Organization. *Ustati*, meaning "standing up," was the root of the word. The founders tried to erect semi-military units of the Ustasha in Hungary, and from 1930 they built training bases for them in Mussolini's Italy. Their weapons originated from both Italy and Hungary, turning the Ustasha into one of Mussolini's executive arms in the Balkans. But in Yugoslavia they remained outlawed, just like any other parties, despite the wide support they enlisted among farmers, the uneducated, and the poor. In 1932 Ustasha units attacked a Yugoslavian army base, which was essentially Serbian, something that triggered retaliation against innocent Croats, who were not involved in the Ustasha raid and denied, from the outset, their unjustified identification with the Ustashas. All in all, on the eve of the war, only some twenty thousand supporters at home could be counted on as the firm kernel and the solid base of the organization. Under the Nazi occupation, Pavelic combined his hatred for the Serbs, his burning ambition for independence, and his contempt for the Communists and the Jews, to concoct an Ustasha ideology that was as cruel, fanatic, anti-Semitic, and murderous as the Nazis'. On April 15, 1941, after he agreed secretly with Mussolini to cede to him the Croatian coast and its islands, Pavelic entered Zagreb with two hundred of his gang in Italian tanks, an indication to his rootlessness and lack of a loyal base in the city that was to become his capital.

The fact that Pavelic had to conquer his own country by force of arms, not in response to an appeal by popular movements to take it over or to rescue it from the foreign occupier, goes a long way to describe the relationship between ruler and ruled. Initially, as the Italians hoped to control the entire Ustasha state, it was founded as an Italian protectorate. Pavelic, in fact, requested that Italian King Victor Emmanuel III should reign over the new state, but the latter appointed his young nephew for the job, which transpired as a futile démarche once the supposedly independent state was divided between two zones of influence under Germany and Italy. While the Italians exercised direct civil and military rule upon their half, the Germans maintained garrisons in the large cities of the Ustasha domain, as of all Yugoslavia, which encompassed Nazi activities on all levels, including the SS, *Einsatz Gruppen*, the *Gestapo*, and departments to deal with Jews under their jurisdiction or within their purview: in Zagreb, Sarajevo, and Osijek in Croatia-Bosnia (the Ustasha state), in Novi Sad (occupied by Hungary), and in Skopje (occupied by Bulgaria). The power base of Pavelic was the headquarters of the Ustasha, while his declared state was no more than a rubber stamp to his authoritarian and often whimsical decisions.

Pavelic immediately declared an all-out war against the Communists, who in those days were identified as Partisans under Josip Tito, and the rest of the "unwanted elements," such as the Serbs, the Jews, the Gypsies, and Croatian dissidents. They were all purged from state service, from the media, the military, and the professions. Systematic murders began at the end of April, when groups of Serbs were hand-picked for arrest. In May, Pavelic ordered his forces to convert Serbs to Catholicism, under threat of expulsion, death, and confiscation of property if they failed. Hitler is said to have encouraged Pavelic to transfer Slovenians to Croatia and Serbs from Croatia to Serbia under a blueprint of "fifty years of national intolerance." In effect, within six months, the Ustasha expelled 120,000 Serbs to Serbia, triggering the flight of many untold thousands of others on their own. It is estimated that some 250,000 were converted to Catholicism, and tens of thousands of others were assembled in camps, notably Jadovno and Jasenovac, and exterminated. But when the Ustasha realized that persecution of the Serbs encouraged them to join the Partisans and the *Cetniks*, the Ustasha regime agreed to treat some of the war injured among those two categories in either Croatian hospitals or even in Germany in grave cases.[3]

Croats and Serbs will argue forever about who did what to whom and when and where. Both carried out massacres and both collaborated with the Germans under various guises and appellations, though extermination camps for the sake of genocide were an Ustasha invention, unequalled and unparalleled by other groups in Yugoslavia. That horrifying monopoly on systematic and organized genocide by the Ustasha regime was directly aided by Bosnian Muslims under circumstances that will be detailed in the coming chapters. On one topic, however, neither of them relented or recoiled from extreme action, namely hating the Jews, persecuting them, and then either exterminating them or delivering them to the Nazis for deportation and annihilation. Once again, it is true that only the Ustasha, of all the main actors in the Balkans, proceeded to exterminate Jews (and others) in special camps erected for that purpose, though all the others (Germans, Serbs, Croats, and Muslims) found a common cause in persecuting their Jews, deporting them, delivering them to Germans, and massacring them; admittedly, though, the camps where the Jews were physically exterminated, were not erected for them specifically, but primarily for the Serbs. It is possible that the Ustasha believed that they could persuade their Nazi patrons to accept those camps only if they saw the added "benefit" for themselves and their war aims in implementing the final solution for the Jews.

Milan Koljanin, who presented at the Jadovno Conference, made the point that it was the favorable political and military circumstances after March 27, 1941, and the aggression of Germany and its allies on the Kingdom of Yugoslavia, that enabled the establishment of the Independent State of Croatia, known as the NDH, thus allowing the program of extremist Croatian nationalists to be fulfilled. Though it was formally within the Italian zone of interest, the Ustasha state was ideologically much closer to the German-Nazi than to the Italian-Fascist model. The new state structure was erected very rapidly, based on the hierarchy of Croatian Banovina (formerly known as *Banska krajina*, *Banija*), which was a geographical region in central Croatia, between the rivers Sava, Una, and Kupa. The main towns in the region included Petrinja, Glina, Kostajnica, and Dvor. The area was almost entirely located in the Sisak-Moslavina county. Later, in the 1990s, the area was to suffer during the Bosnian War, with much of the population fleeing from the war and the economy in distress. In 1941, after a public call by the vice president of the Yugoslav government, Vladko Macek, other members of the elite made themselves available to the new rule. A very important role was also played by the Roman Catholic Church in the support of the new state, just as a crucial role had been played by the Orthodox hierarchy in the Serbian state. In fact, for better or worse, Catholicism had become coterminous with Croatian nationalism, as much as Serbian identity has grown identical with Orthodoxy, and the enmity between the rival faiths has tragically fed into the ethnic controversy that plagues their respective constituencies to this day.

In consequence, at the base of the Ustasha nationalist organization stood first of all its anti-Serbian component, enhanced by its anti-Semitic racism, which pitted it also against the Jews, a component that put it on a par with their Nazi masters. This double-edged ideology immediately became the new regime's policy, which it forcibly and enthusiastically applied throughout the entire existence of their entity. Oppressive legislation lent a pseudo-legal clout to the enforcement of Croatian national and racial policy, which pursued the creation of a homogeneous state of Catholic Croats, with tolerated Muslims, and determined to destroy Serbs, Jews, and Gypsies, as well as political dissenters, such as Communists and other Yugoslav nationalists. To attain those goals, social excommunication, stigmatization, expropriation, and extermination were pursued systematically. Indeed, from the first day of the existence of the Ustasha state, there were obvious attempts to introduce a system and a rationale; thus the creation of a network of camps was given top priority. In regard to the Serbs, the destruction process started in their ethnic areas, mainly in villages, but from late April 1941, and especially from June, most of the executions were conducted methodically and on a massive scale in the newly erected death camps with the center in Gospic. In the network of collection camps, from which the roads led to Gospic, the most important were the camps in Koprivnica and Zagreb (Grand Fair). The destruction process of Jews, which was part of the Nazi-devised Holocaust, was exclusively connected with the newly formed network of camps.

Based on the domicile, gender, and age of the victims of Camp Gospic, the destruction of the Serbs and Jews proceeded in the entire state of NDH. The model of destruction was created in Jasenovac, as the center of a system of death camps that operated until the very end of the Ustasha state, and it was gradually perfected and produced more variants of the models that were established based on Gospic after June 1941. Gospic indeed took the lead in enforcing the policies of mass extermination of ethnic, religious, national, and racial groups within the "new European order" that was inspired and dictated by the Nazis. Germany and its allies at first began to pursue their crusade when they attacked the Soviet Union on June 22, 1941, and launched the systematic killing of Jews in occupied territories, though their death camp system would not start until the end of 1941 and the beginning of 1942. In other words, the NDH death camps based on Gospic, and from August 1941 in Jasenovac, preceded the Nazi death industry, which was centered in occupied Poland. For already in June 1941, the Croatian national and racial policy was on its way to achieving its most important goal: the physical destruction of Serbs and Jews on its territory.

Death camps were the means to carry out the genocide that was decided upon by the policy makers, in both the Nazi and their Ustasha ally chanceries. Without an all-encompassing decision of this sort, which not only approved of the killings, but also aided and facilitated their implementation, no such large-scale genocide could be possible. Vladimir Umeljic offered at the Jadovno Conference a paper on the social and psychological aspects of the phenomenon of genocide. He claims that the time of genocide is an extraordinary state of mind and of affairs that permits, indeed requires, dehumanization of the victims, on the one hand, and injecting motivation into the planned group of executors, on the other, to make the execution and inhuman treatment of the victims easier. In this sense, while the victims remain unchanged in their essence, they are dehumanized in the eyes of their assassins, and the executors must be regimented, changed, and made impervious to humane sentiment in order to permit them to perform their task. Supposedly, the murderers were basically "normal" people who would have no reason to do evil, let alone kill other human beings in cold blood, because they would see in the victims they murder their own spouses, mothers, brothers, and children. Effecting the psychological transformation in the executors, whereby they would no longer see in their victims human beings (and therefore their own actions neither criminal legally, nor sinful religiously, nor immoral ethically), was necessary to pave the way to mass murder.

The author exemplified his point with a personal tale that shows the degree of dehumanization of the target group of victims, in this case Serbs, but also of the perpetrators of the genocide who were effectively conditioned to shed any human sentiment or sensitivity and to treat their fellow men as if they were pieces of disposable furniture or of human waste. He tells about a Croatian woman, Marija Josipova Obajdin, who gave a deposition in court in 1945 about the Serbian genocide of 1941–1945:

> In summer, 1941 I worked as a cook in Slunj. . . I saw them bringing Serbs and putting them in prison cells, and then taking them overnight for killing, after they would rob them. One morning I took a pick and went to dig potatoes. When I got to Lalic forest, I saw a woman sitting beside a hole in the ground into which Ustasha dumped the bodies of slaughtered Serbs. The woman was stabbed many times and she was bleeding profusely. She was trying to speak but I could not understand anything. I approached her and hit her twice on the head with the pick I had in my hands, after which she

fell flat on the ground and did not show any more any signs of life. It was Milka Zec from Zecheva Varosh. Later on I went on digging potatoes. . . .[4]

Mladenka Ivankovic, who also made a presentation at the conference, stressed the point that Jewish intellectuals and students were at the forefront of the victims of the mass executions that were carried out in Jadovno and then Jasenovac under the Ustasha regime. The NDH had undertaken to rewrite the political map of the world in the image of their Nazi mentors. It was a classical puppet state in the sense that it hardly had any characteristics of itself, save the deeply rooted hatred toward Serbs (and Jews, but that was held in common with the Nazis), for, like the Germans, their state demanded racial and national purity and unity. The Ustasha believed that they could build a healthy national entity only if they physically destroyed their domestic and external enemies, the deadliest among whom were Serbs, Jews, intellectuals, and Communists. The critical role of accomplishing national integration was played by the Catholic church, whose superiority they stressed over the "Byzantine" Serbian national "folklore," which was not even worthy of the epithet of a creed, a faith, or a religion. In this worldview, anti-Semitism was a sacred tenet, aimed at ridding the world of that "human waste" and "absolute evil" so that, taking the Third Reich as a model, Aryanization of NDH would be fulfilled as rapidly as possible. All this stood in strong conflict with the deep cultural roots that the Jews had in the Kingdom of Yugoslavia.

Indeed, at a Zionist Congress held in Zagreb in 1919, a unified Zionist organization was created under the heading of "the Union of Zionists of Yugoslavia," which continued to operate successfully between the two world wars. In the same year, a central Jewish youth organization was founded, dubbed "the Union of Jewish Youth Associations." Some groups, who were not members of these associations, were nevertheless liberal Zionists on the left. Prominent among them was the student Zionist organization at Zagreb University, which in time assembled all Jewish organizations at the university under its wings and formed the University Committee of Jewish Communist Organizations, which naturally championed anti-racist ideals and combated anti-Semitic trends. No wonder then, that along with Serbs, Jewish intellectuals and students were crowded into Jadovno, as soon as it opened its gates, since they were identified as "elements that dissolve the Croatian nation." Together with those intellectuals, who were the most productive and challenging in national culture, the Ustasha also arrested 165 Jewish youths, mostly students and sportsmen, including the entire membership of the Maccabee Club in Zagreb, as recounted in the following Jadovno chapter. Thus, in an ironic twist of history, the genocide of the Serbian population, which was no great lover of the Jews initially, went hand in hand with the implementation of the Holocaust, Ustasha-style, first at Jadovno and then in Jasenovac.

A harrowing description of that genocide and its underpinnings was delivered at the conference by Nicola Zutic, who focused on the "bloody summer" of Lika, which will be later covered in the chapter about Jasenovac, from documentation extant in the archives of the Italian occupiers of that Serbian city, which was annexed to the Italian zone. Zutic pointed out the fact that Croatian hostility toward the Serbs had emerged since the nineteenth century, aided by the anti-Serbian demagogy of the Vatican and the Roman Catholic Church of Croatia. The hate campaign against the Serbs in Lika was also supported by anti-Serbian ideologists from Lika, such as Ante Starcevic, Andrija Artukivic, Mile Budek, and others, some of whom went over from propagating hate theory to perpetrating genocide while serving the regime in the Gospic complex of death camps, including the horrible island of Pag. The reason for the enthusiastic subscription of the population to the acts of genocide, in addition to its loyalty to the Roman Catholic Church, was inherent in its mentality and character of accepting and submitting in its daily contacts and confessions to its priests, with their rhetoric and conduct, denigration and contempt toward the Orthodox Church, which was dubbed "heretical, heterodox, and schismatic." Those nonbelievers, which also included the Jews, dissidents, intellectuals, and liberals, were the main victims of the Ustasha genocide.

As in Serbia, the attitude toward Jews under the Ustasha was the obverse of the collaboration of the local authorities with their Nazi masters. There was certainly a great difference between Croat Pavelic, the head of the "Independent State" of NDH, who like his Quisling and Petain counterparts, run an autonomous state, in close collaboration with Nazis and under the limitations they imposed, and Serb Nedic who worked directly under the daily and close German supervision by the Nazi commander of the Yugoslavian front located in Belgrade. In some sense, German presence in Serbia was much more felt in its streets than in the towns and villages of Croatia, but there the Italians filled this gap. So, on the one hand, the Ustasha acted as dedicated

Nazis as the Germans themselves, but the support of the populations to their policies was not evident, especially due to Italian presence, which somehow softened the burden of the Nazi virulence. Thus, paradoxically, where ideological virulence was at its apogee under the Ustasha state, it was mainly the minorities, like the Serbs, the Jews, the Gypsies, and Croatian dissidents who suffered the most. In fact, the camps of Jadovno and Jasenovac, which were erected by the Ustasha themselves, were in accordance with Nazi will, and later a replica of similar death camps were constructed in Eastern Europe. But on the other hand, the fact that Nedic was a Serbian nationalist, though with anti-Semitic biases, forced him to play the role of an efficient manager of Serbian affairs, which some researchers have compared to a *Judenrat*, under Nazi control, therefore he did not erect death camps, though he collaborated, or turned a blind eye on the extermination practices of the Nazis on the territory he theoretically controlled. These are two different states of affairs and states of mind, which have to be constantly taken into account when one compares, reviews, criticizes, or judges the comparative situations, including genocidal practices, across the borders between those two subjugated entities, which were later united under one federal government, and then again divided in bitter and poisonous rivalry during the war of the 1990s and thereafter.

While the Nedic government held the anti-Masonic exhibit in Belgrade, which was in effect mainly anti-Semitic, geared to dehumanize the Jews and justify their annihilation by the Nazis, the Ustashas too opened their own anti-Semitic display to justify their own decimation of their Jewish communities designed to counter the alleged Jewish domination of American press and finance, particularly the control of *The New York Times*. This type of anti-Semitic propaganda was useful for showing how art and propaganda posters, in particular, could help create the other. Jews were both capitalists and Communists at the same time, and the alleged secret force that dominated all aspects of European, indeed world economic life. Norman Cohn, the renowned British writer and film producer (d. 2007), has described this as a "warrant for genocide." The long lines before the ticket office, during the entire three-month run, were another indication of that mood. One of the posters advertising the exhibit, with a hideous serpent representing world Jewry, was accompanied by a catalog full of hatred, bigotry, and scary stereotypes of the Jews, certainly not designed to attract sympathy and compassion toward them. The exhibit showed the development of Jews and their "destructive actions" in Croatia before the April 10 coming of the German saviors. It explained that the "solution of the Jewish question" in the Independent State of Croatia was exhibited between May 1 to June 1, 1942, at the Zagreb Pavilion of Arts at Strossmayer's Square. In harrowing detail, it elaborated upon:

1. *The Jews in ancient times.* Examples that prove that in those days they were of the same importance as they are today, and how they penetrated the other nations.
2. *Jewish settlement of the country of Croatia.* After the destruction of Jerusalem in AD 70 through the "Tolerance Patent" in the eighteenth century,[5] they enslaved the Croatian people, slowly but surely.
3. *Jews in Croatia between 1782–1918.* The sudden strengthening of the Jews in Croatia, how they penetrated into the ranks of nobility, and how they Judaized the Croatian public.
4. *Days of freedom.* Explaining how the Croatian Ustasha solved the Jewish question.
5. *Jews in other countries.* Now the Soviets turned from favorite allies to sworn enemies of Hitler, the fall of the Soviet Union in "the chains of Jewry" had to be expounded, as well as to tell how English nobility came to mix with Jewish blood, and the United States became led by the Jews, who took over its politics and economy.

On the pages of the accompanying catalog, one could read a revision of Jewish history over two millennia, as a tale of the inventors of slave trade and prostitution, and of the destroyers of all ancient civilizations. It also proudly stated how Croats mostly saved themselves from Jewish disaster till the times when the Gypsy Dynasty of Karadjordjevics handed them and their land over to Jewish greedy hands. The most interesting claim was that the "entire nation" helped Pavelic's propaganda office to prepare this exhibit. At the end of the catalog were coupons to allow visitors to watch, free of charge, German movies like *Eternal Jew, Rothschild, and the Jew Suss.* "Educational Units" were appended, such as *"Are the poor Jews harmless?"*—with elaborate answers in the negative, as could be expected. Only in 2012, when the remnants of Sarajevo Jews organized the exhibit "*The Jews Remember: 1942–2012*" in the New Temple of Sarajevo, to commemorate the seventieth Holocaust anniversary, could one perceive and read beyond the propaganda import of that catalog. Yeshayahu Jelinek, a writer on the Jewish Holocaust in Yugoslavia, had written long ago:

> I feel that the destruction of Croatian Jewry has not yet been exhausted from the historiographical point of view; nor has it found its ultimate historian. Croatia, despite the comparatively small size of its Jewish population, is unique in Holocaust history.[6]

It was claimed that part of the Ustasha ideology was rooted in the Roman Catholic Church, something that could be corroborated by such prominent clerics, who committed mass murder in their clerical robes, such as Miroslav Filipović in Jasenovac (see the relevant chapter following), and the statement made by Dionzije Juricev, a priest and a cabinet minister of the Ustasha state, in his role as the head of the State Direction for Renewal, on October 22, 1941:

> In this country, only Croats may live from now on, because it is a Croatian country. We know precisely what we will do with the people who do not convert. I have purged the whole surrounding area, from babies to seniors. If it is necessary, I will do that here too, because today it is not a sin to kill even a 7-year old child, if it is standing on the way of our Ustasha Movement. . . . Do not believe that I could not take a machine-gun in hand just because I wear a priest's vestments. If it is necessary, I will eradicate everyone who is against the Ustasha state and its rule—right down to babies![7]

This declaration, which includes a justification for killing children for the Ustasha cause, must have been baffling even to the most fanatic supporters of that evil regime, whether they dubbed it Fascist or semi-Fascist, or proto-Fascist, and whether they recognized or denied the existence of Ustasha nationalism, since there was no Croatian state or nationality before the war. Moreover, many decent and good-willed Croats claim today that most of them were not supporters of the Ustasha regime, therefore they resist the equation Ustasha = Croat. I suppose that their position is similar to the Germans who refute today the equation Nazi = German, and they claim that most of them were not Nazi. What created the appearance that those two equations were valid during the war was the circumstances surrounding them. Take, for example, a man, whose family was German aristocracy prior to World War II, and owned a number of large industries and estates. When asked how many German people were true Nazis, the answer he gave can guide our attitude toward fanaticism. "Very few people were true Nazis," he said, "but many enjoyed the return of German pride, and many more were too busy to care. I was one of those who just thought the Nazis were a bunch of fools. So, the majority just sat back and let it all happen. Then, before we knew it, they owned us, and we had lost control, and the end of the world had come. My family lost everything. I ended up in a concentration camp and the Allies destroyed my factories." Many Croats would easily subscribe to this wording today with regard to the Ustasha domination of their country.

If so, when today's Germany is no longer accused of Nazi tendencies, even though some neo-Nazi and skinhead groups can erupt here and there, it would be extremely unfair to continue to accuse Croats today of anti-Semitic and Fascistic propensities just because the Ustashas toed that line during the war. What makes the difference is the government policy today: skinheads, neo-Fascists, and neo-Nazis do exist in both countries but exert little or no influence on public opinion, carry no weight in the polls, and are combated by the governments in place, while in the 1930s and up until the end of the war, they were the government, they made the law, and their conduct and deeds were considered the norm.

There is no doubt that the Ustasha state was both nationalist and Fascist, though both terms merit definition. One can argue that even though there had been no sovereign Croat state since 1102, when Croatia was subsumed under larger political entities, this does not mean that Croatian particular identity cannot reemerge. In fact it did, both under the Ustasha and in the post Yugoslavian era, if one is to judge by today's insistence on the Croatian language, literature, and culture, which was until recently part of the unifying Serbo-Croatian tongue and civilization. Or take the Jews, who were deprived of nationalism for millennia, but they revived it (Zionism), retrieved their ancient homeland (Israel) and reconstituted their nationalism and national tongue. The fact that the Croatian ideal of nationalism, which was created in the nineteenth century, and was not sustained by a well-defined territorial possession, far from diminishing the Croat identity, on the contrary augmented it, again like the Jews who were homeless for two millennia, except for their millenarian dream about Jerusalem, and their idea of a definable territory grew together with the modern national idea, instead of being a condition to it. But modern Croats have been all imbued with the idea of self-identity and sovereignty, and the Ustasha revolutionaries among them also entertained ideas of ethnic supremacy, to the detriment of other groups, something akin to the Nazi Aryan theories and the Nuremberg Laws, while other nationalists, like the Peasant Party, did not advance these Nazi-like theories and were willing to operate within the Yugoslavian federal state.

It is true that the Ustasha drew on Catholicism as an expression of their identity, but that in no way diminished their Fascism; the same had happened before with the Romanian *Iron Guard*, the Spanish *Falange*, the Afrikaner *Ossewabrandwag*, and to an extent with Pierre Jumayyel's *Phalanges* in Lebanon. Furthermore, the Ustashas tried to emphasize themselves as an organic part of the Croatian culture and history. By placing Catholicism within the cosmology of the totalitarian state, the NDH wanted people to worship its party program of June 1941, which asserted that in "the Ustasha state, created by the *poglavnik* and his Ustasha, people must think like Ustasha, speak like Ustasha and—most important of all—act like Ustasha. Namely, the entire life in the NDH must be Ustasha-based." However, this was, at the same time, a secular, not a religious, regime that appealed to the ancient Croatian traditions of Roman Catholicism to legitimize its rule. For Croatian Fascists, placing the state before God meant that religion was a constituent part of the Greater Croatian nation, which was intended to be purified through violence. However, as noted in Feldman's essay,[8] even though Ante Pavelic adopted the title *Poglavnik*, probably calculated to parallel the German *Fuhrer* and Italian *il-Duce*, he was not a demagogue of the type of Hitler and Mussolini. Unlike the two Fascist senior brothers, who had a period of peace to consolidate their regimes before they launched their respective and joint offensives, Pavelic's regime was born in war and sustained only as long as war lasted, mainly against the *Cetniks* and the Partisans; directed at the genocide of the Serbs and others, it waned at the end of the war. So, he did not have the time to educate, cultivate, and convert a citizenry that would constitute his power base, hence perhaps the small nucleus of diehard Ustashas, which belied the lack of massive popular support, compared to the Fascist mass and youth movements that were cultivated by Germany and Italy. Those popular mass movements endured only as long as the expansive and successful wars bore fruits, and they died out when the popular anger against the leaders arose as the futility of their delusions came to the fore.

Be the Ustasha regime mainly secular or mainly Catholic, we can neither exonerate the individual clerics who participated in the murders, arguing that they performed under their secular Ustasha affiliation, nor universally blame the Catholic establishment in wartime Croatia for the horrors committed under its aegis, by reason of their Catholic commitment. It is evident that many Catholics, within and outside the Catholic Church, behaved inhumanly, but there were also many Catholic priests, and more so Catholic laymen, who joined the Partisans and fought Fascism. As Feldman argues, "though the Church hierarchy made a long-awaited Faustian bargain for political sovereignty in 1941, that does not mean that all its institutions and priests are guilty." He says that since the 1930s, when the royal dictatorship reigned supreme, the politization of Catholicism in Croatia brought it more closely to the idea of the Croatian state sovereignty, probably a parallel process to what happened with the Orthodox Church in Serbia, though, admittedly, the latter was far from associating with mass murders of conceived enemies. When Catholics in Croatia were faced with the choice between supporting a paralyzed Yugoslav federation and an independent Croatian state, the clergy, from Archbishop Stepinac on down, placed themselves on the side of Croatian sovereignty, that is the Ustasha rule under the circumstances of 1941. Feldman also claims that the mass murder, launched by the Ustasha in summer 1941, caused most of the clerics to rethink their support for the regime, though their early support, for the sake of sovereignty, not for the purpose of mass murder, cannot be discarded either. The bottom line is that more than two hundred Catholic clerics joined the ranks of the Ustasha, blessed its flag, and took part in their funerals and ritual masses, and fully 124 of them were decorated for their service to the NDH.[9]

If we focus on the Ustasha state mistreatment of the Jews, we must go back to the Milan Ristovic seminal essay, extensively cited above.[10] The determining factor here is that the Ustashas willingly collaborated with the Nazis in the final solution, while the Serbs explain their own collaboration as "constraints of the occupation" or deny it altogether. But Croats had also developed an ideology and praxis of their own, at times surpassing, in its religious zeal and enthusiastic implementation, even the worst of the Nazis. So, without incriminating all the Croats for this horror, it is important to recall that in their eternal debates with Serbs on questions of culpability, they cannot gain the upper hand when they try to minimize what was done by their compatriots on their national territory during the war. The distinctly horrifying attitude of the Ustasha state and its auxiliaries toward the Jews (equally toward the Serbs and Gypsies too), began upon the declaration of its establishment on April 10, 1941, and lasted for four disastrous years until the end of the war and the destruction of Nazism and its NDH state. Their genocidal policy applied not only directly to the territories of NDH per se, but also to the areas of Serbia that were added to the Croatian state, like Srem, or indirectly to other areas of Serbia that fell under German administrators that were open to be aided in their genocidal designs by their Ustasha like-minded and obedient allies.

Of course, the main genocidal operational effort of the Ustashas was concentrated in the two major camps of Jasenovac and Jadovno under their jurisdiction, which are at the center of this study. However, when Serbian Zemun and eastern Srem were surrendered to the Ustasha, their rule of terror against the Jews (and others) was immediately enforced: plundering of Jewish property, eviction of Jewish families from their homes, the use of unlimited violence against them, imposition of forced labor, extortion and blackmail of the Jewish communities, destruction of synagogues and cemeteries, and deportation of Jews en masse to the extermination camps, including the Jews of Zemun, who were rounded up in the night between July 26 and 27, 1942. Before dawn, the arrested men were transported to Jasenovac, women and children to Stara Gradiška. The majority of the 573 Holocaust victims of Zemun, as well as other parts of Srem, were killed in those Ustashi camps. Thus, out of the total of 2,800 Jews who lived in Srem prior to the war, some 2,500, or nearly 90 percent of them, were murdered, making Srem—the one area of Serbia controlled by the Ustasha—the region with the highest rate of Jewish victims.

It is noteworthy that the NDH, which was created on April 10, 1941, preceded the capitulation of Yugoslavia by a week; by immediately becoming an ally of the Axis, the NDH turned its arms against its compatriots and launched its own genocidal program against the Jews (and the Serbs). Her racial laws also started immediately and developed in May, and in a way were applied at a faster pace than Germany's in the rest of occupied Yugoslavia. Her extermination programs were inaugurated in May 1941 in the concentration system of Gospic, several months prior to the application of the same program in occupied Yugoslavia. The latest estimations speak about some thirty thousand Jews exterminated by the Ustasha within their jurisdiction, in spite of the fact that some top Ustasha leaders had close family relations with Jews. Pavelic's own wife, Mara, was of Jewish descent, as well as Olga, the wife of Slavko Kvaternik, the military commander of the state, whose son, Eugen, played a role in the establishment of the security apparatus that terrorized the Jews (as well as the Serbs and the Gypsies). Somewhat as in other totalitarian states, like Communist Soviet Union, Jews, who were victims of the regime, including Trotsky, Zinoviev, and others, were first accused of betraying the revolution that they had kindled, and then, when that regime collapsed, they were blamed for having invented and established it in the first place. In new Croatia some claims were insinuated that Jews were running the NDH, meaning that they are accused of their own destruction.

The estimated figure of about thirty thousand exterminated Jews under the Ustasha does not include the Jewish refugees from other countries who were temporarily stationed in the NDH, nor the seven hundred Jewish victims who were active members of the Yugoslav army (and were "guilty" of serving in that Serbian-dominated military force), or later in the Partisan force, something which helped justify their "criminality" by reason of their "Communist" leanings as they enrolled in Tito's ranks, which was their only recourse for evading the Nazi and the Ustasha roundup and elimination. Given that 80 percent of Yugoslavian Jewry lost their lives in 1941 and 1942, the quasi-totality of them in concentration camps, either Nazi in Serbia or Ustasha in the enlarged NDH, the greater Croatian state became, statistically, the local authority that directly exterminated more Jews than did the Germans in occupied Europe.[11] In all other places, including Serbia, Poland and France, while local authorities may have collaborated with the Nazis, either willingly or compulsorily, the Germans were encumbered to do the dirty work of extermination themselves. In fact, while the Ustasha state acted in full steam to annihilate the Jews they had incarcerated, they also urged the Germans to deport as many of them as they could to the camps in the East, once the final solution blueprint was activated after Wannsee. After they "Aryanized," namely confiscated or destroyed all Jewish property, the Ustasha made their first request to the Germans, in October 1941, to deport the Jews that their much slower extermination machine did not have the time to deal with as yet. In August 1942, five thousand of them were shipped eastward.[12]

In December 1942, one of Eichmann's assistants estimated that the Croats still held two thousand Jews in Ustasha camps, and in April–May 1943, the Germans transported them to their death camps. The last thousand inmates in Jasenovac liberated themselves with their bare hands on April 22, 1945. Only 129 of them survived this rebellious break out and transmitted their memoirs. Most of the liberated surviving victims spoke of the unique extermination practices of the Ustasha, which have been immortalized in such books as *Smell of Human Flesh*, by Cadik Danon-Braco, and *Witness to Jasenovac Hell*, by Ilija Ivanovic (both in Serb-Croatian and unavailable in English translation). A prominent Belgrade Jew and writer, Jasa Almuli, wrote that Jasenovac was worse than Auschwitz. It is perhaps hard to imagine how anything could be worse than hell or "another planet" as Elie Weisel has depicted Auschwitz. Almuli, who had no way to compare between those two versions of hell, of course meant the Ustasha direct, manual, bloody-handed operation of personally slashing the throats of victims or stunning them with sledgehammers before they were thrown into pits or into the river by their assassins, compared with the quick, industrialized, and impersonal mass executions by gas and crematoria of the Nazi-operated camps. To support this datum, statistics have found that while the death rate among the inmates of Auschwitz was 84.6 percent, in Jasenovac it amounted to an 88 percent mortality rate.

Another unfortunate aspect of the Ustasha death camps was that the ways in which they tortured and then murdered their victims by hand had become notoriously shocking even to their Nazi masters. Another unique characteristic of the Ustasha was that they killed more non-Jews (mainly Serbs and Gypsies) than Jews, which amounted to the entire Gypsy population under their jurisdiction and hundreds of thousands of Serbs, as claimed by the latter, many less according to their own reckoning, though the numbers remain disputed. Of course, one can argue that there were simply many less Jews and Gypsies than Serbs, therefore the latter's numbers are necessarily larger. What remains intriguing is how such a small and new state, not particularly advanced, could embark on such a large scale genocidal operation, in proportion to its small population, which remains almost unique in the annals of wartime Europe, compared to the horrifying larger scale, "chain-production," industrialized operations of mass murder in Germany and its occupied territories. Killing on that scale cannot be done by individuals, who can commit murders or massacres, but not genocide or mass murder, which require state power and organization and an ideology of murder to lend justification or rationalization to it. Yet, a higher percentage of Croatian than of Serbian Jews survived World War II. That was primarily thanks to the Italian army, whose occupied territory offered a much higher chance to survive than in either the NDH or in German-occupied Serbia. It is estimated that up to ten thousand Yugoslavian Jews survived the war by hiding, escaping, or living in Italian captivity. Some 4,500 of them survived thanks to their participation in the Partisan movement, and about 1,200 stayed alive by hiding in Croatia, while some 500 survived in German POW camps.[13]

Notes

1.   For the details of that ethnic cleansing, see Marko Attila Hoare, *The Ustasha Genocide, 1941–1943*, Oxford University Press, 2006.
2.   This passage is based on Philip Cohen, op. cit., especially chapter 4.
3.   Ibid., 88–91.

4. Cited by Umeljic during his presentation at the Jadovno 1941 Conference in Banja Luka in June, 2011.
5. The Patent of Toleration was an edict issued in 1781 by the Holy Roman Emperor, Joseph II of Austria. The Patent extended religious freedom to non-Catholic Christians living in Habsburg lands, including Lutherans, Calvinists, and the Greek Orthodox. It was followed by the Edict of Tolerance in 1782. The edict extended to Jews the freedom to pursue all branches of commerce, but also imposed new requirements. Jews were required to create German-language primary schools or send their children to Christian schools (Jewish schools had previously taught children to read and write Hebrew in addition to mathematics.) The Patent also permitted Jews to attend state secondary schools. A series of laws issued soon after the Edict of Toleration abolished the autonomy of the Jewish communities, which had previously run their own court, charity, internal taxation and school systems; required Jews to acquire family names; made Jews subject to military conscription; and required candidates for the rabbinate to have secular education.
6. Yeshayahu A. Jelinek, *Historiography of Slovakian and Croatian Jewry* in Yisrael Gutman and Gideon Greif (eds.), *The Historiography of the Holocaust Period*, Yad Vashem, Jerusalem, 1988, 363.
7. Cited by Matthew Feldman, "Genocide Between Political Religion and Religious Politics,"*Internet*, www.tandf.co.uk/journals/pdf/papers/FTMP_NDH_conclusion.pdf , 7.
8. Ibid., 11–12
9. Ibid., 1–19.
10. Milan Ristovic, op. cit., 24 ff.
11. Dragan Cvetkovic, " Holocaust in the Independent State of Croatia" (in Serbian), *Istorija*, No 20, January, 2011, 163–181.
12. Jozo Tomasevich, *War and Revolution in Yugoslavia, 1941–1945: Occupation and Collaboration*, Stanford University Press, 2001, 595.
13. Milan Ristovic, *In Search of Refuge: Yugoslav Jews Fleeing the Holocaust*, Belgrade, 1998, 345 ff.

3

The Jadovno Complex[1]

In view of the Ustasha ideology, it is natural that one of the first and principal pursuits of its government when it was constituted in 1941, at the height of German success in Western Europe, under Nazi tutorship and guidelines, was to handle the perennial and thorny issue of the Serbs, who were present in the southern part of Croatia, known as Krajina, which is immediately adjacent to the northern part of majority Serbian Bosnia around Banja Luka, as well as in eastern Bosnia, which is contiguous to Serbia. All in all, the Ustasha state, which encompassed Croatia, Bosnia-Herzegovina, and parts of Serbia, came to extend its rule over about one million Serbs, a population with which the ruling Croat nationalists did not have much love lost. In view of the practical impossibility of exterminating so many people, though there is little doubt that they would have loved to do so, they emitted in public, as a threat, a warning and probably an expression of wishful thinking, without much visible embarrassment, their design to eliminate one third of them, to convert (into the Catholic Faith) another third, and to expel (into Nazi-occupied Serbia) the rest.

To respond to every part of this general and ambitious plan, concrete and purposeful steps had to be taken and measures adopted. Elimination, the main course of action, needed places of execution, preferably not too exposed to the outside world, where a systematic gathering, incarceration, maintenance, deception, and murder of the victims could be pursued more or less covertly. In this regard, they could take a page from their Nazi mentors and their collaborators, who had been massacring hundreds of thousands of Jews, Poles, and others and burying them in ditches in the middle of forests, like in Baby Yar, in the Ukraine, or throwing them, dead or alive, into rivers or into the sea, like into the Danube in Hungary. All this, well prior to the Wannsee Conference (January 1942), where the final solution was devised for the Jews under the Third Reich, while the Jadovno enterprise was launched six months earlier, in June 1941. But there is little doubt that the idea of incarcerating perceived enemies or rivals, with a view of liquidating them, without any due process as would befit the civilized world, and exclusively because of what they were and not for what they did, was easily adopted by the Ustasha from their mentors, for if the great German nation could go down that path, why not its Croat apprentices? Moreover, one has to assume that the Ustasha thought, probably under their mentors' instigation, that in the midst of the massive massacres of millions, caused by the Nazis and their collaborators, anything done by the Croats in their territory would be so marginal and diluted within the larger world events and slaughters, that hardly anyone would notice. And if you add hundreds of thousands Serbs to the millions of perishing Jews and other conquered Europeans at the hands of the Nazis, who will care?

In addition to the almost innate hatred of the Serbs among the Croats (and vice-versa), which must have facilitated in their minds the mental transition from abhorrence to liquidation, the Ustasha who equally despised the Jews for different reasons, saw a great opportunity to lump together the implementation of their ambition to see the Serbs disappear with the service they rendered to their German mentors in the physical elimination of Jews and Gypsies, exactly as their counterparts in the Baltics, Poland, the Ukraine, and Central Europe had excelled in doing in the footprints of the Nazi advance. Countless victims of many nationalities were then drowned in the Danube or the Visla, or buried dead or alive in the forests of Poland and the Ukraine, or ended up eventually in extermination camps. Similarly, the Serbs, the Jews, and the Gypsies of the Balkans were sent to the bottom of the sea at the island of Pag; thrown into the Sava, after they were knocked down by coarse and primitive tools; choked with ropes or strangulated by bare hands; or strung together in dozens and forced live into bottomless pits, where the first in the human chain pulled into the abyss the others behind him. Only one who has seen the remnants of those skeletons, trying desperately, and in vain, to climb out of that underground cliff to safety, can begin to understand the cruelty of the overzealous Ustasha and their Bosnian Muslim collaborators in carrying out their harrowing task, to the point that their Nazi overlords had to ask them to attenuate their enthusiasm for killing.

The occasion to go to visit the Jadovno complex, and learn firsthand something of its gruesome hidden history, did not open until recently, when inquisitive minds, of locals and foreigners, especially the few survivors from that hell and the families of the victims of the camp complex, first investigated on their own to satisfy their restlessness and to try to learn and understand what had happened to their loved ones. The two-day conference (June 24–25, 2011, in Banja Luka, the capital of the Republika Srpska) was the implementation of the dream of such an individual: Dushan Bastasic, a Bosnian Serb, who was motivated by an uncontrollable drive to investigate the horrors where many members of his family perished at the hands of the Ustasha government and its Bosniak collaborators. For many years, since Communist Yugoslavia emerged from World War II under Tito, the genocide in and by the Ustasha state, which was established in 1941 by the Nazis to serve their occupation in the Balkans, was pushed to the margins of history by a government that was aware not only of the horrors, but also of the delicate ethnic and religious balance between the various groups that made up the new Communist state based in Belgrade. So, in spite of the harsh reprisals that Croat Tito took against his compatriot Usta-shas for their subservience to the Nazis, he kept their genocide of the Serbs, the Jews, and the Gypsies under wraps, and he did not permit the enmities to disrupt the outer harmony of the Yugoslav federation.

The *Encyclopedia of Yugoslavia* says about the Jadovno camp:

> The prisoners in Jadovno had to work the whole day till exhaustion with almost no food. Five kilometers from the camp was a pit where prisoners were murdered and dumped. The last group of 1,500 inmates was killed by the machine guns of the Ustashas. New victims were taken to Ostarije (a village on the Gospic-Karlobag Road) where they were thrown into a pit at a small village called Stupacinovo. It is calculated that the Jadovno camp and its surroundings swallowed more than 35,000 victims.

> The nearest pit to the camp is the Saran Pit, which is situated about one kilometer from the camp where the 35,000 victims have perished. But there are other pits, which are known today and some others, which aren't known as they were filled up with earth, concrete, and leaves in order to erase any trace of the crimes. Hence the figures are probably much higher than the mentioned 35,000. It is estimated that the total number of killed victims in Jadovno must be around 50,000–60,000, which ranks Jadovno under Jasenovac. The Slano and Metajna camps on Pag Islands were shut down in mid August 1941 as the area was occupied by the Italians. Many of their remaining prisoners were taken to pits at Jadovno, called Saran at Stupacinovo near Ostarije (where most of the Jews had been gathered before they were executed). Some were thrown into other pits or were murdered in Pag, so that no trace of a crime was left on the island.[2]

Tito's death in 1980 and the disintegration of the federation caused that hell of hatred to break loose into a civil war that lasted some three years, producing more harrowing demonstrations of mutual hostility and evidence of more outbursts of genocide on all sides. Only after the Dayton Agreement was mediated and imposed by the United States in 1995 did Bosnia settle into a new reality of a ticking bomb, where no one is at ease, and a sentiment of uncertainty and of unsettled accounts still prevails. The old grievances begin to surface, independent investigations take place, and instead of just hurling accusations at each other, a database is being erected by all parties concerned, each presenting the best face and pushing the uglier sights into oblivion. The Jadovno Conference of 2011 was part of that process. Before it was convened, much individual work was undertaken, more by Serbian and Jewish investigators, who were the victims, than by Bosnians and Croats, who have no particular interest to illuminate that black hole in their history, and have every interest to keep it under cover, while, on the contrary, throwing light on the misconduct of Serbs then and now. Hence, there were many Serbian (and Jewish) participants in the conference but no Croats to mention; though the conference included some straightforward valuable research, peppered at times by apologetic Croatian scholarship, and many semi-scholarly and publicistic and outright propaganda writings, which have been accumulating lately and struggling to occupy their space in the world of printing. Numerous were also Jews from various nationalities, including Israel, Serbia, Italy, and the United States, who contributed the fruits of their private investigations over the years. Some of them have descended to the bottom of the fifty meter deep natural pits where thousands of the victims were pushed, live or dead, to their final burial place. The study of the skeletons retrieved revealed something of the final suffering of the dead while they were living their last moments.

No one argues the fact that the Ustasha government acted cruelly and inhumanly; the question under dispute remains the numbers, between eighty thousand and seven hundred thousand of Serbian victims. But even the smallest numbers of these victims advanced in this debate, and the mode of their execution, are still horrifying enough to deserve the epithet of genocide all the same, as long as they were exterminated solely because they were Serbs. The annihilation of some thirty thousand Jews and similar numbers of Gypsies, are not a topic of disagreement, and fell in line with general Nazi policy. The systematic annihilation of Serbs, however, was a specifically Croat-Ustasha

enterprise. It is said that the Nazis did not quite comprehend this hatred by Slavs (Croats) to other Slavs (Serbs), and they often reproached
their overzealous Ustasha clients for their eagerness to kill and their
thirst to slaughter. The first camp in Jadovno was opened for a few
months only in summer 1941, until it was closed when the Italians
moved to that area. Its substitute, the much larger Jasenovac, on the
Sava River, operated for four years until 1945 and increased the pace
and the scope of the murders of masses of Serbs, Jews, and Gypsies by
the end of the war, earning the epithet of the "third largest in Europe,"
probably after Auschwitz and Treblinka.

This chapter will dwell in some detail on that early period of three
months in the summer of 1941, when the inexperienced Ustasha regime
was acting hectically, recklessly, and in a hurry to complete their task,
as long as the Nazis' preponderance permitted their collaborators to
act at their whim. In that short period, Serbs, from their concentra-
tions as indicated above, and Jews, of the main cities of Croatia and
Bosnia, within the confines of the Ustasha regime, notably Zagreb
(Croatia) and Sarajevo (Bosnia), were hurriedly herded together and
brought either to the island of Pag, which was not far from there, or
to the Jadovno complex to be executed one way or another. While the
conference participants were visiting Jadovno, for a first ceremony
commemorating the seventieth anniversary of the mass executions,
many mind-boggling stories were told by the thousands of elderly (pre-
sumably Serbs and a few Jews) who were present and hardly staggering
on their feet. It was hard to reconcile the painfully detailed descriptions
of the massacres, by the people who remembered them as eyewitnesses
or from stories they heard, with the contrastingly serene landscape on
top of that picturesque and forested mountain, where tall and antique
trees stood witness to the eternally misleading and treacherous history
buried under its rocks. Particularly moving to us was the description
of the Jewish members of the Maccabee Sports Club in Zagreb, who
were rounded up in one of the first raids of the Ustasha against the
Jews, brought to Jadovno, strung together to one chain, and then forced
into a fifty-five meter deep pit, where they all perished in horror. To
erase any trace that the Jews may have left behind, the two synagogues
of Zagreb were razed, burned to the ground, while their worshippers
were being thrown into those dark and bottomless pits where their
memory, it was assumed, would perish for eternity.

Maybe due to the organizational mind of the Germanic people,
their raids against the Jews, the thousands they loaded on trains, the

hundreds of thousands they temporarily absorbed in death camps before or for the sake of sending them to crematoria, were all documented and accounted for. Even the inmates in those camps, most of whom would ultimately perish, were tattooed with indelible ink on their arm, so as to carry on their bodies at all times their transitory identity, in the form of a number, which permitted their tormentors to keep count of them and to report to their superiors, at any time, the pace and volume of their "production" capacity. Survivors of those death camps have kept that number incrusted in their skin, permanently crying out to the world their mark, both physical and more so psychological, that was left forever to distinguish them from the rest of humanity. Maybe the Slavic collaborators of the Germans, notably the Ustasha, were less inclined to impeccable order, to writing reports, to concluding summaries, to accounting for their "accomplishments." For them, the "delight" of throwing a Jew or a Serb into a pit; or knocking them off, before they were drowned in the river or in the sea; or torturing them and observing as their human traits receded, as they were reduced to animal instinctive motions, when they begged for bread, for their lives, or for the lives of their children or of the old and the sick, filled their very petty and miserable beings with the satisfaction and purposefulness that they needed.

For the German killers, the prisoners in their wards were anonymous, small, and insignificant parts of an enormous machine, brought in dead-alive, and as almost inanimate and agonizing souls, who used to be human but have been extinguished since. The Germans dispensed of them through their crematoria chimneys, without giving them a thought, beyond allocating to each of them a rubric and a number in the interminable lists of the murdered, but the Ustasha and their collaborators were of a different brand. Though their victims also remained anonymous, they were treated individually, as if their assassins were reluctant to lump together all those little masochistic pleasures of seeing each Serb or Jew or Gypsy suffer separately, languishing in hunger and suffering in terror and deprivation, and they elected to live and relive the murder of each victim separately, continuously, and repeatedly. That was sadism at its epitome, for how could any human being face the execution of so many murders, so many times a day, day in day out, and yet retain his human sentiment and his operational sanity? Perhaps their way of handling mass murder, severally rather than collectively, had emanated from their upbringing as pretty primitive small farmers, who could not think big or organize enterprises on a large scale. They had been accustomed to work with hand scythes, sickles, pitchforks, spades, shovels, hammers, wooden mallets, ploughs, and other simple farming implements, and to tie things together with ropes, fit them in, or discard them apart with a brutal knock. They had nothing of the German organization, sophistication, and efficacy of mass and chain production, no understanding of mechanization, no delicate approach to advanced equipment, no know-how to operate machinery, and no planning constraints, and they had all the time in the world to enjoy their murderous orgy without undue and unnecessary haste.

Thus, we will find the modus operandi of these coarse brutes very much tied to their customs, capacities, and savoir faire. A victim, whose turn had come to satisfy their murderous pursuit, was either knocked on the head before execution; or stabbed multiple times until he succumbed; or left to be consumed agonizingly slowly by hunger, terror, or illness; or pushed into a pit, over the cliff, or into the sea or the river, along with heavy stones attached to his legs, to precipitate his drowning; or linked to others with ropes or chains, so that each served also as a weight to hasten the drowning of the others, and to leave them no hope of escape or rescue. To manage the murder of so many, these merciless assassins must have stretched to the limit the varieties of immolation that they had used for animals in their rural experience. They apparently saw no difference between a sheep, a Serb, a pig, a Jew, or a Gypsy, except that the animals could be consumed and made good use of, while humans were pure waste of no value at all. The corpses of the victims (and they counted in the many thousands) were either thrown into the deep pits, where no trace or scent of them remained hanging around, or thrown into the sea and the rivers. (If only the Sava could talk, how many restless souls could we count floating over its constantly flowing and precipitately changing waters and the treacherous serenity they conceal?) But most were buried, mostly dead though some also probably alive, in enormous ditches dug within the confines of the camp for dissimulation.

Small wonder then, that it has been so difficult after the war to reconstitute a full picture of what had happened there, especially that, for the nearly forty years of the Communist existence, it was taboo to raise these explosive questions, and therefore, until recently, nothing close to what was done in the protracted and painful data collection at *Yad Vashem* in Jerusalem has been attempted in Croatia and Bosnia, the arena where these crimes were mostly concocted and executed.

The immediate ramification of this mammoth failure has been the paucity of data and of impartial research on either side, hence the predominance of narratives and accusations, and the flourishing of many contradicting histories, instead of allowing fewer but more authoritative, comprehensive, and synthetic histories to predominate the agenda. One of the absolute imperatives for anyone who cherishes the memory of the departed, and wishes to cultivate it and to bequeath it to the new generations, is not only to collect every bit of documentary evidence from the survivors and their families and friends, but also to compile a list of names of the murdered (there is no better or more convincing evidence of the validity of the numbers that are hurled around), to institutionalize the Memorial Day that was inaugurated in June 2011, and especially to strive to open, without reserve, the old archives of the Ustasha and their allies and collaborators. Without all those measures combined, not much progress can be made, and no breakthrough can be effected into this vast virgin territory that cries for research, opening, recognition, tolerance, historical consciousness, and curiosity to know and to learn. If nothing of this is done, then at least we are duty bound to respond to the cries of the tortured souls of the victims to be recognized, accounted for and commemorated by their descendents, fellow citizens and countrymen, and plain human beings.

The comparatively small area of Jadovno was probably chosen because of the abundance in that landscape of grottos, caverns, and bottomless pits, where the murdered victims could be thrown without leaving a trace. It was abandoned after merely three months due to the fact that the Italians had expanded their occupation zone to encompass Jadovno and its immediate surroundings; the murderers feared that the genocide they were bent upon possibly did not quite accord with Italian policy and conduct in their occupied areas. Therefore, they decided to transfer their genocide of Serbs, Jews, Gypsies, and dissidents out of those crude facilities to Jasenovac. But within those three or four months (April–August 1941), tens of thousands were massacred, including thousands of Jews and seventy-three members of the Serb Orthodox clergy, namely one third of the total in NDH, the acronym for the "Independent State of Croatia," otherwise known as the Ustasha state. Like the Nazi camps of the same nature, Jadovno was erected in close proximity to a railway station (Gospic, in this case) to facilitate the easy access and quick delivery of the victims from other parts of Yugoslavia, and on a river bank or a seashore (here in Velebit and Pag), to expedite evacuation of corpses, debris, and traces of genocide. Branches of this vast complex existed from June 25 to August 20 on the island of Pag.

Chronologically, these camps preceded the large known concentration camps in Germany, and were soon established, with the help of the Germans and the Italians. (This seems to have contradicted Italian policy, but apparently differentiation was made within the Italian Command between bearing responsibility for death camps, under their direct occupation, and lending a hand to their other Fascist allies in the logistics of building facilities under the Ustasha.) This means that the Ustasha had launched their ethnic cleansing operations as early as summer 1941, while Auschwitz and Treblinka were not readied until early 1942, and the mass murders in gas chambers were inaugurated in July of that year. Under the Ustasha, as under the Nazis, a Serb or a Jew did not need to be indicted and convicted for anything. Being a Serb or a Jew was conviction enough, which required capital punishment, regardless of race, gender, faith, age, and nationality. Jews and Gypsies fell clearly within the Nazi racist policy to which the Ustasha subscribed. But Serbs were their own innovative addition, and it underlined their own innate anti-Serbian grudge that for centuries had been allowed to accumulate hatred, wrath, and scorn. Serbs, Jews, and Gypsies were rounded up in all parts of NDH and transported to the Gospic concentration camp, at the rate of three hundred daily. According to this pace of extermination, if nothing else, in the space of about one hundred days, the camp could have "processed" about thirty thousand souls. Above the abyss of the pits, column after column of tied, mutilated, helpless, and tortured people would be knocked by mallets, knives, or otherwise, or brutally pushed with a bunch of other horrified or numb people at the head of the column, head first into the dark pit to their certain death, dragging all the others behind them.

The extant disorganized and unsystematic reports and memoirs, which are being culled from the few survivors who are still around, in no way do justice to the memory of the murdered. This situation was allowed to become almost incorrigible because throughout the duration of Communist rule, which held Yugoslavia together, the federal state paid no attention to collecting the details and commemorating them, under the pretense of cultivating unity and fraternity between the peoples and territories of its component parts. Conversely, the families of the victims were taught to forget and forgive those horrible events. But when the federal state tottered under the weight of its own contradictions, the hatreds and jealousies entertained by its peoples, and the rapidly bifurcating narratives that instigated rival nationalisms, especially between the Serbs, the Croats, and the Muslims, rapidly came to the fore. The study of the Ustasha state saw a tremendously revived new interest, especially by the Serbs, in its history and persecution of the Serbs (and Jews as a useful appendix), and in the constitution of the death camps on Ustasha land, which to their mind dramatically exemplifies the "ethnic cleansing" and "racial purity" drive that are part and parcel of modern Croatian nationalism. Even though the Serbs have later demonstrated during the Bosnia War (1992–1995), their capacity to apply the same repulsive policies toward their Croat and Bosniak rivals, a policy that turned that war into unbridled savagery in the heart of Europe, others do not feel the accounts settled. Hence the continuation of mutual hostility between the parties, and the nearly impossible task of reconstituting war records, collecting data about the victims, and opening the official records for unselective and uncensored scrutiny by impartial scholars and researchers.

Milan Ljustina, who spent time in the Gospic camp from its inception on June 22 until its liquidation on August 21, estimates in his statement that around 120,000 people in total were massacred at Jadovno: 118,000 of them Serbs and 1800 Jews. There are, however lower estimates, like the one appearing in the census of 1964, amounting to 1,794 victims in total, which clearly reflected the desire of the authorities to minimize the numbers, out of fear for how they might inflame the interethnic situation. But the census itself was understandably criticized for disorganization and partiality in its attitude, and insincerity and dishonesty in terms of the pursuit of truth. Those distortions were based on the claim that in that census, the names of 3,127 Serbian men, women, and children from the former Gospic and Perusic counties had been registered, and 3,063 of them were murdered in the camps of Jadovno, even before there was a Serbian uprising against the Croatian state, which could have tentatively justified the massacre. Franjo Zdunic Lav, who lived in Gospic in 1941 and later researched Ustasha crimes, stated that a total of 37,660 people were murdered in Jadovno. He claims that he got this approximate number from the analysis of daily transports through Gospic to the execution sites.

Another eyewitness, Terka Gojmerac, claimed that during the period of one month alone (July–August) in 1941, around twenty-five thousand inmates went through the penitentiary of Gospic, not counting those who were taken directly from the railway station to the execution sites and did not sojourn in the main camp. In his opinion,

Franjo Zdunic had erred when computing only the days of June to August as part of the average making up the total amount of the murdered, while in fact the arrest and execution of the victims had begun on April 11. Therefore the actual numbers must be much greater than in Zdunic's estimates, perhaps a double of what he says. Fikreta Jelic Butic estimates that in August 1941 alone, eighteen thousand inmates were murdered in Jadovno, while an Ustasha report speaks of twenty-five thousand victims. To her mind, culled from numbers given by survivors in 1942, after the Camp was shut down, the total numbers of the Jadovno victims vacillated between thirty thousand and forty-eight thousand. The author of the entry in the *Encyclopedia of Yugoslavia*, Ljubo Boban, cites a military encyclopedia, from which he got the number of seventy-two thousand, with the Saranova pit alone devouring half that amount. Another former inmate, Duro Medic, states that in the less than three weeks, between August 3 and 20, 1941, namely when it became known that it was going to close down, 35,000 people went through the camp; and yet another, Drago Svjetlicic, stated that 18,000 Serbs were incarcerated in Velebit during those sixteen days in the month of August alone. Ustasha sources, which have certainly no interest to inflate the numbers, report for the same month, the figure of deported and murdered as 28,500 Serbs. Indeed, Sergeant Markovic, who served in an Ustasha unit, also confirmed that number.

All this is to say, that while there is no orderly archive where the numbers were registered; there is also no particular enthusiasm on the part of the Croat government to reveal to the public authoritative numbers it possesses. The opportunity was lost decades ago to undergo a systematic, impartial, and objective data collection when Yugoslavia existed and was capable of launching such a research, if it had had the political will to do so. There are nevertheless today many honest, courageous, conscientious, fair, and truly caring individuals, in all quarters, who would do what they can under two dominant constraints: first, that what was lost is irretrievable, and second, that what can still be distilled from lies and propaganda, may, against all odds, still be partly rescued. This is the task that this volume is dedicated to. Naturally, what we have is scattered, intermittent, fragmentary, and inconsistent, for each piece of data we can lay our hand on represents only the point of view of an individual (biased or impartial), during a limited period of time and at certain places.

Our task remains, then, even if we should succeed in gathering enough data, to piece them together; to verify them for authenticity; to compare and cross-check them with other sources; to test them in their historical, local, and international context; to try, at best, to present the lacking puzzle to the reader; or at least, and most likely, to present a general sketch of events, with the remaining blanks to be filled by further research or according to the research experience and creative imagination of the writers on this sensitive topic. Since the range of bottom-line estimates, culled from both Ustasha and survivors, does not vary as greatly as it could have, one can take, as the working total figure, thirty thousand to forty-eight thousand exterminated Serbs and Jews in Jadovno; the great majority, probably 90 percent or more, were Serbs. The numbers will increase manifold when we get to the much more massive Jasenovac camp, which was in operation for a full, four-year period, until the end of the war, and on a much grander scale.

Similarly, the death machine on the island of Pag operated from June 25 to August 21, 1941. Again the estimates are based on eyewitnesses, partly inmates, partly residents of the island; Italian documents, which took note of many of the horrendous murders briefly after they were perpetrated, and even *post-factum* statements by a large number of the murderers themselves. For example, Pavle Lvric and many other residents of Pag claim that 18,600 persons, of all ages, were imprisoned on the island. Emerik Blum, who spent thirty days there out of the fifty-seven days it existed, stated that there were ten thousand inmates in the Slana Camp on the island, comprising nine thousand Serbs and a thousand Jews. His statement was supported by others. The author, Ratislav Loric, tells in his book, *Conspiracy against Serbs*, that 4,500 Serbs, 2,500 Jews, and 1,500 Croats were killed on Pag. Another researcher, Duro Zatezalo, disputes these figures because they are not sustained by any other evidence, archival or otherwise.

An unexpected source of information was Priest Josip Felinovic, who reported on the Italian military commission, which burned corpses of victims in the Slana camp on Pag a few days after it was evacuated by the Ustashas in August 1941. He claims that based on what he saw and what he was told by Italian officers in the area of Furnaza, eight thousand corpses had been found in place. One month later, on September 22, a report written by a Dr. Stazzi admitted that only 791 corpses had been incinerated. But one of the Ustasha murderers, Luka Barjasic, stated that the "Ustasha on Pag had killed 6,500 men, women, and children, mostly with hammers and daggers." Other people who were supposed to know what was happening in the Slana camp on Pag, such as Ivo Bilic and Tomo Dodoja, state that to the best of their knowledge, some six thousand persons were thrown into the sea to their death. Once again, based on these testimonies, press articles, and bits and pieces gleaned here and there over many years of inquiry and research, we can estimate that about six thousand persons in all perished in Pag. In all, the Jadovno complex, including Pag, was the burial area of some 42,246 individuals during that period of 132 days between April 11 and August 21, 1941. The numbers are neither certain nor accurate, but the scope of the murders, the pace of the killing, and the cruelty of the pitiless executions, leave no doubt as to the almost unparalleled hostility and cruelty of the Ustashas toward Serbs and Jews, and occasionally even toward their Croatian kin, whose "crime" probably was either reluctance to participate in the massacre, or they may have expressed human bouts of courage, decency, compassion, and assistance to the doomed victims. Zatezalo obtained these figures going through NDH archival documents, interviewing survivors and some of the criminals, and adding up reports of railways stations and police departments from various counties. Inaccurate and incomplete as they may be, they can stand as universally agreed working numbers until refuted or confirmed by other sources.

Two periods are distinguished by this most thorough, comprehensive, and caring about the truth Zatezalo report: the first seventy-four days, between April 11 and June 24, 1941; and from there another fifty-eight days to the closure of the camps on August 21. During the first period, at the rate of 180 victims a day, 13,346 people were incarcerated and massacred; in the second period, at the accelerated rate of 498 Serbs and Jews daily, some 28,900 inmates were extra-judiciously arrested, deported, and criminally executed. Of that total one ought to deduct, however, the surviving 2,123 individuals that the Ustashas did not have the time to obliterate prior to the Italian takeover of the camp. That leaves us with the harrowing total of 40,123 murdered persons in the Jadovno complex, over the limited period of less than four months, the majority of whom (32,103) were killed on Velebit and the rest (some 8,000) on Pag. One can only imagine how many more lives would have perished had that rate been maintained to the end of the war. But as we shall see, that vacuity would be more than made up in Jasenovac. At any rate, on average, 320 prisoners were transported every day aboard cattle train cars to Gospic, and 304 of them were executed, on average, every day.

Between August 19 and 21, just before the Italians landed in Jadovno, the Ustashas pushed 2,123 prisoners that they did not have the time to exterminate, as yet, into cattle train cars and transferred them to Jastrebarsko. In the final transport of August 21, there were nine hundred Serbs, who were then forwarded to the newly opened Jasenovac camp to become its first inmates. Others were sent to other camps, pending the regular opening of Jasenovac to the routine arrivals, incarceration, and execution of the new inmates. By the end of the 1990s, more than ten thousand names of victims were identified. But, paradoxically, the breakdown of the Yugoslavian state, which had prevented an open and unlimited inquiry into the horrors of wartime Croatia, now constituted a novel obstacle in the pursuit of such investigation, due to the rising local nationalisms and the developing diverging narratives, which by necessity restrained the amount of information each rival nationality wished to release to the others. Thus, for half a century, the horrors of Jadovno and Jasenovac remained under wraps in the forests, islands, and rocks of the bygone Ustasha state, or in the depth of its pits and mass burial sites. What we know for certain is that the rate of the Serbian population in what used to be the Ustasha state, went down from 12 percent, at the outbreak of the war, to just over 4.5 percent at its end, something that gave rise to the claim that the missing 8 percent, amounting to about seven hundred thousand Serbs, were exterminated in those camps. Granted that many Serbs died at the hands of Germans, either under direct German occupation, or within the ranks of the Partisans, and that more Serbs had found their way out of the war zone for other reasons, it remains that the numbers of Serbian victims in the camps is quite staggering. Even according to the minimal claims of the Croats, the thousands who perished in the two camps remain a grueling figure on the scale of a genocide.

Since the Jadovno 1941 Conference was devoted specifically to that complex of death camps, and most of the papers presented dealt with one aspect or another of that chilling reality, it is essential before we bring this sad chapter to its close, to sum up some of the new contributions that were brought up during those deliberations. Foremost among the presentations was Duro Zatezalo's, who has been repeatedly referred to above, due to the meticulousness of his research and the striking accuracy and apparent emotional detachment with which the author presented the data he gathered during his lifetime search for the facts and their interpretation. His delivery of his findings, nonetheless, was not devoid of passion, the passion of the scientist who can at long last cry out his *"eureka!"* at the end of a long process of search and frustration. First of all, he spelled out the gory topography of the Velebit pits, the Gospic camp and its camp Ovcara appendix, another camp near Risova Glava, the execution site Slana and another Metajna on Pag, yet another named Stupacinovo near Baske Ostarije, and a collection point for victims at Gospic railway station. All these hidden encampments were erected by the Gospic County authorities and police administration in April 1941 by Ustasha Jurica Frkovic, with the assistance of members of the Catholic clergy, army, and police, all under state sponsorship, who raided, arrested, and delivered any Serbs and Jews they could lay their hands on, as well as decent Croatian anti-Fascists who refused to collaborate in the destruction of innocent victims.

Significantly, this complex was hurriedly erected already on the second day of NDH's existence (April 11), before any resistance could develop to this Nazi-Ustasha creation under Ante Pavelic, geared to achieve the elimination of Serbs in Croatia and Bosnia, as a specific implementation of Croat ambition to attain a pure Croat-Catholic state, and the genocide of the Jews of Yugoslavia as part of their Holocaust in Europe. The elimination of fellow human beings was conducted under the most inhuman and cruel conditions, and it included, in addition to Serbs and Jews as detailed above, also eighty-eight Croats, eleven Slovenians, nine Muslims, two Hungarians, two Czechs, one Russian, one Romanian, and one Montenegrin. The author concluded that the Ustasha surpassed, in their grueling murderous practices, the German Nazis in the Jewish Holocaust and the Turkish genocide against the Armenians during World War I. Not only were the victims hit on their heads before they were pushed into the abyss of the pits, but rocks were attached to their bodies to avert any possibility for them to seek rescue. Ustasha savagery and apparent sadism raised question marks among the Nazi Germans and the Fascist Italians, who wondered at the Ustasha blood thirst and delight in murdering in cold blood. One of the most poignant documents cited by the author is a report by Nazi Zagreb chief of defense, Arthur Heffner, to Berlin on April 24, 1942, which is one year after the beginning of the genocide, expressing shock over the terrible crimes of the Ustasha toward Serbs and their property, against "People who had been living there from time immemorial."

Heffner wrote, *inter alia*, that he could not believe that most Catholic priests supported these crimes, and he cited the Sarajevo Archbishop Saric, who wrote in a Catholic paper on May 11, 1941: "I visited our Ustashas in North America. I sang with all my heart our Ustasha hymns with tears in my eyes. We have always accorded loyalty and fealty to the Homeland. More Croats! More Catholics! God and Croats!" He also stated unabashedly that he was an Ustasha. Heffner also reported that Franciscan monk Francetic ordered a primary school teacher to separate Serbian Orthodox children from the rest, to have them later murdered, in front of their teacher and schoolmates,[3] while other Catholic priests gave detailed instructions on how to cleanse the NDH from Serbs, Jews, and Gypsies. But in spite of the depth, the scope, and the gravity of these crimes, what happened in Jadovno was kept under wraps, an indication in itself of the recognition by the Ustasha of the unforgivably wicked moral and legal offenses they committed and of their fear, lest they be caught, indicted, and convicted as war criminals. Moreover, efforts were constantly made by the criminals to erase any traces of the horrors, and even the humble memorials, which were erected in place over the years subsequent to the war, were destroyed in the years 1990–95. The cries of helpless despair of the victims, while they were executed, went with them to their collective tombs without leaving a trace or a memory. Due to their mode of extermination, they were never exhumed, their body count never effected, their individual identity never revealed, and their decent burial never executed. Thus, although the monstrosity of those harrowing acts was never equaled, let alone surpassed, by anyone else anywhere else, since the grueling massacres by the Mongols in the medieval world, the memory of the murdered was never commemorated. The pretext was in the name of the pretended "unity and brotherhood" between the component parts of Yugoslavia, which elected to let "the bones rest where they were" instead of investigating the crimes and persecuting the culprits.

Alexander Necak, of the Union of Jewish Communities of Serbia, addressed precisely this question of preserving the memory of the deceased. Knowing one thing or two about the Jewish tragic experience in the Holocaust, he distinguished between individual and collective memory of the dead, the former performed within families and private circles, the latter by states annually for their murdered nationals. At times one hears the chilling absurdity that a memorial day was "successful," because many participants attended, including representatives of those who had perpetrated the crimes and who pretend to have "repented." Memorials are usually matched and backed up by public monuments that are erected to replace the missing living souls with inanimate stone structures, which do not tell the story and do not even hint at the enormity of its incomprehensible atrocities.

For example, if one walks by the *Staro Sajmiste*, the old fair grounds in Belgrade, the location where *Judenlager Semlin* was placed, no one can begin to guess or imagine today, seventy years later, the amount of horror that gripped the 6,800 Jews, mostly women and children, who were raided, assembled, detained, and deported to their death by the Nazis; though there, unlike in Croatia, the job was done by the Nazis themselves. There are two monuments for anti-Fascist fighters, but not a mention of the Jewish innocent people who perished there. Thus, the moral, historical, educational, and humane dimension of these memorials is sorely missing, save when they are constructed in Israel, which emphasizes specifically those aspects.

An extraordinary document is extant in the Belgrade Museum, titled "Group Jadovno," which encompasses 229 names of Jews who were murdered in Jadovno, out of the at least 1,998 who perished there. That was a statement written by Dr. Bela Hohsteter and signed in front of witnesses, which confirms that the authority in the camps of Danica, Jadovno, and Gospic was in the hands of the Ustashas, and that the massacre of the inmates in Jadovno was committed between July 30 and August 3, namely prior to the Italian takeover of that region. Dr. Alexander Blivajs confirms these observations and the fact that the elimination of inmates in the camp was the Ustasha's doing, regardless of the attempts made today by the murderers to whitewash the NDH Holocaust and World War II track record, by presenting Croatian anti-Semitism as mere Nazi import (although the Ustasha had their own racist and ethnocidal ideology and theory as well as extermination practices[4]), and to convince the public that Serbs actually were worse than Croats. Some consider Cohen's[5] book, *Serbia's Secret War* as the "culmination of this strategy."[6] They believe that the distortion of history was achieved now, not by using lies, but by omitting any "inkling of the actual societal impact of these manifestations of anti-Semitism in Serbia," and by abstaining from determining "whether they were marginal or dominant."[7] Dennis Reinhartz, a professor of history, said in his review of Cohen's book that *Serbia's Secret War* belongs to "the current popular-historical and journalist literature that seeks to demonize and condemn more than to chronicle and elucidate fairly."[8] He also added that the book was in danger of degenerating itself into an irrational conspiracy history and belongs to those history works of the Balkans that contribute little to our understanding of past events and their impact on the present.[9] Indeed, Serbia and Serbs were presented as the cause of all evil, implying that there was no need to say explicitly that every action against Serbs, in the past and the future, was and will be justified.

Out of this maze of contradictory statements, evaluations, prejudices, personal involvements, and scholarly inquiries, it will never be possible to sort out truth from accusation. Since I have to raise my hands in submission in the face of these contradictions, and since I have no axe to grind in shifting evidence and good sense from one side to another, I have elected to leave these truly hard nuts uncracked, because of my inability to unravel them, not because of my unwillingness to clarify them. I have therefore followed the track of the Holocaust researchers, who viewed this entire issue from the Holocaust studies standpoint, namely how, how much, and in what form, did the proportional part of the Croats, the Serbs, and the Muslims in former Yugoslavia contribute to the genocide of the Jews in Europe, under the overall Nazi blueprint. Viewed uniquely from that standpoint, the findings will certainly not do justice to the parties concerned, but they will certainly summarize and bring to the fore the suffering, the sacrifices, and the victimization of the Jewish people under all principal actors. Thus, Philip Cohen may have been right to say that "the last victim of genocide is the truth," but the overall truth that Jews were persecuted and eliminated by all parties, attempts to whitewash *post-factum* that history, by all murderers notwithstanding, will stand as a blazing and a blaring fact for all generations to come.

A chilling summary applying to the genocide of Serbs in the area of Bosanska Krajina during the entire duration of the war (1941–1945), was provided by Jovan Mirkovic, drawn from the database of the Museum of Genocide in Belgrade. It says that the area in question constituted 11.23 percent of the NDH territory, with a total population (based on the 1931 census) of 659,701. Of these, 63.9 percent were Orthodox Christians, namely Serbs; 12.1 percent Roman Catholics, that is Croats; 23.84 percent Muslim; and 0.76 percent others. It is estimated (no census was conducted during the war) that by 1941 the total population had grown to 804,835. The roll of victims recorded in that area during that period was 105,624, which was 23.16 percent of the total list of victims in the NDH and 13.12 percent of the estimated population in 1941 in that area. Out of the 105,624 people who died, 24,537 of them were children up to the age of fourteen, or 23.23 percent of the victims. That included 13,184 preschool children, up to the age of seven, 5,614 or primary school children, and 5,739 older children. Along with the children, the elderly over sixty, who were fit neither for work nor for military service, their numbers among the victims totaled 6,239, or 5.91 percent of the lot. That number could grow considerably if we add to it the persons of unknown age who perished. Data of the Jadovno camps victims were compared by the author with Duro Zatezalo's book on this topic, and both bottom lines are equally devastatingly inhuman.

Notes

1. Most of the data reported in this chapter originate from the papers presented in the Conference of Jadovno 1941, convened in Banja Luka in June 2011; from the field visits to the Jadovno camps, in the same month, and previous visits to Jasenovac; from the scant literature published on this topic; an illustrated booklet prepared for the Conference by Jovan Mirkovic, senior curator of the Museum of Genocide Victims in Belgrade; and from author Duro Zatezalo, who published his *Jadovno Complex of Ustasha Camps in 1941*, which was copiously cited by Mirkovic in the distributed prospectus of the Conference.

2. See Jadovno entry, the Encyclopedia of Yugoslavia, the Yugoslav Lexicographic Institute, Zagreb, 1960, volume IV, page 425.

3. *St Anthony's Herald*, issue 7–8, 1941, 8081. Cited by Zatezalo, Ibid.

4. Nevenko Bartulin, *The Ideology of Nation and Race: The Croatian Ustasha Regime and Its Policies toward Minorities in the Independent State of Croatia, 1941–1945*. A thesis submitted in fulfillment of the requirements for the degree of Doctor of Philosophy, University of New South Wales, November 2006.

5. Serbian and Croatian speaking readers can experience *déjà vu* reading this book because of its similarity with Ljubica Štefan, *Od bajke do holokausta, Ministarstvo vanjskih poslova*, Zagreb, 1993. [In English: *From a Fairy Tale to Holocaust*, published by the Croatian Ministry of Foreign Affairs in 1993.] It deals with "collaboration of Serbia and occupiers, and Serbs genocide against Jews."

6. Marko Živković, *A Wish to Be a Jew: The Power of the Jewish Trope in the Yugoslav Conflict*, in *Cahiers de l'URMIS* 6/2000, 76, quoted in Jovan Ćulibrk, *The Holocaust Historiography in Yugoslavia*, in Serbian, *Holocaust u Jugoslaviji*, Beograd, 2011.

7. Ibid., 76, 78, quoted in Jovan Ćulibrk, *The Holocaust historiography in Yugoslavia*, in Serbian, *Holocaust u Jugoslaviji*, Beograd, 2011.

8. Dennis Reinhartz, *Serbia's Secret War: Propaganda and the Deceit of History*, Philip J. Cohen, in Holocaust and Genocide Studies 2/2000, str. 302.

9. Belgrade Jew and author of several books on the Holocaust in Serbia, Jaša Almuly, stated to the press that he doubts that an American doctor [dermatologist] was able to write such a political propaganda pamphlet, and that he believes that it came from the Tudjman's kitchen in Zagreb, in the form of institute organized to work as propaganda machinery. He asked in public: what misfortune, or perhaps benefit, made an American Jew participate in such a dishonorable deed?

4

The Middle East Connection

In June 1941, the prospects were grim for the British and their Allies in the war arena, while the Nazis were at the peak of their stunning accomplishments in Europe and North Africa. They had smashed Poland in the East, France and its surrounding satellites in the West, and had stationed their *blitzkrieg* hero, Erwin Rommel, in North Africa. Rommel, in conjunction with his Italian partners, threatened to overrun the British forces in the Middle East and reach the strategic Suez Canal, which ensured the link between the British-dominated Mediterranean and India. The main worldwide battle was waged by Germany to subjugate the British Empire, the only obstacle that stood, at that time, in its way to dominion in Europe, while the Japanese, Germany's allies, were making headway in the Far East and conquering British colonies, such as Singapore, Burma, and Hong Kong, thus weakening the empire that was equally faltering in the West.

The British, who were and felt quite isolated, in addition to being constantly bombarded and harassed by the Germans on their island, were desperate to reinforce their hold on their Middle East colonial positions, which were centered mainly on Egypt, Palestine, and Iraq, knowing full well that if they were forced to retreat there too, the Mediterranean would become a German lake, much to the detriment of the Allies. At the same time, they realized that the Middle East and North Africa, being essentially Arab, had to rely, more than they would have chosen to, on whom they still regarded as their "Arab allies." However, they had also understood that the rapid successes of the Germans in North Africa, and the fall of Morocco and Algeria to the Vichy regime, which was the Nazis' new ally after the capitulation of France during the month of June 1940, had helped to shift the Arab public opinion in German favor, once it became apparent to them that a Nazi victory against the British would place them solidly on the victors' side. Moreover, since the British were the colonizing power in the Arab world, the anti-British adversaries in the war, that is the Nazis, were automatically conceived as the prospective liberators, hence the interest to ally with them and assist their war effort.

In Palestine, which had been under a League of Nations Mandate since 1922, the British had a particularly hard time to balance between their original commitment in the Balfour Declaration, to ensure the growth of a Jewish National Home in Palestine, in concert with the demands of the Zionist Movement, and the pressures of the Arabs on the colonial power to rescind that obligation and to sustain their counterdemands for an Arab/Palestinian state to conform with the Arab majority of the population. The Arab revolt of 1936–1939, which triggered anti-British and anti-Zionist riots initiated and led by the mufti of Jerusalem, Haj Amin al-Husseini, the progenitor of Palestinian nationalism, had burst out in the wake of the Peel Commission, which had made the first major recommendation to partition the land of Palestine, ceding most of it to the Arab majority of over one million, and leaving to the smaller and more fragile Jewish community of a couple of hundred thousand, a small sliver of land along the Tel-Aviv coast. Like with subsequent partition proposals, the Jews were jubilant over the prospect of acceding to a Jewish independent entity after two millennia in dispersal and persecution, but the Arabs rejected the idea lock, stock, and barrel, and launched the revolt.

The British had hardly succeeded in squashing that rebellion, when the clouds of war started to gather over the skies of Europe, and the German Nazi war machine's political arm, based in Egypt and other parts of the Arab Middle East, began to spread anti-British and anti-Jewish propaganda, partly in accordance with their own worldview and partly to lure the Arabs into their camp. When the war broke out, Haj Amin was already firmly entrenched in the camp of the Muslim Brothers, who had been founded in 1928 in Isma'iliyah, Egypt, and embraced a clearly pro-German, pro-Palestinian and anti-Semitic agenda, and he was invited to Berlin to launch a broadcasting program to the Arab and Muslim world, under the aegis of the Nazi propaganda machine of Dr. Goebbels. The British at first issued one of their "white papers," to placate the Arab rage against the recommendations of the Peel Commission, to the effect of limiting or even banning Jewish immigration to Palestine, precisely at the time when Jewish refugees in the thousands, fleeing Europe from the Nazis, were knocking on the gates of Palestine and had nowhere else to go. Unwilling to lose completely their Arab constituencies, precisely as the Nazi propaganda and achievements on the ground were escalating, the British put themselves on the defensive, doing the best they could to control their damage, thus totally blocking their ears and their sights, and rejecting all Jewish pleadings and supplications to open the gates of Palestine for shelter.

However, at some point the British panicked in the face of the stunning Nazi advances and of their own losses on the various battlefields, and they began to prepare for an eventual evacuation of the Middle East, the like of the Dunkirk debacle a year earlier on the French coast of the Channel. The Jewish *Yishuv* in Palestine, which was so desperate, though disillusioned by the cruel attitude of the British, who continued to reverse the flow of Jewish refugees back to European ports for certain extermination, nevertheless emitted the public message, to wit: "we shall fight the Nazis as if there were no White Paper, and we shall fight the White Paper as if there were no world war." On a practical level, considering the probability of a German takeover of Egypt, the Suez Canal, and Palestine, and the withdrawal of the British defenders, in view of the swift advance of Rommel in the Western Desert, the Jewish *Haganah*, which acted as a self-defense militia, determined to establish a new elite body, made out of permanently recruited and well-trained companies, to assure the building of a new defense line along the ridges of the Carmel mountains in northern Palestine. That new force, dubbed *Palmach*, the acronym for *Plugot Machatz* (strike forces), recruited six companies at first, which also acted in the service of the British in guerilla warfare and were trained to harass German forces behind their lines and to disrupt their logistics and supplies.

Those forces were to double and treble in May 1948, when the state of Israel was declared and five Arab armies invaded the fledgling Jewish state, and they became the skeleton of the newly organized field brigades that rescued Israel from extinction. Some of those recruits participated, under British guidance, in operations against the French Vichy troops in Syria, in one of which Moshe Dayan, later the Israeli war hero, notoriously lost his eye. But in 1942, upon the reversal of the fortunes of the war, with Rommel defeated by Montgomery in al-Alamein, the Germans repulsed from North Africa, the Americans landing in Casablanca, the quelling in Iraq of the pro-Nazi Rashid Ali revolt, and the Nazi invasion of the Soviet front in the previous summer, which caused the diversion of considerable forces from Europe and the Mediterranean eastward, the usefulness of the *Palmach* for the

British became obsolete. Parallelly, Jewish volunteers were recruited by the British to parachute over German-occupied Central Europe, notably Hungary, in order to harass Nazi troops behind their lines. Most notable among them was the young and audacious Hanna Senesch, who was caught when dropped over Hungary, tortured, and executed; she became a folk heroine in fledgling Israel. Thus, the two sides were crystallized, with Arabs and their Palestinian mufti supported by the Nazis and actively aiding their war effort, while the British were bolstering Jewish guerilla forces both in Palestine and in Europe, but at the same time they heartlessly prevented desperate Jewish refugees from Europe from attaining the safety of Palestinian shores. Wars do indeed convene together strange bed-fellows.

It is impossible to grasp the depth of British anxiety in its confrontation with Nazi Germany, which if it were not for the extraordinarily visionary and bold wartime leader, Winston Churchill, would have converted into utter despair, if one does not comprehend first the significance of its setbacks in Egypt, the Middle East, and North Africa, which forced it to move its troops and then withdraw from the Balkans and leave the entire Mediterranean sea to the merciless Nazis. As if confronting the Germans and the Japanese worldwide were not enough, Churchill had also to deal with the contradictory claims of the Jews and the Arabs in Palestine, which had been placed under a British mandate by the League of Nations since 1922. The Jewish side was a minority of a couple of hundred thousand in Palestine, stateless and harshly persecuted by rising Fascism in Europe, and threatened by the winds of war, which forced it to seek shelter in Palestine due to the Western universal reluctance to lend it refuge ("none is too many," became the infamous response of Canadian immigration officials who were probed about the numbers of Jewish refugees they would accept). Britain, as a result of the Arab rejection of the partition plan of the Peel Commission and eager to avoid the wrath of the Arab community if it accorded any favors to the Jews who accepted the plan, issued the White Paper in 1939, limiting immigration into Palestine, which made the situation even worse, even more hopeless for the Jews, who were counting on British generosity to let in all the stateless Jewish refugees flocking in from Europe.

The Arabs could not care less about Jewish extermination in Europe, in fact their chief Palestinian mufti, Haj Amin, started collaborating with the Nazis, leading the two parties to share the idea of the final solution. The White Paper had been issued by Neville Chamberlain, the coauthor of the Munich Agreement, a few months before the outbreak of the war, and stipulated that seventy-five thousand immigration certificates would be authorized by the mandatory power to incoming Jewish refugees, in spite of the exile from the land, since 1937, of the Palestinian leader who already was seeking collaboration with Nazi Germany. According to Walid Khalidi, one of the senior scholars of Middle Eastern affairs, when that quota was exhausted, further Jewish immigration would be contingent upon Arab agreement, "which clearly would not be forthcoming,"[1] because, since the beginning of the Zionist settlement in Palestine, the Arabs had been dead set against Jewish immigration. It was supposedly the memorandum written by Musa Alami and George Antonius, two of the prominent Palestinian leaders, in the absence of Haj Amin, and signed by all Arab senior officials and submitted to the British high commissioner in Palestine in 1936, which complained about British unjust policies in Palestine, that started to tilt that policy toward the issuance of the White Paper. Musa Alami joined the Palestinian delegation in 1939 to the London Round Table, which directly triggered the publication of the White Paper.

The White Paper had also come on the heels of the Arab Revolt of 1936–39, during which Nuri Pasha of Iraq mediated a truce between Haj Amin and the British, which held together only until the Peel Report was published in 1937, and the second phase of the revolt exploded in more violence and vitriol because of the report's partition recommendation. The outburst of renewed violence caused the banning that year of the Arab Higher Committee, and Haj Amin, its head, fled to Lebanon, where the ruling French tolerated his continued fight against the British in Palestine. Only when the war broke out, were he and his colleagues, who were in exile with him, asked to leave. They all sought refuge in Iraq and associated with a coterie of military and political leaders who supported the Palestinian cause. The British sent emissaries to Haj Amin so as to cater favor with the Arabs and to convince him to endorse the White Paper. Nuri Sa'id Pasha, the prime minister of Iraq, was instrumental in convincing Haj Amin and his colleagues (Musa Alami and Jamal Husseini), and he also agreed to put Iraqi forces at the disposal of the British in their war against the Axis, if a deal was worked out with Haj Amin. But apparently due to Churchill's opposition, the deal fell through. As a result, Haj Amin became soon involved with the Iraqi pro-Nazi Rashid Ali (Kilani) and his coconspirators, backed by the Muslim Brothers in Egypt (see next chapter), and so a front of anti-British and pro-Nazi actors was formed in April 1941, which put in direct jeopardy British domination of the Middle East. When the British sent troops and reentered Iraq in May to quell the revolt, Haj Amin (and Jamal) fled to Iran, thence to Turkey and then to the Axis countries and Nazi Germany, which he served until the end of the war.

But the crushing of the Rashid Ali coup only escalated Arab animosity toward Britain on account of its Palestinian policy, despite the White Paper and the London Round Table, which were basically a positive response to Arab demands. So, the British, and their loyal ally Nuri Sa'id, wished, in the absence of exiled Haj Amin, and after his short-lived conspiracy with Rashid Ali, to see in the secular, liberal, and highly intellectual and respected Musa Alami, the substitute leader of the Palestinians with whom they could do business, but the Alami-Nuri Pasha collaboration created Palestinian resistance, that was rooted in the pre–1936 Rebellion. The politically active Palestinians had been then divided into two camps: the councilors, who backed Haj Amin and sat in his council, and his opponents, led by Raghib Nashashibi, the patriarch of the century old rival family to the Husseinis in Jerusalem. During the Arab Rebellion, particularly in the second phase that generated the Peel Commission and its report, scores of the Nashashibis were assassinated, and that created widespread hatred and retaliation between those two clans. The assassinations, guided by the mufti from his exile in Lebanon, as part of his struggle against the British and the Jews, were calculated to eliminate his compatriot Palestinians, who were suspected of collaborating with either of his perceived enemies, of passing information to them, or of mediating the sale of lands to the Jews, which the mufti had prohibited in a *fatwa* (religious verdict). Assassination had been established in Arab and Muslim lore as a persuasive comment against opponents on disputed policies since the times of the first Caliphs, most of them murdered by dissidents.[2]

Of course, the opposition put the blame for those murders directly on Haj Amin, but his status as the most popular leader of the Palestinians, in spite, or perhaps because of his exile, was not diminished, precisely as the British were struggling to shore up their reputation among the Arabs and to tarnish the image of their bitter Nazi enemies. Churchill could not recall any period when the stresses and the onset of so many problems, all at once or in rapid succession, bore more directly on him and on his colleagues than the first half of 1941. He reminisced that

The scale of events grew larger every year; but the decisions required were not more difficult. Greater military disasters fell upon us in 1942, but by then we were no longer alone, and our fortunes were mingled with those of the Grand Alliance. No part of our problem in 1941 could be solved without relation to all the rest. What was given to one theater had to be taken from another. An effort here meant a risk there. Our physical resources were harshly limited. The attitude of a dozen powers, friendly opportunist, or potentially hostile, was unknowable. At home, we must face the war against the U-boats, the invasion threat and the continuing *blitz*; we had to conduct the group of campaigns in the Middle East; and thirdly, to try to make a front against Germany in the Balkans. And we had to do all this for a long time alone.[3]

There could be no more eloquent statement of the constraints that shackled Britain's wartime conduct in the Middle East and the Balkans and the link between them. Confident in his ability to repel any German landing in Britain, Churchill gave priority to beefing up British troops in the Middle East and the Mediterranean and its littoral, including the Aegean Sea and the Balkans. He thought that Africa was the only continent where he could face his enemies on land; therefore emphasis was lent to the defense of Egypt and the Suez Canal, where he built up a front against the Fascists in the Western Desert between Egypt and Libya where the Italians predominated. Already in early 1941, the British reoccupied Kassala in the Sudan; had Tobruk in their sight, when they foresaw the rapid demise of the Italians in Cyrenaica, under the unrelenting counterattacks of General Wavell; and invaded Eritrea, at the same time that reports accumulated regarding German movements toward their Balkan campaign. In April, 1941 the British counted on their ten to twelve divisions available around the Nile Valley to provide the necessary security for East Africa, Egypt, and Palestine. At the same time, Britain aided the Greeks to resist the Italian onslaught, and it was prepared to slow down Wavell's advance toward Benghazi, once Egypt's western flank was secured, in order to give higher priority in air and naval support to the Greek takeover of Valona.

On January 6, 1941, well before the German invasion of Yugoslavia, Britain's foreign secretary, Anthony Eden, wrote that he was certain of Nazi intervention in order to avert a total defeat of Italy in Albania, and he urged, echoing his prime minister's concerns, that the victories in North Africa, should in no way decrease British attention to Turkey and Yugoslavia.[4] Thereupon, Britain indeed took the daring decision of reducing its troops and air force in North Africa, in spite of their propitious success there, in order to sustain the Greek front. This trend of thinking was enthusiastically confirmed after General Wavells' successes in Cyrenaica predated by several weeks the set target of March for implementing that decision, and prompted the prime minister to conclude that as soon as the Western Desert front was secured, much of the force deployed in Egypt could be rerouted toward Greece, so imminent the Nazi invasion seemed, and so assured seemed British victory in Libya and North Africa.[5] But since the Greek Command lost heart in the originally planned resistance to Germany, with some assistance by the British, because they hesitated about their capacity to arrest the Nazi advance almost single-handedly, the British were also constrained to alter their plans, in spite of their own General Staff's misgivings about sullying the reputation of Britain if it should retreat from its offer of aid and from assurances to the king about their joint partnership in repulsing the Germans. But the British also concluded that losing Greece and the Balkans was not a disaster after all, as long as Turkey remained neutral. The British resolved that having so little to offer to the Greeks, they could not encourage them to fight to death all alone and bring about the ruin of their country.

In Yugoslavia, a period of political disintegration was ushered in after the assassination of King Alexander in 1934, and internal stability was directly affected by the hostility between Serbs and Croats. Macek, the leader of the Peasant Party of Croatia, stuck to his policy of noncooperation with the Belgrade government, at a time when Prince Pavel, the regent over the minor heir apparent Peter, overshadowed the monarchy. Pro-Fascist Croats, protected by Italians and Hungarians, worked from there for the detachment of Croatia from federal Yugoslavia. Belgrade, instead of pursuing the interwar cooperation within the Little Entente of the Balkan Powers, opted for a rapprochement to the Axis powers and the signature of an Italo-Yugoslavian Pact in 1937. But in the elections of 1939, a new prime minister, Cvetković, was elected, who sought to appease the Nazis, just like his counterparts in London and Paris, had in Munich the year before. When in August 1939 Macek entered the Belgrade government, followed by the German-Soviet astonishing pact, which though instinctively drew the Serbs' sympathy to their Russian fellow Slavs, still seemed to deliver the Balkans to the Germans, precisely when the capitulation of France in June 1940 seemed to deprive Yugoslavia of its traditional protector. The regent was hesitant to move into any formal commitment that violated his neutrality, lest it would provoke the Nazis to launch a decisive attack on his country.[6]

Churchill attests to the fact that in January 1941 a mood of fear reigned in Belgrade, which prompted Prince Pavel's refusal to accept a visit by Anthony Eden. There was one exception in that ambience and that was an air force general, Simovic, who represented the nationalist elements in the Yugoslav (namely Serbian) armed forces, and whose office at Zemun had become the center of opposition to Nazi penetration of the Balkans and to the inaction of the Belgrade government. To prevail upon the Yugoslav government to accept adherence to the Tripartite Pact, Hitler encircled the country by enlisting the support of Bulgaria and Romania and threatening to invade Greece. The regent undertook to join the Tripartite Pact, but in his cabinet the opposing view was rife, with Simovic remaining firm against capitulation and Churchill directly calling upon Cvetković to resist surrender to the Nazis, and to form a joint front with Turkey and Greece to defeat the "Huns." But the Yugoslav prime minister and his foreign minister stole out of Belgrade and secretly signed the pact with Hitler in Vienna on March 25. When the act was reported to the Cabinet the next day, three ministers resigned, and Churchill ordered his representative in Belgrade to "pester, nag, and bite" the Yugoslavs that they ought to detach themselves from Nazi designs.[7] On March 27, the conspirators acted, as already stated before, they arrested the prime minister, forced him to resign and took over without bloodshed, and cited the young heir apparent Peter as their source of legitimacy.

The coup at first was received by chants in Belgrade where Serbian nationalists were elated for the choice of war over the pact of surrender. The British and French flags were displayed again in the streets, and the Serb national anthem was sung by the delirious crowd. The young king was crowned amidst popular acclamation in the Belgrade Cathedral. Hitler was furious and resolved to act in view of his design to invade Greece in anticipation of the Barbarossa Campaign that was looming on the horizon. The decision was then taken to destroy Yugoslavia militarily and as a national unit, for there was no more time for diplomatic coaxing or brutal ultimatums. The Germans assumed that the Croats would come to their side, for which they would be rewarded by the fulfillment of their long aspiration for autonomy. Territorial rewards were also promised by Hitler to the Axis allies who would participate in the onslaught: Italy, Hungary, and Bulgaria, while Romanian military help would be reserved for the Russian front. Orders were given to the Nazi air force to destroy Belgrade in attacks by waves. While Hitler was acting swiftly to shore up his suddenly altered Balkan plans, Churchill expressed his elation to his Conservative Party Central Council for what he thought was a Yugoslav revolution that enabled that nation to "find its soul," once the ministers who had signed away its honor, integrity, and freedom to Germany were under arrest.[8]

At that point (March 28, 1941, one day after the Belgrade coup, which instilled in Churchill great hopes and illusions), weighing the odds of Germany's invasion of the Balkans, he thought that in view of Britain's good standing in North Africa and the Middle East, he could still come to the aid of the three major Balkan countries—Greece, Yugoslavia, and Turkey—if they stood together and created a bulwark against any further thrust of the Nazis to the Aegean and the Mediterranean. Indeed, in his message to foreign secretary, Anthony Eden, who was first visiting Malta and then Athens, he suggested that:

> If Germany, notwithstanding the objections, attacks in the Balkans, we must play our part there with all our available strength. If, on the other hand, she pretends that she never wished to bring war into the Balkans, and to leave Greece, Yugoslavia and Turkey alone, then we might turn our forces to a strong summer and autumn campaign in the Central Mediterranean, including Tripoli [Libya], Sicily and the Italian toe. We should have a good pad in our right hand to protect our Middle Eastern interests, and take smart action on a medium scale with our left in the Central Mediterranean. . . .[9]

On April 6, the German war machine struck, and Belgrade was mercilessly bombarded, leaving seventeen thousand civilians dead. But at the same time, the sure maintenance of the desert flank in North Africa, which had allowed the Balkan delusions of Britain to shape up, had also collapsed, turning the war map upside down. The Seventh British Armored Division, under General Wavell, which had constituted the backbone of the British sweeping victory in Cyrenaica and allowed the destruction of the Italian army there, was withdrawn to Egypt for rest and eventual transport to Greece, and so was the Sixth Australian Division, and they were replaced by reduced formations of less trained and less battle-hardened troops. Already at the end of February, British field commanders in North Africa were warned about the arrival of German armored formations, reinforced by some, less formidable and less threatening, Italian troops, in Tripolitania, under the command of highly reputed general, Erwin Rommel, just west of the front line the British held in Benghazi and Tobruk. He indeed arrived in Tripoli on February 12, and in March began to push eastward and shake the British hitherto held lines of defense in Cynenaica, taking full and rapid advantage of the British complacency, which had allowed the thinning down, in quantity and quality, of their deployed forces, given the inefficiency of their Italian rivals and the priority they gave to the reinforcements they intended to rush to the Balkans. The weakened Brits began to retreat, on that front, and the glamour of Wavell to be tarnished by his unceasing withdrawals, which had followed his long string of easy victories over the Italians in the same war theater, thus undoing British war plans in the Balkans and the Mediterranean.

Wavell thought that the sweeping German counterattack in the desert was a major diversion timed to precede the Nazi invasion of the Balkans, which was a correct reading of the war map. The British leadership was even more concerned about the negative image a withdrawing Britain in the Middle East would project in other fronts, like the Balkans, where the legendary might of England elevated it to the degree of a reliable ally, even a savior. It was feared that a retreating fighter, who cannot stand up to Nazi aggression and arrogance, can no longer be held as a hero and cannot be valued as an ally. To make matters worse, the two main British field commanders in that front, Generals Neame and O'Connor, fell incidentally prisoners of war in a silly incident off the front line. As the British were discussing whether the new line should be held in Tobruk if possible, news struck of the Nazi invasion of Yugoslavia on April 6, as Wavell was making plans for the next line of defense at Marsa Matruh, close to the Egyptian border. It was when these dark clouds were gathering on the Western Desert theater, that the Iraqi revolt broke out, which strained to the limit British capacities to stand by its plan to assist Greece and Yugoslavia and provide them with air and maritime backup. Churchill himself had come to regard the worsened situation in the Middle Eastern front as a "disaster of the first magnitude," not only for its own sake, but also for the dire repercussions it would have for other theaters, especially the Balkans.

The extent to which Churchill was personally involved in the unfolding events in the Middle East, and his global view of the war where any arena had its impact on all the others, are key to understanding the little leeway left to him in those dire days of the worsening situation on all fronts. England had signed the Anglo-Iraqi Treaty of 1930, which provided that in time of peace, Britain could maintain air bases in Basra, the second largest city in the south, and in Habaniya, in the Iraqi desert. In time of war, it could make use of all facilities, including airports, seaports, railways, roads, and rivers for the passage of its troops. When the war broke out, Iraq severed relations with Germany, though it did not declare war. But when Italy joined the Axis, Iraq did not break relations with it. Thus, the Italian Legation in Baghdad became the chief center of the Axis propaganda and for inciting anti-British sentiment, in par with Cairo and Jerusalem as we have seen above. In addition, since the mufti of Jerusalem had fled from Palestine during the Arab Revolt there shortly before the outset of the war, he found shelter in Baghdad and was instrumental in fanning the anti-British mood. When France collapsed in 1940, and the Axis Armistice Commission arrived in Damascus, which had been a French colony before the war, Britain's standing was at its lowest and caused great concern in Churchill's mind.

The scarcity of British troops in the area, due to the large forces tied up in North Africa, and the British commitment to rush to the aid of Greece and the Balkans if the situation improved on the African scene, precluded any British response by force to those developments. In March 1941, Rashid Ali, who worked for the Germans, became prime minister and mounted a conspiracy with three Iraqi officers, styled as the "Golden Square." The Pro-British regent fled Baghdad. Because of the growing sense that the Americans needed an air base in the Middle East, to enable them to deliver directly military supplies, Churchill prevailed on the viceroy in India to dispatch a division to Basra and to divert there other British forces that were on their way to the Far East. Churchill nevertheless stressed that because of the existing restraints, no troops would be dispatched immediately, either to Baghdad or to Palestine. Rashid Ali, who had been assured of German land and air assistance, tried to resist British new landings in Basra by first attacking the British airbase in Habaniya, where the flying school was based, which had absorbed the British families that flew out of Baghdad for secure refuge. On May 2, Iraqi forces attacked the perimeters of the base.

Though General Wavell, the British supreme commander of the Near East had consistently refused to commit any of his forces from Egypt or Palestine to rescue the situation in Iraq, Churchill thought that this measure had grown inevitable, because of the common border between Iraq and Turkey, which it became necessary to defend in view of the German air supremacy in the Aegean that had to be circumvented and avoided. But Wavell actually warned against that policy, because he was afraid that the prolongation of fighting in Iraq might endanger the defense of Egypt and Palestine, which were in turn a key to blocking the Germans in North Africa and the Middle East. Churchill insisted that British forces in Habaniya and Basra should hold out, even against all odds, as the stakes in giving up those bases were unbearably high. But after a few days of battle, the Iraqi forces withdrew under the harassment of the Royal Air Force, which did not let up despite the rapport of force that was not in its favor, and the siege of Habaniya was lifted. Churchill continued to press a reluctant Wavell for pursuing the success by sending a column from Palestine to Baghdad to put down the rebellion itself before the Germans sent air and ground forces to its aid, for there was no question for him of negotiating with Rashid Ali. Indeed, by the time the advance guard from Palestine reached Habaniya, in mid-May, the first German aircraft had arrived in Mosul, northern Iraq, but the valiant and rapid attacks by the British forces ultimately prevailed, reaching Baghdad on May 30. Rashid Ali fled to Iran from the British advance, accompanied by the mufti of Jerusalem and the Axis diplomats in Baghdad who had incited the trouble. The Iraqi worries were finally off Churchill's table.

Another headache loomed instead for the British leadership, replacing Iraq with Syria. After the collapse of France in June 1940, Syria was one of its overseas territories that submitted to the Vichy government and made efforts to prevent any French deserters from joining Free France and crossing into British Palestine in search of an allied base. German and Italian agents started to stir anti-British and anti-Zionist troubles among the Arab population there, in accordance with the grand Nazi design to disinherit the Brits and take over their positions. With German control of Syria, both the Suez Canal and the oil refineries in Abadan in the Persian Gulf came into the range of operations of the *Luftwaffe* by March 1941, as the British command was preparing to defend their Middle Eastern possessions and to rush aid to the Balkans. On May 2, 1941, Rashid Ali in Iraq appealed to Hitler for urgent support against the British, and the Germans prepared to rush war materials to him via Syria. During the month of May, some hundred German and twenty Italian aircraft landed in Syria, en route to Iraq. At that time, the British had to evacuate Greece and then Crete, respond to the Rashid Ali rebellion, lend the top attention to the defense of Egypt and Palestine, and attend to all other home and overseas fronts. Finally, on June 8, British and Australian troops, aided by Free France's armies, entered Syria to prevent further German penetration there, and they captured Damascus on June 21, after some reinforcements arrived from Iraq following the quelling of the Rashid Ali rebellion. The success in Syria greatly improved the British strategic position in the Middle East and paved the way for "Battleaxe," the code name of the crucial British counterattack in the Western Desert against Rommel's forces, which, it was hoped, would signal "the end of the beginning" in the fortunes of the allies for the better, and in the fortunes of the Axis for the worse.

Churchill attests to the fact[10] that the Western Desert weighed in his strategy much more that the evacuation of Greece and the other troubles in the Middle East that he had to overcome. He and his field commanders were of one mind that crushing Rommel and regaining Tobruk by far outweighed all the sideshows that were imposed on the British by the Axis powers and their allies in Syria, Palestine, and Iraq. It was a tremendously risky operation to send across the Mediterranean to Wavell the three hundred tanks he needed to reconstruct his force toward the great and fateful counterattack, before the dreaded German Fifteenth Panzer Division arrived in full strength to the frontline. But the attempted attack in mid-May did not go as well as hoped, while the German reinforcements were getting to the front and making the challenge ever greater. Battleaxe was launched on June 15. By the end of the month, Churchill came to the courageous conclusion that Wavell, who had been for months responsible for some five different theaters, was a tired man and needed to be relieved of his command. General Auchinleck was appointed in his stead, and a new strategy for the Western Desert offensive was devised, when it was recognized that only by reconquering the lost airfield and port in eastern Cyrenaica could the fleet and air force resume effective action against the enemy seaborne supplies, on which Rommel's offensive depended. Unless, of course, the Germans took the northern route, via Turkey, Syria, and Palestine, to attack Britain's Middle Eastern positions, and that threat was also being considered under the new command, who was quite reluctant to launch the awaited Western Desert offensive until meticulous and time consuming preparations and reinforcements were completed.

Churchill kept pushing the Middle East Command to launch the Western Desert operation, using the lull accorded to the Allies by the German entanglement with Russia, to restore the situation in Cyrenaica, as "the opportunity may never recur."[11] Churchill also pressed that General Maitland Wilson, the architect of the Syrian success, should be put in charge of the confrontation with Rommel in the Western Desert, but that appointment was resisted by Auchinleck, who preferred General Alan Cunningham, and who anyway could not see his long-expected offensive launched before November 1, under the code name "Crusader." The Germans were strained too, owing to the British presence in Tobruk, whence they could sally at any moment to impair Rommel's long and indefensible logistic supply lines. But they too waited for forces to be assembled before they could launch their decisive sweep of Libya and then on to Egypt and Palestine. On November 18, Cunningham attacked, but within days and because of heavy losses, withdrawal was ordered, and this second offensive, postponed for many months to make the necessary precautionary preparations, ended again in frustration for the Brits. Inevitably, Cunningham was relieved of the command of the Eighth Army, and the grand offensive to eliminate Rommel had to be postponed once again.

In February 1942, the British army in North Africa was once again in one of its lowest points of the war, and an urgent injection of energy and hope was direly needed. Rommel renewed his attacks, and the British Eighth Army, now commanded by General Ritchie, gradually withdrew and partly capitulated to the Germans, notably in Tobruk, who seized large stores of food, water, fuel, and ammunition, which would allow them to pursue the Brits and their subordinates into Egypt and on to the Suez Canal. At the end of June 1942, Rommel had crossed the border into Egypt, while the British Eighth Army had retreated to Marsa Matruh, soon to set the new line of defense in al-Alamein, where the battle of destiny would be decided soon thereafter. Auchinleck took again the direct command of the army, because of its failures, and he held valiantly against Rommel, who was exhausted by the long and costly engagements with the British all the way from Tobruk to the outskirts of Alexandria. After Churchill's visit to Cairo and to the Alamein battle arena in August 1942, it was decided to appoint General Montgomery to the command of the Eighth Army so that Auchinleck could go back to his overall command of the Middle East theater. On that occasion, Churchill also decided to change the structure of command of that theater, by dividing it into two: the Near East Command would comprise Egypt, Palestine, Syria, with its center in Cairo, and with the Eighth and Ninth Armies at its disposal; and the Middle East Command, comprising Persia and Iraq, with its center in Baghdad and the Tenth Army under its orders.

Now Auchinleck was to remain commander in chief of the Middle East, with a reduced scope of action, and General Alexander was appointed to head the Near East Command, which encompassed the Western Desert operations, the hottest and most crucial arena under the circumstances. These changes, including the appointment of Montgomery as the chief field commander, under whose orders was placed the Eighth Army, which faced Rommel, were geared, in Churchill's words to "impart a new and vigorous impulse to the Army and restore confidence in the Command," which if achieved in August or September 1942, might have a decisive effect on all other fronts.[12] The fateful Battle of al-Alamein, deep within Egypt, signaling the sweeping and threatening German penetration toward the Suez Canal thus far, and the British desperate determination to repulse it back into the desert, and squeeze it between the "Torch" operation in North Africa, where massive American landings would mark their entrance into the war in the European arena, and their own thrust from Egypt, code-named "Lightfoot," would finally defeat the invaders and erase them from the balance of power in the Mediterranean.

In the days and weeks leading to the great offensive, the British forces were beefed up with fresh divisions, and the tank force, the airpower, and the artillery were reinforced in quantity and quality, including with American matériel, on a scope never possible before, and a strict regime of training was undertaken aimed at both enhancing physical and organizational capacities and raising the spirits and morale. The air force started the battle immediately, sinking German supplies of fuel, food, and ammunition, and the fatal land attack on which the entire course of the war depended, was launched on October 23, 1942. Montgomery had ten divisions at his disposal, three armored and the rest infantry. The plan for deceptive measures worked perfectly, and the effect of surprise as to the timing and the concentration of troops, was total, precisely when Rommel was absent in Germany and his command was taken over by his deputy, who died from a heart attack, forcing the legendary German commander to relinquish his hospital bed and rush to the front upon Hitler's instigation. Twelve days of heavy fighting sufficed for Montgomery to inflict a definitive defeat on Rommel's forces, thus signaling the reversal of the fortunes of the war on other fronts, too, though at the price of thirteen thousand casualties on the British side. As Churchill said: "Before Alamein, we never had a victory, after Alamein we never had a defeat."[13]

It is evident then, that while the worsening situation in North Africa in 1940–1941 had prevented massive British help to Greece, Yugoslavia, and the Mediterranean islands, the great victory of Alamein at the end of 1942, the entrance of the United States into the war in Europe and North Africa, and the Russian counterattack in Stalingrad had not only reversed the fortunes of the war, but also issued a death verdict against Hitler and his Reich. True, this was done at the price that the Balkans, except Greece, fell into the Soviet orbit as a result of the Allied victory over the Nazis, with the consequence of forty-five years of Communist rule, which crushed their economies, enslaved their peoples, and oppressed any democratic and freedom-yearning tendencies that grew there. In Yugoslavia, Tito's desire to hold together so many ethnic groups, which hated each other, generated the policy of suppression of war memories, which were liable to deepen domestic contradictions instead of soothing them. Jadovno and Jasenovac were not fashionable topics of research or public discussion in those years, but as soon as Tito's yoke passed into history, outbursts of freedom, democracy, and yearning to remember came to light, which made this study possible.

Notes

1. Walid Khalidi, *Journal of Palestinian Studies* Vol. XXXV, No 1, Autumn 2005, 60–79.
2. Ibid., 70–71.
3. Churchill, op. cit. Vol. 3, 3–4.
4. Foreign Minister Anthony Eden to Prime Minister Winston Churchill, January 6, 1941. Ibid., 14–15.
5. Prime Minister Churchill to General Wavell, February 12, 1941. Ibid., 64–65.
6. Amidst the controversies among historians about who did what to whom, when, and where, Winston Churchill still sounds as a lone lucid voice, dedicated to defeating the Nazis and to rescuing as much of Europe as possible from their claws. This discussion is based on his wartime history. Ibid., Vol. 3, 156 ff.
7. Ibid., 160–161.
8. These were Hitler's orders to the German High Command, retrieved in the Nuremberg records and cited by Churchill. Ibid., 163–167.
9. Prime minister to foreign secretary, March 28, 1941. Ibid., 169–171.
10. Ibid., chapter 19, 333 ff.
11. Ibid., 403.
12. Prime minister to deputy prime minister, August 5, 1942, Churchill, op. cit. Vol. 4, 459–464.
13. Ibid., 603.

5

The Muslim Connection and Haj Amin al-Husseini

There was also the other determining element that converged with these momentous developments, which was the rise of the Muslim Brotherhood in Egypt. Of course, the story is long, and we don't need to narrate the entire intricate and fascinating tale. Suffice it to record here that the Muslim Brotherhood was created in Egypt in 1928 by Hassan al-Banna, who had all kinds of ideas that he introduced into Islam. He did not generate or invent Islam, but he updated it, so to speak. For example, he added to the Islamic usage two or three major terms, which injected perhaps a new life into to the very operation of modern Islam. He addressed jihad, the holy war, which had been taken before by Muslims around the world, as a striving, as an aspiration to be a better Muslim. That's precisely what it means, for jihad means aspiration, self-strengthening, or making an effort, which can also be intellectual, not necessarily military. From now on Hassan al-Banna said that, as of old: "jihad *is* an instrument in order to battle against the enemy." The problem is to identify who the enemy is. And the enemy is, he said, first of all the British, who were occupying Egypt, and second the Jews, who were coming to colonize Palestine, and who were battling against the local Arabs, Muslims, and Palestinians for the same land, and therefore Muslims are duty bound to help the Palestinians against the Jews. And the second term was *shaheed* or martyr. He said that whenever a Muslim dies in this battle, it's not just death as one is killed in other combats. This is the death of a martyr, because then one is assured to go straight to paradise, and therefore not only were people who volunteered for the Muslim Brothers not afraid to die, they were eager to martyr themselves in battle for the cause of Islam and in the Path of Allah, and so take the shortcut from this tormenting life into eternal paradise in the entourage of Allah.

When Hassan al-Banna spoke on those terms, he revived a terminology which had not been operational since medieval times, when
Islam was great and victorious. He was impressing upon the Muslims
of Egypt that: "We are under obligation to help other Muslims," that
is to say those in Palestine, and not only to wage jihad against the
Jews and the British, but also not to be afraid to die, because those
who die are assured of their second life in heaven, in the afterworld.
Now one can understand how the Nazi Germans picked up the same
ideas, realizing that this was the great occasion they were looking for,
quite a great opportunity to penetrate the Islamic world. They had
been trying to create in Egypt an office for propaganda, for their own
cause. Previously, the Egyptian population rejected that propaganda of
hatred, because they had reasonably good relations with the Jews, who
had lived there for many centuries. There were some eighty thousand
of them in Egypt then. There was even a very famous trial, when the
Germans published in French an anti-Semitic book by their Nazi office
in Cairo, speaking about the threat the Jews posed to Germany. They
used Nazi propaganda to warn the Arabs that: "Jews are not only a
threat against Europe or against Germans, the Aryans, but are also a
threat against you." And Jews in Egypt sued that Nazi office in Cairo,
and they won the case. And therefore the whole idea was dismissed
in public opinion, showing how Egypt was ill-prepared for a negative
anti-Semitic propaganda attitude toward the Jews at that time. But here
the propaganda machine of the Nazis in Egypt and later in Palestine,
together with the Muslim Brothers in Egypt since the 1930s, combined
with the efforts of the mufti of Jerusalem, Haj Amin al-Husseini, simply
changed attitudes in the Middle East toward the Palestine and Jewish
problems, whose consequences we suffer from to this very day. The
Germans, who understood exactly what it was all about, jumped on the
opportunity to tell the Arabs, and Muslims in general, that as a matter
of fact both Germans and Muslims shared a common ideology. Both
of them wanted to eliminate Jews, for both of them thought that Jews
were treacherous in character, and so on, therefore, it was only natural
for them to join their efforts and to collaborate in their elimination.

Against this background, we can understand that as soon as the war
broke out, the mufti of Jerusalem, Haj Amin al-Husseini, was invited
to Berlin. He established together with sixty more Arabs and other
Muslim broadcasters and translators, a broadcasting service, which
operated from Berlin until the very end of the war. And in the middle
of the war, when more and more German divisions were needed for

the eastern front, when Stalingrad went awry and the whole situation on the war front started to deteriorate, the Germans became very short on manpower, and therefore they resorted to the thirty-eight divisions of *Waffen-SS* that they recruited to fill the ranks. *Waffen* means armed, the armed SS. The SS was created initially as a police unit, some kind of elite unit, and later they were needed for battles, for selected battles. Therefore their numbers and their tasks expanded from three battalions of police at the very beginning, into thirty-eight divisions of fighting troops at the end of the war. Most of them were German, but since they ran short of recruits they started to enlist others: Lithuanians, Ukrainians, Romanians, and of course, Yugoslavs and Albanians, and so on. So, the concerned Nazis flew especially the mufti of Jerusalem—who was settled in Berlin—to Bosnia, with the task to convince the Muslim population there of his newly acquired militant Muslim Brother ideology, which he had adopted as a tool to achieve his goals in Palestine, and which prescribed that it was good to fight against the Jews, who deserved elimination, and the British because they supported the Jews, and that if one fought that war, it would be considered jihad, and any casualty would be regarded as a martyr, hence his automatic salvation is guaranteed to eternity when he goes to heaven to dwell in the vicinity of Allah. The mufti went from place to place in the large Muslim agglomerations of Bosnia, especially the cities, where in 1941 the Imams of the major Muslim communities of Sarajevo, Tuzla, Banja Luka, and Mustar had issued *fatwa* decrees, a sort of religious verdicts, forbidding the Bosnian Muslims to collaborate with the Ustasha government of NDH, which had encompassed their country under German and Italian accord. And here comes the mufti of Jerusalem, the great spiritual authority with the reputation and prestige of his city, and representing both the Nazis in Berlin and the Muslim Brothers in Egypt, and telling them: "No, no, no, forget about that. That verdict is not valid anymore." And in 1943, when he visited all those four cities, he convinced the local religious leadership to come out in support of the Muslim recruits, thus mobilizing some twenty-one thousand people to serve in the Waffen-SS Division Number Thirteen, notoriously known as the *Hanjar* Division, which in Turkish and Arabic means simply "dagger," as a symbol of the war itself.

Some elaboration is needed nonetheless on the Islamic element, not only in itself, within which a Hassan al-Banna in Egypt and a Haj Amin in Jerusalem, in Berlin and in Bosnia would naturally find common cause against Jews and Zionists, but especially on the ideological and political juncture that would allow both to act in concert to achieve a genocide against the Jewish people in the Middle East, and in Europe to aid the Axis powers against the Allies. And after the war, the banner of virulent anti-Semitism would definitely pass from Europe, with Nazi Germany at its centre, to the Islamic world led by the Arabs, and by fundamentalist Muslims like al-Qa'ida and Iran, since the end of the twentieth century. The writer who detected and researched the ideological link between Islamic fundamentalism and Nazi Judeophobia is the German Matthias Kuntzel, a political scientist and a student of anti-Semitism, in his book published in German, English, and Hebrew.[1] The only drawback in this seminal volume is that the author follows today's vogue among Western scholars, who differentiate between Islam and "Islamism," as if they were two different religions or systems of belief, attributing the built-in hatred to Jews only to the latter, while the former seems to be generally exonerated. The problem is that it is becoming more and more difficult to differentiate between the two, if there ever was a difference, since the Muslim Brothers have moved to the international Muslim consensus, and what used to be considered as fanatic "Islamism," is now the accepted norm.

It is true that those called "Islamists" are more radical and vocal about their hatred toward the Jews than the common Muslims, and this has given rise to the spurious claim that the abuses of Islam, including anti-Semitism and terrorism, are only the lot of those "radical," "fundamentalist" Islam, usually quantified as some 15 percent of the 1.5 billion world Muslims. In fact, we are talking about the same one creed, which upholds Sharia law to various degrees, and those who do not follow it to the letter, as in any other religion, are not adepts of an alternative "moderate Islam," the one that is sometimes dubbed "religion of peace," to distinguish from the faith of aggressive "extremists." The truth of the matter is that no such Islam exists, though there are certainly many truly moderate Muslims, who have broken away from the bloody road of jihad, especially when they have conveniently moved to the West and can from a safe distance criticize the killing in their original countries of those dubbed "apostates" or "traitors," or the phenomenon of the Islamikaze[2] bombers against Westerners and Israelis, or the culture of death, which is cultivated in many Muslim lands, or indeed the unbridled anti-Semitic calumnies that are rife in their culture. But they have yet to produce an alternative doctrine and worldview that could rival official Islam and posit a creed and a set of rules that can tempt Muslims to relinquish the Sharia and embrace a different path. If they did, they would no longer be Muslims in the eyes of established Islam, that is, they would be accused of apostasy, which is punishable by death.

In short, anti-Semitism has been built into Islam from its inception. Any one of the numerous autobiographies published by people who grew up under Islam, whether Muslim themselves like Ayaan Hirsi Ali, who was brought up in Saudi Arabia,[3] and certainly Jewish individuals who lived under the yoke of Islam,[4] can attest to the phenomenon. Therefore, there is no need to attribute anti-Semitism to "Islamists," as if mainstream Islam were different, exactly as jihad, the violent aspect of Islam, has been a common tenet of all Muslims, though some of them practice it less than others. This is the reason why the Muslim Brothers are so popular among Arabs and Muslims in the world, and one need not be an Islamist to be a member. Similarly, hatred of the Jews has been universal among Palestinians, and there is no difference, in that regard, between the Palestinian Authority, which is considered "moderate," and the Hamas, who are said to be Islamist. Thus, the common enmity of Muslims toward Jews was not discovered on the eve of World War II, nor was it an innovation that was due to the Nazi propaganda, though under those circumstances of the prewar, the Nazi machinery knew how to incite the Muslim populace, which at some times and in some places had lived harmoniously with the Jews, to rise against them when they could free themselves from the restraining shackles of Western colonial powers, like Britain in Egypt and Palestine, and France in Morocco.

In Islamic writings during the war, like those of the Brothers and of the chief mufti of Jerusalem, thoughts of violence of the Nazi type started to creep in, coupled with paranoid conspiracy theories that attributed to the Jews both an evil nature, capable of causing damage to all nations, especially Islam, and a satanic ability to carry out those schemes. It was necessary, when the moment of anti-Semitic action had come, to operationalize the evil attributes of the Jews, as the Germans did, in order to render them an easy prey to the people they dwelt with, and to facilitate their exclusion, persecution, discrimination, and ultimately their removal and physical extermination. Kuntzel's seminal innovation is that he traced the roots of the historical collaboration between Islam (that he called Islamism) and Nazi ideology and practice, and why in the postwar era, when Nazism was wiped out, it was Islam that inherited that questionable clout and raised the banner of anti-Semitism as one of the first items on its agenda. Kuntzel also claimed that it was not the Arab-Israeli dispute that caused this anti-Semitic trend to gain strength, but on the contrary, it has been the radicalization of Muslim anti-Semitism, as among the Hezbollah in Lebanon; the Hamas among the Palestinians; the Muslim Brothers and their affiliates in Pakistan, Africa, and Asia; and then al-Qa'ida and its Taliban and other sister movements, which enabled them to dominate the Islamic discourse, aggravate the already difficult hostility to Jews and Israel, and make that conflict all the more intractable. It is not the Middle Eastern conflict that causes virulent Islamic anti-Semitism, claims Kuntzel, but like in Europe, it is the overt and covert anti-Semitism that sharpens the anti-Zionist and anti-Israeli attitudes worldwide.

This is the reason why at the time, when Nazism was universally condemned in Europe, west and east, except for the Axis powers, which stood to gain directly from it, in the Arab world it not only won currency, but it was regarded as both the savior of the Arabs from the yoke of British colonialism, and from Jewish settlement in Palestine, which the Arabs/Muslims considered exclusively theirs. Moreover, they viewed in the Nazi final solution an ideal platform and blueprint to reverse, not only to arrest, the Zionist great strides made in Palestine, that no other available plan, not even the British White Paper against Jewish immigration to Palestine, could undo. No wonder then, that after the war, Nazi officials found shelter in the Arab world, and the remnants of Nazi ideology could find their echo among Muslims. Shoah denial, which has spread almost universally into the Arab and Muslim world to this day, is one manifestation of these surviving vestiges of Nazism, which at one and the same time seek to avoid worldwide criticism of the regime they had supported in Germany during the war, and to avert any support or sympathy to the Jewish victims of the Nazis. Kuntzel's unquestioned accomplishment has been tracing the stunning persistence, even escalation, of this violent brand of anti-Semitism in the Islamic world today, and more and more within the growing Muslim communities in the West, which is often latently acclaimed and supported by the world media, and sometimes by the authorities of the rest of the world.

Kuntzel's focus on the Muslim Brothers in Egypt not only interpreted that movement as the beginning of modern radicalism in Islam, but he found extraordinary organizational similarities between it and Nazism and Fascism in general, for example, the subordination of the individual to the collective will, the worship of iconic leadership, hostility toward liberal and democratic principles, vitriolic rejection of Communism, extreme opposition to capitalism, and a strong ambition among Muslims to establish a universal Muslim state, ruled by the Sharia, similar to the Germanic thousand-year Reich that Hitler had in mind. In this ambience of continual fighting under strict rules of conduct and their relentless enforcement, the predominance of men was paramount, the submission of women obvious, as was martyrdom for the sake of the collective, and above all, a common contempt, hatred, and obsession with the Jews, who were simultaneously feared and despised. Hence the need to fight to the finish, both the Jews and the British, the only nation that stood up against the Nazis at the opening of the war and confronted them fearlessly under Churchill. These similarities and affinities between the two ideas and nationalities emerged during the 1930s and contributed to the forging of the alliance between the two by the time the war broke out. It was the Muslim Brothers (MB) who translated Hitler's *Mein Kampf* into Arabic and distributed it throughout the Arab world and helped channel to Haj Amin in Palestine, who was facing similar challenges, arms and funds from Germany, which sustained him in his major revolt against the British (and Zionism) in Palestine during the lead-up to the war (1936–1939).

The Islamic connection peaked when Haj Amin, who escaped British wrath during the Arab Revolt by moving to Iraq and aiding the short-lived Rashid Ali's Rebellion, which was also prominently anti-Semitic, as it was mainly directed against the Baghdadi Jews in what was known as the *Farhood* Pogrom, and escaped to Germany in the heat of the war (June 1941), met with Hitler in person, and harnessed his energies, his prestige as the mufti of Jerusalem, his hostility to the British and the Jews, and his skill as a propagandist to enhance the German war effort. Unlike the general ties, sympathetic exchanges and assistance in weapons and funds to face the Brits in the Middle East, which the Nazis had forged with the MB since they began their relations and collaboration, Haj Amin went a step further by proving himself to the Nazis as a practitioner. First of all, he lived in Berlin throughout the war and broadcast in Arabic over shortwave to the entire Arab world, and in other languages spoken in the Islamic world, like Turkish, Iranian, and Urdu, to try to enlist the support of much of the Muslim world to Hitler and his Nazi enterprise. From the mufti's point of view, perhaps the summit of his "achievements" was his string of meetings with the highest German hierarchy, to persuade them to scuttle any attempt of any deal to rescue Jews from the German claws in Europe, and to make sure that they were sent to their execution in the Nazi death camps. In that regard, he participated directly and heartlessly in the decimation of thousands of Jews who could otherwise have survived that fate, not least of all by fighting their entrance into Palestine.

Of course, the center of gravity of Kuntzel's interest in the MB was not only their inspiration by Nazi doctrine, but their extended influence on Haj Amin and Palestinian Arabs, which facilitated the mufti's close collaboration with Hitler. That caused him to move to Berlin during the war and after the war to invite some MB troops to participate with the Palestinians in their war against the Jews in 1948–49. Historically, the fact that the Palestinians are still struggling today to establish a state of their own, is the fruit of their and their Nazi allies' failure to wipe out the Jews of Palestine during the war, who stood after it as their main and victorious competitors. Under Nazi instigation, the Palestinians elected to claim all of Palestine undivided, instead of compromising over it with the Jews, so they ended up losing it all for more than six decades and entering the future with uncertainty, for it is very difficult to turn the clock back today. Kuntzel also laments the fact that the victorious allies, instead of punishing the MB and their supporters, including Haj Amin, after the war, for their collaboration with the Nazis and for concocting with them the ruin of Britain, on the contrary came to view their restored good relations with the Arab world as outweighing any doctrinal "deviation" by the mufti and his MB allies, who continue to this day to declare their abhorrence of the West, to profess virulent anti-Semitism, to vow the destruction of Israel, to advocate Holocaust denial, and to hardly hide their admiration for Hitler and the Nazis. In the current unrest in the Arab world, that has been wrongly dubbed the "Arab Spring," some of those themes are reemerging. Britain and the West, who were prepared to sacrifice their long term interests for a temporary rehabilitation of their positions in the Middle East, may be now be paying dearly for that momentary lapse in their thinking. Indeed, with British and American silent consent, France had permitted the mufti, back then, to run away from her territory and so avoid his trial as a war criminal, and seek refuge in Egypt, which had become, just like Syria, Argentina, and Paraguay, a shelter for Nazi criminals after the war.

In spite of the many differences between Nazism and Fascism, on the one hand, and the authoritarian regimes in the Arab and Islamic worlds, on the other, there is a lasting red (now green) thread that continues to connect between the two, long after the former has waned away in Europe and the latter has begun to shake off the unbearable regimes that have oppressed Arab peoples for so long. These connections persist, in spite of the doctrinal reversals that have gripped the Arab world since the end of the war and caused them to attribute Nazism to Israel. Devout Muslim radical practitioners, like the MB, the Hamas, and Hezbollah and similar movements, indeed often attempt to wash themselves clean of Nazism by projecting it on Israel and accusing her of having adopted it. What truly unites these movements with bygone European Fascism are indeed their common enchantment with modern technology (today it is Internet, satellites, up-to-date television and radio broadcasting, and the most modern weaponry, including weapons of mass destruction); their fascination with violence and war, and the cultivation of supreme sacrifice, to the point of encouraging self-immolation, like the Islamikaze (that are wrongly viewed in the West as "suicide bombers"); and the rejection of democracy and liberal values. And perhaps above all, the obsession that refuses to die, with eliminating the Jews wherever they can be found.[5] No wonder that spectacular acts of international terrorism, like 9/11, the London and Madrid mass killings in civilian subways, hijacking airplanes and killing their passengers, or the Bali and other senseless bombings, have all an element of fanatic madness in them, reminiscent of the abuses of the Nazis. Even the Twin Towers' attack is strikingly identical to Hitler's similar fantasy to see Manhattan burning.[6]

Kuntzel's book explains what happened in Egypt in the years 1925–45 to turn the pro-Jewish sentiment in the early years of Zionist activity in Palestine, which was thought to benefit the entire area, into a hostile ambience that kindled the violent eruptions against the Jews thereafter. He attributes the radical change to the rise of the MB in 1928 that later impacted drastically the developments in mandatory Palestine, the relations between the Arabs and the Nazi regime, and ultimately the alliance between the mufti of Jerusalem and Hitler in person. He rightly observes that in the beginning of that period, amiable relations existed between the Muslim majority and the successful and well-to-do Jewish minority. But lest anyone believe, or come to the conclusion, that the Jews had always been privileged in Egypt at all times, and in general in the Arab and Islamic world, let us remember that when the state of Israel was founded in 1948, and the Jews found a shelter for themselves, the almost totality of the million Jews who had lived in the Arab and Islamic worlds emigrated either to the Jewish state or elsewhere in the West. American and European Jews did not leave, and there must be a reason. The reason was that Jews had lived under the discriminatory and humiliating status of *dhimmis*, and there were periods that under particularly strict and harsh rulers, like the Almohads in North Africa and the Mamluks in Egypt, or under the fanatic Shi'ites in Iran, Jews were persecuted, massacred, forced to convert to Islam, expelled, or constrained to run for their lives elsewhere.

Kuntzel speaks about contemporary Egypt, and it is there, under the pressure of the MB since 1928, on the eve of the world depression, which they could easily impute to the Jews, that the Jewish condition veered to the worse and had a direct impact on the situation in Palestine, and on the increasingly close relations between Arabs and Nazis. It was then and there that the Islamic connection to the Nazis and the Balkans began to burgeon, and it was then and there that the seeds of modern Muslim radicalism were sown, whence they would spread worldwide, under different appellations, to this very day. The membership of the MB, under its charismatic leader until 1940, Hassan al-Banna, grew from eight hundred in 1936 to two hundred thousand merely two years later, and half a million in 1948, with a military arm of about forty thousand. Ostensibly, the growth and the rhetoric were directed against the colonizing power, the British, who were not forthcoming on their promise to grant full independence to Egypt. Al Banna took advantage of the post–World War I socioeconomic dislocations, and the building tensions with the British, to announce and promulgate his brand of conservative and restorative *Salafi* Islam, which professed a return to the roots, as in the times of the Prophet. He taught that Islam had lost its prestige and impact on daily life in Egypt, due to Western intrusion, which lured people to secularism and to the abandonment of religion, and he propagated the return to the divine law that is incorporated in the Qur'an and the Sunna, which gave clear and detailed guidance to all needs of life.

The MB advocated a return to religious orthodoxy as the panacea not only for moral and social ills, but also for regaining the moral high ground that was lost to the West, by internationalizing the movement and attracting to it wide constituencies, especially of young people, and not only in the countryside where Islam had always kept its grip on the people, but also to reconquer the cities, which had fallen to the secular, westernizing, and modernizing bourgeoisie. They recruited the foreign Muslim students, who were studying in Cairo, to train them as their representatives when they returned to their countries of origin. Thus, they very early established branches of the Brothers in Lebanon, Syria, Transjordan (later Jordan), and in 1940 the Palestine Committee was set up, which encompassed the entire Middle East, and then the Far East Committee to cover the Muslim countries of Asia, and prophetically they even established the European Committee which has served its purpose only when Muslim immigration has intensified to Europe in the postwar period. Domestically, and following the European Fascist pattern of Germany and Italy, the MB demanded the dismantlement of all political parties and the abolishment of liberal democracy in Egypt. This is the main reason, though there are also others connected to Egyptian, Arab, and Muslim traditional order, why in the 1920s Egypt, and possibly also Iraq and others, were far more democratic and dedicated to women's rights than ever since, but all of them embraced varying degrees of authoritarianism following the military coups that plagued them for almost a century, until the 2010s when their "Spring" at last permitted them to talk about democracy if not to achieve it.

The Party of MB platform proposed a new political organization modeled on the medieval universal Caliphate, based on Sharia law and obeying the global Caliph, much along the lines of the thousand-year Reich, just with another content to its ideology albeit with a similar organizational philosophy, which also prohibited any other competing all-encompassing theory like Communism. The MB soon began to pursue an organizational praxis, by penetrating Communist ranks and denouncing them to the state security apparatus. In this endeavor, too, the MB felt they were treading on the Nazi's heels, launching a spreading pattern of confrontation that pitted Islam against Communism everywhere. Since in most Communist parties in the Arab and Islamic worlds, Jews (and Christians) were more prominent than in other local political parties, due to their preferred adherence to an atheistic political entity where Islam played little or no part, Communism became also a channel to rationalize the growing hostility toward Jews, in both the MB and the Nazi political organization. Economically, the MB treaded its unique route when it forbade interest (which countered any ambition to establish a modern banking system), and created a commonality of interest between capital and labor, while at the same time recognizing, like in Nazi Germany, the significance of technology, industrialization, and work ethic, as a condition and prerequisite to gaining military preponderance and running a world Islamic regime.

The MB, again like its Nazi model, also professed a social and moral Puritanism, which sought to control individual desires and ambitions by strictly adhering to conservative modes of conduct, avoiding material temptations, and aspiring to spirituality, a controlled asceticism that lent priority to satisfying the needs of the collective before turning to address personal necessities. In this light, or rather obscurity, one has to reconsider *Kristal Nacht* and other abuses by Nazi thugs toward their Jewish victims that they wished to subdue by terror and violence, as well as the violent outbursts of the MB then and the Hamas today, which burned down night clubs, brothels, and movie theaters, inherited from the Palestinian Authority in Gaza. Similarly, the Islamic Revolution of Iran, in February 1977, was triggered by the arson of a theater in a coastal city, by Muslim radicals who falsely claimed that a pornographic film was being shown, which justified the burning of the hall with its occupants inside. Since the MB, particularly their prominent leader, Sayyid Qut'b, who inherited the clout of Banna after his assassination, saw Jews as the evil of the world and the cause of its misfortunes, then, of course, all acts and institutions of immorality, such as theaters, movies, prostitution, drugs, corruption, and the deterioration of manners and values in all societies, were due to the Jewish management of world affairs. The MB could outdo the Nazis in their obsession with anything Jewish, and in the hatred they instigated them in their constituencies as a result, so much so that they naturally concocted plans together to wipe out the cause and reason of these troubles by methodically exterminating that race. Those ideas have become so rooted in general Islamic and Arab culture that one can still detect them, without much effort, more than half a century after Nazism was routed and eradicated.

However, nothing illustrates the great doctrinal breakthrough of the MB as the operationalization of the idea of jihad, from a dormant ideal, whose time had evolved, to an active tool to combat present-day enemies, binding every individual Muslim, not only the Muslim *Umma* as a whole. The rationale was that when the house is burning, it was incumbent on each individual Muslim to carry a bucket of water and contribute to the extinction of the fire the best he can, regardless of what the state, the public or the community does or refrains from doing. The idea was that the Qur'anic tenet of jihad, which had been the driving force of Islam at its inception, and the engine of its expansion, and had become over the years mostly viewed as merely an endeavor for self-striving and improvement, for example by spreading and propagating Islam, ought to be revived and Muslims ought to convert the use of force from self-defense into propagatory activity. In other words, jihad, as a mere educational value, ought not to predominate and it should be developed into an active tool, as of old, to spread the word of Islam worldwide. Al-Banna gave this idea a very active twist, as in the times of the Prophet, essentialized in the popular slogan that is still central to MB affiliates like the Hamas: "Allah is our aim, the Prophet our model, the Qur'an our constitution, jihad our path, and death for Allah the sublimest of our ambitions." By promising eternal martyrdom to the casualties in battle, he turned death for the cause not only into something that does not inspire fear and abhorrence, but into a desirable ideal that every young Muslim can and should embrace, thus avoiding the torment of this worldly life and taking the shortcut to the eternal hereafter under the blissful protection of Allah. The revival of MB and *Salafi* Islam in the Arab and Islamic world following the "Spring" of 2011–2012, attests to the tenacity of this thinking.

The dominating issue of the day for the MB as the world war storm was gathering, remained to identify the enemy against whom it was worth dying. That could initially be the British, the colonizer from whom the MB wished its constituencies to disengage. But as the Palestinian issue loomed on the horizon of the MB in the 1930s, and as Nazi anti-Semitic propaganda focused on the Jews, it was only natural and expectable that the two trends would converge into one, and the ultimate enemy of both be identified as the Jews. This did not happen all of a sudden, but was the fruit of evolution and development, as Kuntzel shows. At first, as already mentioned above, the Egyptian civilian constitution of 1923, in that first manifestation of democracy in the Islamic and Arab worlds, which did not last, had proclaimed full equality to all citizens, and no religious loyalty was referred to as a matter of state concern, for faith remained the private domain of each individual, and the reigning monarchy was declared "constitutional." During that period, under the political domination of the Wafd Party, Jews were part and parcel of the social, economic, and political system, and they were welcome in all walks of life. Though a branch of the Zionist movement was established in Egypt in 1924, Palestine seemed remote, beyond the wilderness of the vast Sinai Desert, and Pharaonic and democratic Egyptians did not sense the Palestinian issue as an inseparable part of the adjoining Arab world, which they despised. The Jews were then a mere domestic issue, as one of the three important denominational communities in the country, and no attention was yet paid to the international issues of world Jewry, nor to Zionism's struggle in Palestine. Nor was Palestine very noticeable to the Egyptian rank and file.

The rise to power of the Nazis in Germany generated mass demonstrations in Egypt that were understandably led by the local Jewish community, which was eighty thousand strong. In March and April 1933, more anti-Nazi demonstrations took place in many Egyptian cities, and many German products were boycotted. But the Germans reacted: Alfred Hoess, Rudolf's brother, whose family had settled in Alexandria in the previous century, founded the Egyptian branch of the Nazi Party, which organized without delay the free distribution in Egypt, in Arabic and French, of the German manifesto *"The Jewish Question."* A local Jewish businessman obtained a ban on its distribution on the grounds that it constituted racist incitement and disturbance of public order. So, the Germans turned to the official governmental channel, and capitalizing on Egyptian dependence on its cotton export, they hinted that they might boycott it in the future. King Farouq's government, which was pro-German, picked up the hint and began to work hard to discredit the Jews and to dismantle the boycott of German goods. The court ban on the dissemination of Nazi anti-Semitic literature was reversed, and within three years Egypt was rewarded when Germany became its second largest trade partner (after Great Britain).

The change of ambience toward the Nazis also facilitated the emergence in Egypt of new semi-military movements like "Young Egypt," the "Young Muslim Association," and the MB, whose members watched on movie screens the pomp and circumstance in which similar movements held their processions in Germany, with uniforms, strict discipline, and total doctrinal dedication to their cause and leadership. Thus, the street made its appearance, beside the monarchy and the parliament, as a third political power to be reckoned with. The growing pro-Third Reich public sympathy, which was launched at first as a manifestation of the rising anti-British nationalist sentiment, was soon veered toward an anti-Jewish jihad, once the Nazis diagnosed the situation in Palestine as a focal point of potential antagonism between Muslims and Jews, and decided to act in consequence. Their attention was thenceforth turned to transplanting the Palestinian controversy into Egypt and to harness the Egyptian Muslims to aid their coreligionists in Palestine against the Jews there and against world Jewry. The new campaign was to hinge on the mufti of Jerusalem, whose hatred to the Jews competed with that of the Nazis, and whose program of crushing Jewish immigration to Palestine, and of banning land sales to the

Zionists, coincided with Nazi plans to diminish the Jews, exterminate them, and close all the avenues that might help to rescue them and to allow them into Palestine.

Perceptively, it was the Nazis themselves who triggered the explosion in Palestine of the conflict between Arabs and Jews that would serve as a German pretext to intervene and transplant that dispute from Palestine to the rest of the Islamic world. Due to the rise to power of the Nazis and the escalation in Jewish persecution throughout Germany, a steady stream of Jewish refugees, to whom other countries, including the most "liberal" and "humane" among them, had closed their gates, headed to Palestine, where the British, in retaliation, imposed the White Paper limiting Jewish immigration, and the Arabs, under the mufti Haj Amin, launched the Arab Revolt (1936–1939) against both the British mandatory power and the Jewish Zionists. The Revolt afforded the MB the first opportunity to link their new interpretation of jihad with the contemporaneous battle in Palestine. It was in those years that membership of the MB had soared to two hundred thousand, some of them volunteering to go to the aid of Palestinians under the banner of jihad. Thus, the active battle of the MB against the Jews was transplanted to Palestinian soil, much to the delight of Nazi propagandists who wished to see all those anti-Jewish manifestations as part of their worldwide blueprint to exterminate what they viewed as the "Jewish race."

While the MB urged Egyptians to boycott Jewish businesses, they also set up the "Central Committee to Aid Palestine," which became their bastion of anti-Jewish activity, involving not only genuine fund raising and aid to Palestinian Arabs, but also boycotts against Jews in Egypt and dissemination of leaflets in mosques and work places, warning of British and Jewish intentions to destroy Muslim holy places in Jerusalem (claims that have persisted over the past sixty years), to tear the Qur'an to pieces, and to trample over it. The Peel Commission, and especially its recommendation to divide Palestine into an Arab and a Jewish state, raised the ire of the Palestinians and their supporters in Egypt, while the Egyptian government reverted to the utopian idea of establishing one state in Palestine, where everyone can live in "peace and harmony," something never attained in that land, and seldom elsewhere, if we take Yugoslavia's history as a guide. These manifestations of moderation and readiness to compromise were violently rejected by the MB throughout Egypt, which expressed itself in student demonstrations, "Down with the Jews!" and "Jews, get out of Egypt and Palestine!" Reflecting the Nazi propaganda that diffused in Europe the hoax of the "Jewish threat" in those days, leaflets of MB in Egypt also cried and shouted the "imminent danger of Egyptian Jews," attributing to them all the evils of the world.

Again, mimicking what had been unfolding in Nazi Germany, young Egyptians were urged to buy only Muslim goods, to prepare themselves for jihad to "defend the Al-Aqsa Mosque," and to donate for the benefit of Palestine anything they might receive as presents. Muslim ladies began proclaiming to the media their readiness to sacrifice their sons in jihad in Palestine, and at the same time Jewish synagogues and residences were bombed, a testament to the extent that MB propaganda, fanaticism, and anti-Semitism had predominated the public agenda in Egypt, though other organizations also participated in the anti-Jewish "festival," and were aided and financed by Nazi funds. While previously many Egyptian media had refused to participate in anti-Jewish incitement, by the outbreak of World War II in 1939, the Egyptian public, as well as its government and media, had embraced a clearly anti-Zionist inclination that would lead it directly into its disastrous involvement in the 1948 War, from which it emerged badly broken and bruised. The MB crowned their incremental propaganda successes in Egypt with the convening in Cairo in 1938 of an "Inter-Parliamentary Congress of Arab and Islamic Countries" where not only the Egyptian government took an anti-Zionist stance, but so also did the other participants, thus internationalizing the Palestinian question and bringing it to the attention of Arab and Muslim peoples other than the Palestinians and the Egyptians.

The Muslim connection between the war in Yugoslavia and the Muslim world was calculated very intelligently and skillfully by the Nazis as they brought into the loop the mufti of Jerusalem, Haj Amin al-Husseini, himself an adept of al-Banna, in the process of their rapprochement with the MB. The Arabs in general, showed a deep appreciation, which grew into open admiration, of Hitler's National Socialism. They were quick to produce an Arabic translation of *Mein Kampf*, to cultivate the belief that Arabs and Nazis shared enmity toward Britain and France, and also to promote the idea of *Volk*, which identified a people/nation not on the basis of borders and sovereignty, but on innate common traits like language, culture, history, and blood descent, hence the Arabs of Palestine were the business of the Arabs elsewhere. The Arabs in fact differentiated between *qawmiyyah*, their equivalent to the German *Volk*, which can be interpreted as ethnic/

cultural/linguistic loyalty; the word *qaum*, meaning originally a tribe; and *wataniyyah*, loyalty to a territory, or a homeland (patria). So they were able to accommodate both their general Arab identity and their attachment to a particular Arab locale (Morocco, Syria, Palestine, etc.). When Anton Sa'adeh founded in 1932 the Syrian People's Party, it readily adopted some Nazi paraphernalia, including the Nazi salute and a flag sporting a likeness of the swastika. The Phalangs, which were founded by the Lebanese-Christian Pierre Jumayyel, shortly thereafter, also adopted the same molds of conduct. Iraq did not lag far behind when *al-futuwa* youth movement was established to mimic the German *Hitlerjugend*, not to speak of the Egyptian "Young Egypt" already mentioned above. In other words, the Arab world of the 1930s was well disposed toward the rising Third Reich. Delegations from the Arab world participated in the Nuremberg marches of the Nazis, during the 1930s, and expressed their common disgust toward the Jews and their joint accusation of the Jews as the "scum of humanity" and the reason and source of all corruption and cultural degeneration in the world.

All these elements and more played a crucial role in the process of rapprochement, which threw the mufti of Jerusalem, Haj Amin, into the Nazi lap. Already in 1933, the mufti confided to the German Consul in Jerusalem that he and his flock welcomed the rise of Hitler in Germany and looked forward to the spread of Fascism in Europe. He also launched his own youth movement under the heading of "boy scouts," adopting Fascist-style uniforms and distributing propaganda materials bearing Nazi slogans and symbols. Upon the publication of the racist Nuremberg Laws in 1935, Hitler received greetings from the entire Arab world, from Morocco to Palestine, where Nazi propaganda had taken root. A meeting of minds between Nazis and Arab nationalists was achieved, with both sides proclaiming their anti-Zionist agenda, using the same rhetoric that accused Zionism of "dispossessing the aboriginal inhabitants of Palestine to create a purely Jewish land." The Nazi argument that since Jews cannot be creative, they would be unable to establish a state, and all they needed is a physical base to lead their international conspiracies, was enthusiastically welcomed by the mufti and his followers. This position was adopted by the Nazis in 1937, when the recommendations of the Peel Commission rendered the possibility of a Jewish state relevant. Foreign Minister Von Neurat stressed that a Jewish state would not conform to German interests, as it would create a base for international Jewry that would be given to the protection of international law.

Thus, Germany identified its interest as lying with the Arab world, which was the most dedicated and vocal in its opposition to the idea of a Jewish state. In consequence, many Arab students were invited to study in Germany, German companies took in Arab interns, Arab political leaders were invited to attend the annual marches and processions of the Nazi Party, and senior Arab military officers were invited to attend maneuvers of the *Wehrmacht*. In Berlin an "Arab Club" was founded, which became a center of propaganda for Palestine and against the Jews, and later a center for the Arab and Muslim broadcasts under the Nazi regime during the entire extent of the war. The Nazi Ministry of Propaganda, via its representative in Jerusalem, Dr. Franz Reichart, maintained close relationship with the mufti, and channeled monies to Arab media and agents. In 1937, an SS delegation, where Adolf Eichmann was a member, went to the Middle East for a study tour, followed by many other high-level delegations. In Damascus, they set up in 1939 an "Arab Club" that served as a clandestine base to train "volunteers" to the Arab Revolt, which was raging in Palestine against the British Mandate, and to undo the project of the Jewish National Home in that land. The Germans responded positively to the urgings of the mufti and supplied weapons and funds, which maintained the momentum of the Revolt during its last two years (1937–1939).[7]

As the British were striving to put an end to the Revolt, the Nazi press was enraged about the "cruelty with which the British were quelling Arab freedom fighters." So much so, that the active support lent by the Nazis to the mufti, against the Brits and the Jews, was taken by some as a general rehearsal preceding the real war.[8] The British, who were eager to preserve their good relations with the Arabs in view of the approaching war, looked with horror at the rise of radical Islam in Egypt, Iraq, and Palestine, and at the extraordinary convergence of this movement with European Fascism, especially the effort deployed by Nazism to aid the Arab cause and thus jeopardize British positions in the Middle East. So, as the Arab street was boiling hot with anti-British sentiment and pro-Nazi demonstrations, and as Jewish synagogues were being torched on *Kristal Nacht* (November 9, 1938) throughout Germany, Britain was caught in panic under its spineless government, which sold off Czechoslovakia to Hitler in Munich, and it resolved to abolish the recommendations of the Peel Commission, cancel the first Partition Plan for Palestine, and put a sweeping ban on Jewish immigration under the infamous White Paper. That happened precisely as Jewish immigration was coming to its apex (in 1931, only four thousand Jewish immigrants, in 1935, sixty thousand), as their dispossession in Germany was accelerating, the rest of the world was rejecting their plea for shelter, and the rebellion in Palestine was gaining momentum.

The mufti's almost innate anti-Semitism did not need Nazi encouragement to express itself. Already in the 1929, unrest in Palestine unfolded, where Palestinian crowds, led by the young mufti, were incited to kill and maim fellow inhabitants of Jerusalem, Hebron, and others cities, for no other reason than their being Jewish, even before there was any mass immigration of Jews to the land. The mufti, as the president of the Supreme Muslim Council, also held the highest religious function in the land, and in that premodern society, religion was the main source of power and authority. He lent to his national struggle against Zionism a religious and a pan-Islamic character, inasmuch as he also loathed the Jews for being a harbinger of westernism, modernism, secularism, and liberalism in the Middle East. He regarded the modern media, notably cinema, theater and some Western papers and magazines, as agents of corruption that undermined Islamic culture and destroyed morality, especially among the Muslim youth. For example, he viewed liberated Jewish girls in Palestine, who filled pioneering jobs in the fledgling Israeli society, adopted liberal fashions of dress and mixed with men who were not their spouses, as a debilitating process of degeneration, which by exhibiting themselves in the public square were likely to lure Muslim youth away from their restrained mores. In his extreme puritanical conservatism, he found an ally in German Fascism, so that as soon as the Rashid Ali Revolt in Iraq was crushed by the British, he turned to Berlin, where he became a loyal servant of the German cause and stayed there to the end of the war. But when the Americans landed in Morocco in 1942, he declared that they were subservient to the Jews, therefore they were by definition the enemies of Islam and the Arabs.

The mufti's clout, both as a Muslim cleric and as the loyal servant of the Nazis, was fully exploited by the Germans, first when he was fully mobilized, together with sixty broadcasters in various languages, translators, and administrative and technical staff, to the task of broadcasting Nazi propaganda in Arabic, Turkish, Persian, and Urdu. In the years 1939–1945, his station near Berlin, which broadcast round the clock Arabic music, Islamic programs, news about the war viewed in Nazi eyes, and an incessant flow of German propaganda, was the most listened to in the Arab world. The mufti's involvement in the programs became predominant since he moved to Berlin after the Baghdad fiasco in 1941 and stayed there until the final Nazi rout. In 1940, he worded the draft of a joint German-Italian proclamation recognizing the right of Arab countries to solve the Jewish problem in the same fashion those two Axis powers did, and from 1942 onward, he was involved in the permanent presence in occupied Athens of a special SS unit, which stood ready to move to Palestine and undertake the extermination of its Jews, with local Arab help, after the victory by Erwin Rommel in the Western Desert came to pass, which seemed a certainty. In 1943, when Himmler initiated, both as a propaganda measure and as a means to obtain the release of twenty thousand German POWs, an idea that would allow the rescue of five thousand Jewish children from German crematoria, Haj Amin, who believed in his ruthless and cruel Allah, fought that decision tooth and nail, and succeeded in abrogating it by interceding with Himmler, his close friend, and so he could add to his bloody credit the gassing of those innocent victims of the Nazi-Muslim hatred of the Jews.

The blood-thirsty mufti, who hardly fit the conduct that is expected of a cleric, did not stop there. When he got word that Bulgaria, Romania, and Hungary consented to allow Jewish children and their guardians to find shelter in Palestine, he wrote to the Bulgarian foreign minister and prevailed upon him to prevent the emigration of Jewish children from his country to a place where they would escape any supervision upon them. He suggested sending them instead to a place like Poland, where they could be more closely watched. The emigration permits were abolished, the kids were exterminated, and the Palestinian hero could add another feather to his headgear. In 1947, after twenty years of close collaboration between the mufti and the MB's al-Banna, which had started even before the MB was officially established in 1928, the mufti was appointed as al-Banna's deputy and the leader of the MB in Palestine, in preparation for the 1948 invasion of fledgling Israel by the Arab armies, with the active support of MB troops that were dispatched to Palestine, to overwhelm the Jews, and possibly to carry out the extermination plan that the mufti had in mind, once his blueprint for the final solution in conjunction with his Nazi allies had fallen through. In his calculus of the upcoming war, the "armies of Allah" were bound to crush the "armies of Satan." But this time Allah was less alert, less combative, and less determined than the mufti and his followers had expected and hoped.

In the fall of 1942, Himmler asked Hitler for the green light to recruit one Bosnian- Muslim SS division, to deal with the Partisans and other Yugoslav dissidents, so as to free German troops for the foundering Russian front. By Christmas of 1943, some hundred thousand Bosnians, almost 10 percent of the total, had been killed in the war, and a quarter million more were displaced, mainly by *Cetnik* Serbs. Himmler fantasized that he could capitalize on those data to mobilize the Bosniaks, in addition to the fact that he thought they were by nature and training very obedient to their superiors, due to their fearlessness and eagerness to die as *shahids*. Himmler and his ilk also theorized that Bosniaks, who were the descendants of the ancient sixth century Goths, had shown their bravery in World War I as part of the Austro-Hungarian army. Himmler thought to capture and revive that inherited spirit in the new Bosnian SS division, in order to battle against and destroy the growing threat posed by Tito and his awesome and successful Partisans. In February 1943, the plan was approved by Hitler, and Himmler appointed Arthur Phleps, the commander of the Seventh Waffen SS Division, in charge of the recruitment process, which was unprecedented among non-Germans. Karl von Krempler, a SS officer who was regarded as an expert on Muslim affairs, was nominated as the actual recruiter, under Phleps' orders.

The Waffen SS (or armed SS troops), which had started with three battalions when they were founded to replace the SA that was elimi- nated by Hitler when he thought that its commander threatened his own leadership of the Nazi Party, had grown to thirty-eight divisions (most of them ethnically German, and some notoriously manned by Latvians, Hungarians, and Bosnians), who were an armed branch of the Nazi Party, which operated as an elite security force in the conquered territories. They committed many war crimes and their leaders were tried in Nuremberg after the war. Already in 1942, the Waffen SS was becoming a sort of Foreign Legion in the German armed forces, as more and more foreigners joined in. The Thirteenth Mountain Divi- sion, named *Hanjar* (dagger in Arabic), was recruited in Croatia (which included then Bosnia as part of the Ustasha state), Serbia, Hungary, and Romania, with the mission to battle against the Partisans. Some of the recruits were *Volksdeutsche*, namely the small German community in occupied Serbia, whom Himmler had included in the compulsory military service that all Germans were obliged to undergo. From 1943, as the situation on the war fronts worsened, more foreign divisions were recruited to the Waffen SS in France, Scandinavia, the Ukraine, and Galicia. In September 1943, as the Allies invaded Italy and the Germans had to rush reinforcements to hold the line of defense, recruitment of foreigners was scaled up to allow the creation of the Twenty-Fourth Division made up of volunteers from Italy, Slovenia, Croatia, Serbia, and the Ukraine.

In March 1943, the German officer Von Krempler, accompanied by the Croatian Alija Suljak, traveled for eighteen days through eleven Bosnian counties, making use of Islamic symbols, like green banners sporting crescents, against Suljak's best judgment, who would have preferred the use of Ustasha symbols. In Tuzla they met the local Muslim leadership, and in Sarajevo they were introduced to Ra'is al-Alami, the chief Imam of Bosnia, without the presence of anyone from the Ustasha authorities. Much to the dislike of the Croats, who demanded Krempler's removal because he also recruited Muslim deserters and Catholics from the Ustasha army, his standing in the SS permitted him to ignore those reservations about his service and to pursue his operation. In the summer of 1943, the Jerusalem mufti was invited to lend his help to the recruitment of the Muslims of Bosnia, and he was flown from Berlin to second Von Krempler in his endeavor. The main obstacle that the mufti met in his encounter with Bosnian Muslims was the fact that back in 1941, when the Ustasha state was founded, the Imams of Sarajevo, Tuzla, Mustar, and Banja Luka had prohibited their followers from collaborating with the Fascist state under whose aegis they were now placed. But using his clout as the mufti of the third holiest city in Islam, Haj Amin, who now also boasted his close collaboration with Hitler and Himmler, succeeded in convincing the Bosniaks to reverse their position, and to join the new Thirteenth Waffen SS Division that was in the making, since "it was a Muslim military unit intended to operate in the interest of Muslims."

The Croat-Ustasha foreign minister, Mladen Lorkovic, suggested that the new unit be dubbed SS Ustasha Division, so that it be known as a Croatian, with Bosnian, Krajinan, and other contingents. Interestingly, the head of the state, Ante Pavelic, was opposed to forming a Muslim division per se, for fear that it might lead to Muslim demands for independence after the war, while he regarded Bosnia as an integral part of the Ustasha state. At the end, the division was baptized as the Thirteenth Mountain Croat *Hanjar* Division, in spite of the fact that only 10 percent of its recruits were Catholic. The mufti demanded that the division be designed to defend Bosnian Muslims and prohibited from leaving Bosnian borders, a limitation that was later ignored by the Germans once they obtained his blessing for its recruitment. In 1944, another SS division, Kama, was established, probably in the wake of the steady thinning of the German ranks, due to the rumors that *Hanjar* would leave Bosnia to fight for the Nazis elsewhere. In consequence, mass desertions ensued, sometimes of entire companies with their weapons, and Kama's new recruits were used to fill the ranks. The division in fact was sent to occupied France for training, and at the end of 1943 to Germany, to end up in February 1944 in Bosnia once again. It counted more than 21,000 recruits at its peak, 2,800 of whom were Christian Croats and the balance Muslims. Every battalion had its own Muslim chaplain—an Imam—and all the signal personnel were German. One battalion was made up of Kosovar and Sanjak Muslims; it was transferred back to Kosovo in April when the Twenty-First Albanian Waffen SS Division was created.

In September 1943, when the *Hanjar* were in training in Ville-franche, France, one unit took German hostages, executed five of them and rose in mutiny, arguably believing that if most of the division joined them they could switch sides and declare their loyalty to the Allies. But under the impact of their Imam, who claimed that they were "misled," they reversed their position; however, in the skirmishes that ensued some twenty of them were killed. As a result, eight hundred of the recruits, mostly Christian Croats, were released as "unfit for military service" and were dispatched to Germany for "labor service." Only three hundred Catholic servicemen remained in the division when it returned to Bosnia. Those who refused to work were sent to death camps where they perished. Himmler granted the Iron Cross to the Imam who helped quell the mutiny. When Villefranche was liberated from the Nazis in 1944, one of its main streets was named *Avenue des Croates*, and every September 17 the city commemorates the "Croat Uprising." When the Tito government asked after the war that the name of the memorial be changed to the "Yugoslav Uprising," the French refused on the grounds that they were duty bound to "preserve the historical truth."

When the division operated within Bosnia, it was told that its mission was to retrieve Muslim Albania from its occupiers (Italians at that time). In mid 1944, as Tito's fortunes in the war were rising, and the Nazis seemed headed to a total rout, he announced a sweeping amnesty to all members of the division who would desert it. Romania had, in the meantime, switched sides and joined the Red Army, which had crossed the borders of the Balkans in their anti-German sweep throughout Eastern Europe. On September 17, the Partisans seized Tuzla, occasioning a massive desertion from the Ustasha's Twelfth

Brigade to the Partisans. On October 20, the Red Army entered Belgrade, but the divisional Imam led a new mutiny of some one hundred Muslims in Bosnia. In November, the division had grown half-German due to the desertions of the Bosniaks. In May 1945 the rest of the division surrendered to the British, who incarcerated them in Rimini, Italy, as POWs. Later in 1947, the Communist regime court-martialed some members of the division, but few were convicted. The division passed into history and became a remote, if unpleasant memory.

For those who are fascinated or amused by historical fortunes, ironies, improbabilities, and strange turns of event, we reserve the tale of several odd developments. The *Hanjar* Division was revived during the Bosnia War (1992–1995), and Nasser Oric was appointed its head when surrounded by the Serbs in the Srebrenica enclave in eastern Bosnia. In 1994, all units under Oric's command were named "the Eighth Operative Group," and he was promoted to brigadier general. In November 2000, he was indicted for possessing illegal weapons and he was convicted for extortion, but the verdict was later reversed. In 2006, he was convicted by the International Court in the Hague for failing to prevent the killing and torturing of Serbs in the area under his command. The perpetrators of violence shifted from one ethnic group to another, but while hatred persisted from World War II through the Bosnia War of the 1990s, the postwar political settlement has at least limited the scope of hostilities and violence for now.

Notes

1. Matthias Kuntzel, *Jihad and Jew-hatred, Islamism, Nazism and the Roots of 9/11*, Telos Press Publishing, New York, 2007. Much of the following discussion is based on the first chapter of this book.
2. The name coined by this author to designate the so-called "suicide bombers." Islamikaze is a composite of Islam and the Japanese Kamikaze, who come phenomenologically closest to the bombers in Islam. See R. Israeli, *Islamikaze: Manifestations of Islamic Martyrology*, Frank Cass, London, 2003.
3. Cited in R. Israeli, *Muslim Anti-Semitism in Christian Europe*, Transaction, New Brunswick, 2009, 4–5.
4. See e.g., Bat Ye'or, the *Dhimmi*, Fairleigh Dickinson Press, Madison and London, 1985; R. Israeli, *Back to Nowhere: Moroccan Jews in Dream, Nostalgia and Reality*, Lambert Academic Publishing, Saarbrucken, 2010.
5. See R. Israeli, *Muslim Anti-Semitism in Christian Europe*, Transaction, New Brunswick, 2010, especially chapter 1.
6. See Jeffrey Herf's splendid introduction to Kuntzel's book.
7. Kuntzel, op. cit., 40–48.
8. Ibid., 50.

6

Jasenovac: The Routinization of Mass Murder

Jasenovac was a complex of sub-camps, close to each other, some one hundred kilometers south of Zagreb, the capital of Croatia. The women's camp, which was a little further away, but nonetheless part of the complex, was at Stara Gradiška, and was also built in 1941 and operated until the end of the war in 1945. All in all, it is claimed by some estimates that at least a couple of hundred thousand people: Serbs, Jews, Gypsies, and Croat dissidents were arrested, incarcerated, and exterminated there. The Ustasha Police was in charge of the operation, and it channeled its victims there from all parts of the Ustasha state: Zagreb, Sarajevo, and smaller towns across the country. Most inmates were executed near the extermination sites of Gradina and Granik and other places, but those who were skilled at needed professions and trades were employed in services and workshops in the camp until their execution. Like in the camps of Eastern Europe, the inmates in Jasenovac lived under extremely severe conditions: a meager diet, miserable accommodations, and a cruel regime on the part of the Ustasha guards toward their victims. Only during the periods of visits by foreign delegations, like the Red Cross, was there any letup. The acts of murder reached their peak in the summer of 1942, when tens of thousands of Serbian villagers were deported to Jasenovac from the area of the fighting against the Partisans in the Kozara Mountains. Most of the men were executed at Jasenovac, but the women were sent for slave labor to Germany, and the children were taken from their mothers. Some were murdered, but others were dispersed in orphanages around the country and very often raised as Catholics, according to the blueprint of the regime. In April 1945, as the Partisans were approaching the camp, the Ustasha, in an attempt to erase the traces of their crimes, blew up the installations and killed most of the inmates. Few of them survived, and the recollections about the camps are based on those accounts. The estimates of the figures of victims in Jasenovac vary from an underestimate of a hundred thousand to a wildly exaggerated one million.[1]

In both Croatia and Serbia, April 22 was adopted as a Day of Remembrance of Jasenovac—in fact, of all the victims of the Ustasha Independent State. It is the date when the last thousand inmates broke out from Jasenovac, liberating themselves with their bare hands, many of them perishing in the process. But what is remembered is different on either side of the aisle: the Croats tend to minimize the disaster and to include all Croatian victims of war, not just the victims of the Ustasha at the camp; the Serbs and some Jews describe Jasenovac as the focus of evil, where hundreds of thousands of Serbs and tens of thousands of others were murdered in a process of ethnic cleansing. In *Yad Vashem*, the Israeli national Jewish Holocaust memorial in Jerusalem, which has been building a database and documenting in minute detail the war memories of the survivors, the Jasenovac entry says simply:

> This was a concentration and extermination camp, the largest in Croatia. It was in fact a complex of camps down the Sava River, some 100km south of Zagreb. To this complex also belonged the camp for women, Stara Gradiška, which was set apart from all the rest. The camp was established in August 1941 and dismantled in April 1945. Its construction, management and supervision were entrusted to Department III in the Croatian Security Police (*Ustaska Narodna Sluzba*, or UNS), headed by Max Luboric, who was personally in charge of what went on within the camps. Prominent in his cruelty among the dozens of Ustasha officials who served at the camp, was the former cleric Miroslav Filipovic-Majstorovic, who killed with his own hands tens of prisoners. In Jasenovac, thousands of people were murdered. Most of them were Serbs, but also others: Jews, Gypsies, and Croatian dissidents. Most Jews were sent to Jasenovac and murdered by August 1942, when Croatian Jews were dispatched to Auschwitz for extermination. Jews were sent to Jasenovac from all over the Ustasha state: from Zagreb, Sarajevo, and from the smaller towns. Upon arriving to Jasenovac, most of them were murdered in the surrounding killing fields, like Granik and Gradina. Those who were not immediately executed, were needed professionals and artisans like doctors, pharmacists, electricians, shoemakers and jewelers, who were employed in services and workshops at the camp.
>
> The conditions in the camp were very harsh: under-nourishment, a tough regime, and a harrowing conduct on the part of the Ustasha wardens and guards. The living conditions were slightly improved

occasionally, just preceding the visits of journalists in February 1942 or a Red Cross delegation in June 1944. The acts of murder reached their peak at the end of Summer 1942, when tens of thousands of Serbian villagers in the Kozara mountains, a battle region against the Partisans, were brought in. Most men were executed, women were dispatched to Germany for forced labor, and children were taken away from their mothers, and then were either murdered or dispersed among orphanages across the country. In April, 1945, as the Partisan armies approached the camp, the Ustasha sought to cover up their horrors by blowing up all the facilities and murdering all the inmates. A valiant attempt was done by inmates to mutiny in the process, but it was quelled and most of the mutineers perished. Very few survived to tell the story.

That vast camp, which came to earn the questionable epithet of the third largest in Europe, was in the nature of things full of villains, but none of them gained the notoriety of that beastly creature, Miroslav Filipović-Majstorović, whose career illustrates the inhuman insanity of the Ustasha regime, which matched the Nazis and sometimes surpassed them and had to be reined in by them.

In an account based on depositions collected by *Yad Vashem* Cadik I. Danon Braco reiterated that eighty-two thousand Jews had lived in Yugoslavia in 1941, and 82 percent (sixty-seven thousand) of them perished between 1941–1945. He said:

> In Jasenovac and in the Jasenovac camps, the majority of Jews of Bosnia and Croatia were killed savagely. The executors weren't Germans but Croatian Ustashas, in contrast to the Nazi extermination camps in Germany. The Ustashas came in direct contact with the victims, since the killing was committed manually and enthusiastically with a knife, club, dagger, or a bullet. On entering the camps, the prisoners had to put their own valuables on a table. The old and exhausted were killed first. The prisoners were poorly fed (e.g., a simple soup was hot water with dirty yellow cubes, which was not really edible). The village of Gardina was the center of massive executions. The Ustashas said that people who were unable to work could have an "easier job" in picking plums. Many innocent people did volunteer for the job and were never seen again. The victims' belongings were stored in houses of the village. One of the punishments was to tie a naked person to a pole and to pour water on him in the winter, until the man froze to death and turned into a frozen statue. A red-haired sergeant was a dangerous man who killed a Jewish prisoner who was previously an attorney. The prisoner was killed in a very cruel way: stabbed with his hands tied, until he was dead.

If anyone tried to run away in the process, he was executed on the spot in front of everyone. Those who complied had good conditions and were treated better than in the camps. The prisoners were guarded by Ustashas, and most of their work was to keep an eye on the cattle. The prisoners were then moved to Obradovci, and there they were guarded by more than twenty Ustashas, but they were treated better so that prisoners would not try to run away. The Herzegovian wardens were known to be more cruel and brutal. One of them, called Cuza, had beaten one of the prisoners very harshly with a stick all over the body. Once he again approached the same prisoner with his gun, aiming at his head, but the magazine of the rifle was empty. Some Ustasha soldiers were Muslim and joined the Ustashas in order to earn more money. At the beginning, some of them took the job innocently, but then they were trained to be cruel to the prisoners and would be rewarded for their mistreatment of the inmates.[2]

When I (this author) visited the main camp on the Croatian side of the Sava, in November 2011, I saw a different Jasenovac than the one revealed to me on my previous visit to the Bosnian Jasenovac, the former site of Stara Gradiška, where women and children had been incarcerated, tortured, starved, and then executed in the thousands. Two memories, two narratives, two worlds, both full of cruelty and inhumanity, both pretending to commemorate the extermination of innocent civilians, mainly Serbs, Gypsies, and Jews, but in fact aggrandizing their own plight, minimizing their own wrongs and demonizing their rivals. In both, unlike in Auschwitz, Treblinka, Dachau, Mauthausen, and their likes, where remnants of the barracks, gas chambers, and crematoria are kept as testimonies to the coming generations, the entire expanse of the Jasenovac (and Jadovno for that matter) camps was razed to the ground, and the only existing structures that stand erect were built as part of the new memorial installations erected in recent years with a view to launder history, to exonerate oneself and indict others. Only the numbers of victims differ: the Bosnian Jasenovac proclaims seven hundred thousand Serbs and thirty thousand Gypsies and Jews, each, while Croatian Jasenovac advertises at most a total of a hundred thousand victims, eighty thousand of them Serbs. In both places I walked through the vast areas of the camps, seeing the location of the brick house, where many innocent inmates were incinerated live or dead, and where the barracks once stood, where regular prisoners waited for their death, and artists and artisans were employed at producing goods that were marketed by the camp authorities and generated income for their butchers. I walked on the paths treaded by the inmates on their way to execution; I saw the gallows on the river, where inmates were placed before they were knocked out and thrown into the water, or left to hang, or abandoned in the snow to freeze to death; and I could follow the tracks the prisoners took on their way to build embankments in the river, where their exhausted corpses were often incorporated into the structures. I could guess the contours of the immense mass graves where the victims were thrown, either after being knocked out by hammers or having their throats slit by their executors, or being buried alive when their stamina no longer allowed them any resistance.

Apart from the vast green fields, which now cover those flat areas that yield no outside signs of the atrocities perpetrated there two or three generations ago, only the nondescript museums, offices, and some memorial structures (the most imposing of them designed and built on the Croatian Memorial site by a Serb architect under the Tito regime, in the form of a concrete lotus flower) disturb the sinister uniformity and desolation of the landscape. One can review old pictures and some artifacts that are preserved in the museums or scan through the lists of tens of thousands of victims that were identified, collected, and commemorated in a two thousand page directory that contains to date over eighty thousand names. One can guess the ethnic affiliation of the dead only by their names. In the book, they are all "Yugoslavian" without distinction, though that term is no longer valid. This is the basis of the Croatian version, which limits the entire list of murdered victims to a hundred thousand. They seem to take the lack of more evidence, for want of more identifiable names, as evidence of no more victims, though they are making visible efforts to lengthen that list by further research. For the Serbs, who champion the much longer victim list amounting to hundreds of thousands, Croats simply manipulate and minimize their guilt, an accusation mirrored in the Croat claim that their bitter enemies grossly exaggerate their figures to win the hearts of the Jews and the West worldwide. The numbers remain disputed, and one wishes that those mass graves dug in the ground; the destroyed buildings, which used to house the murdered victims; and the placid waters of the Sava, which carried away thousands of their corpses, could reveal their secrets and cry out the true figures of the many tragedies that were buried there forever.

Bogdan Petrovic, who gave a heart rendering testimony of his 135 days in Jasenovac, testified about some of the same atrocities. He was a twenty-one-year-old Partisan when taken prisoner on March 29, 1944, during a battle with the Germans some thirty kilometers down the Sava from Zagreb. He was shipped by his captors to Jasenovac, where he stayed from October 5, 1944 to February 1945; then he was sent to a labor camp in the Reich near Linz, Austria, and was liberated by the Americans on May 5, 1945. He arrived to Jasenovac on a special train, with a group of other prisoners from the jail of Petrinjska; they were all dressed in black uniform and wore the badges of "UO," which stood for *Ustasha Obrana* (Ustasha Defense). His story is quite poignant:

> The train arrived in Jasenovac in the afternoon. . . . They did not hit us or maltreat us. . . . As we reached the camp, I looked at the gates and wondered if I would ever see it on the outside again. . . . It was a Sunday, a day off, and there were not many Ustashas in the camp. We went straight to the reception section. As a captured Partisan, I was dressed in a German uniform and carried a Yugoslav military coat over my arm. I had Italian trekking shoes on me. In the reception, an Ustasha took the coat from me, without asking anything, and threw it onto a heap of confiscated belongings. . . . After the reception we were taken to the barracks, which accommodated the inmates. A man, identified as the supervisor of the barracks, walked out from one of them, while some inmates were cleaning the premises. After some argument, the supervisor started hitting one of the inmates on his back with a stick. . . .
>
> The Sava began to flood and we needed to reinforce the embankment. I left the camp grounds for work, for the first time. There were twice as many Ustashas as inmates, to secure the site. I got fever by reason of the cold wind which blew on the Sava. I was afraid I might have contracted typhoid. . . . I went to the infirmary to see Dr. Bardek, with whom I had been in prison, before coming to the camp. He advised me not to go to the prison's hospital and told me: "Go to work and do not let yourself end up in bed." I struggled to bring down my temperature, and it did after a few days. If I had let it beat me and gone to bed, the disease would have gotten me. . . . The Ustasha frequently emptied the hospital, those who did not work were quickly sent away for execution. . . . Only once I heard the singing of the executioners as they went past our barracks in the dead of the night. . . . They sang: "From Garic to Russia, Jewish hides flutter high!"[3]

Various versions persist nevertheless with regard to Jasenovac in general and the numbers of the murdered victims in particular, which, with the passage of time and the passing away of most surviving eyewitnesses, and the suppression of memories during the Communist years, are becoming harder to collect and ascertain by the day. We will briefly survey here, besides the estimates of Western scholars like Philip Cohen, three main Yugoslav contenders who wrote on this topic: Sborljub Zivanovic, Milan Bulajic and Antun Miletic.[4] Zivanovic, a medical doctor and anthropologist, originally from Novi Sad and currently a scientist and member of the International Slavic Academy of Science, Culture, Education, and Arts in London, a miniature replica of a Yugoslavian UNESCO, had excavated mass graves in the Jasenovac system of extermination camps. He was on a team of forensic anthropologists, who dug on both sides of the Sava River, namely Jasenovac on the left bank and Donja Gradina on the right. The mass graves were excavated in 1964, and some anthropologists had estimated that more than seven hundred thousand Serbs, twenty-five thousand Jews and some eighty thousand Gypsies were killed by the Ustasha between 1941 and 1945. Those findings were certified by the entire team of anthropologists, including Vida Brodar and Anton Pogacnik from Ljubljana (so, it was not a purely "Serbian conspiracy" as some have claimed), but it was never published by Yugoslavian authorities, as part of their policy of hiding the war horrors in order to refrain from instigating interethnic unrest among the components of the federal state, as will be explained below.

Only in 1992 did Predrag Dragic Kijuk manage to recover much of this report in the official archive and published it in *Catena Mundi*. Zivanovic himself published his anthropology book in 2006, where this previously suppressed report was cited. Nevertheless, since Zivanovic was the only member of the team who was also a medical doctor, the part of forensic pathology, in the report that he was alone qualified to sign, had never been published even when other parts gradually came to light in the post-Communist era. They were first presented at the Fourth Jasenovac Conference in 2007. Zivanovic attested, and his testimony as a doctor is somewhat more credible than statements by nationalist politicians who have an axe to grind, that he had in his possession legal documents issued by Bosnian and Croatian courts, against Catholic priests and Muslim executioners, which included their confessions and some photos taken at the time when the crimes were committed. These documents had been published in a separate book in Zagreb in 1946, and another set of documents came to the light of day in Zagreb in 1948 in a book by Victor Novak entitled *Magnum Crimen*. Professor Ante Premeru, himself an ex-inmate and survivor of Jasenovac, who had personally witnessed many of the crimes perpetrated in the camp, as he was forced, with others, to dig up corpses of victims from mass graves and burn them so as to efface the traces of the horror. Later also a forensic expert, he had briefed Zivanovic prior to the latter's excavations as to what he could expect to encounter. Thereafter, testimonies of survivors were published in their hundreds and became largely known, though the suffering of the thousands who perished can never be documented. What is widely known, nonetheless, is that the Ustasha and Muslim executioners of the camps delighted in seeing their victims tortured and suffering, as attested by the survivors.

The methods of killing and torturing were reconstructed in harrowing detail in Zivanovic's expert report,[5] based on the findings of the excavations and the testimonies of the survivors, some of them very credible, many of them repeated in such exactly minute details that they could not have been invented and reinvented by some delusional mind. Those methods included, for example:

1. Many of the victims were killed by starvation and total deprivation of food and water. Part of the suffering of the inmates consisted of watching thousands of others, including children, chillingly diminishing by the day until their death. The cruelty here is that because all of those inmates were earmarked for execution in any case, it would have been better for them to be executed immediately, in one stroke, rather than perish gradually amidst suffering and anguish.
2. Many inmates were exposed to infection and infestation, by lack of sanitary facilities, drugs, and medical treatment.
3. Some of the victims were given "special treatment" by nailing them alive to trees, using long masonry nails. They were then left to die slowly as they bled and went mad from excruciating pain, reminiscent of the Roman crucifixion mode of punishment, in which Jesus Christ, the adored icon of the fervently Catholic Ustashas, had himself perished. While that mode of torture could be ascribed to a vengeance on the Jews who had allegedly "killed the Christ," what about the Gypsies and the Serbs who believed in Christ, though their respective denominations may have varied from Catholicism? During the investigation of Zivanovic, many trees with hammered-in nails of this sort were discovered.
4. Many victims were stabbed in the chest, or had their throats slashed by knives, or had their eye balls extracted from their sockets by their executors. Many pregnant women were stabbed in their stomachs and the fetuses were extracted from their wombs, only to be also stabbed, while their mothers' breasts were cut ruthlessly.
5. In Jasenovac there was a huge furnace, named Picili's Furnace, where victims were thrown alive and burned. That was the Ustasha version of the Nazi crematoria, with the difference that the latter took in bodies of

the gassed victims, while in Jasenovac the furnace at once filled the two functions of killing and burning. Cremated bones were found in Picili, but the remnants did not permit researchers to ever evaluate the numbers of victims.

6. At times, people perished in a regime of hard labor-cum-starvation. Those quickly exhausted and fallen victims were either buried on the spot, while still breathing, or used as logs built into walls, embankments, or dams where the deceased had been worked to death.

7. Thousands of victims were thrown, either alive or after executions, into the Sava River, just as the Hungarians had ended the lives of the Budapest Jews in the Danube. The source of the information here is the few survivors who eyewitnessed; or the notes, photos, and diaries that the murdered left behind; or in the depositions of the survivors in courts after the war.

8. Unlike Nazi Germany, which lumped men, women, and children together for annihilation in gas chambers and then in crematoria, the Ustasha established a special camp for children. Most atrociously, Catholic nuns, or others who pretended to be such, who in other occupied countries often risked their lives to rescue Jewish children, were here instruments of extermination; they murdered the kids under their surveillance, including those who cried at night or could not control their bowel function. They would take small children by their legs and crush their fragile heads against the wall until death. This horror could not be verified or certified twenty years after the war when the report was written, but it was described in detail by survivors.

9. A small number of victims were executed by hanging. This is based on photographs taken by some murderers at the site. Other extant evidence was not found, but this mode of execution was believed to have been used as a warning, a threat, and a deterrence to frighten other inmates who might disobey the rules of the camp.

10. Because ammunition was scarce and expensive, the Ustashas tried to save on bullets and seldom used them, except in cases where that kind of murder, again as in the case of hangings, were to serve as deterrence to others; here, a mass grave of male victims shot, with sometimes the spent bullet and cartridge still lodged in the body or lingering around it, was found during the investigation.

11. Surviving inmates of Jasenovac remember the *Srbosek* (the knife for killing Serbs) that was devised, besides ordinary knives, for the manual and individual slaughter of the Serbs. It was crescent shaped and tied to the wrist of the killer to enable him to cut the throat of the victim without much movement of the hand. The forensic examinations have revealed many cases of cervical vertebra cut by sharp objects, probably such knives. That was the same method used by the murderers to kill animals, which they later adopted for their human victims. While the assassins could kill children easily, due to their weak resistance and fresh flesh, it was more difficult to slaughter adults who would offer a stiffer resistance. So, despite the deep cuts, the victim would not die instantly, and they would be thrown while still alive, into a mass grave. They would often agonize

135

for a while, covered by other dead or dying bodies, unable to move much because of bleeding, much less capable of escaping. Only when the killers cut one of the main arteries of their victims, something they learned to perfection in the course of time, would immediate death rescue those unfortunate and helpless people from their suffering.

12. Another technique that the murderers developed in Jasenovac, after being experimented at first in the early mass murders of the Jadovno complex, was to cause fatal injuries to the skull of their victims by cruelly and ruthlessly beating their heads with wooden sledgehammers, mallets, common hammers, or iron bars. The murderers indulged, in apparent delight amidst their murderous ecstasy, during their orgies of killing. Unconscious, though often not instantly dead, the victims were thrown into a pit or a mass burial place, only to wake up later under a pile of other bodies. Some very lucky victims, who were not fatally hit, could even miraculously escape from the pits and the tombs, survive, and tell the harrowing tales of their torment. Mass graves have revealed that the head injuries were caused mainly in the temporal area, on the right or the left, but much less often on the frontal side of the skull. From survivor accounts we know that the Ustasha killers would tie their victims two by two, hit them simultaneously with mallets on one of their temples, and then throw them into the pit or the mass grave, or sometimes one of them would be hit and would drag the other after him. According to forensic examinations, maybe as high as 20 percent of the victims were thrown to their death with their skulls only partly damaged, so that their death was a slow and agonizing process.

Zivanovic comes to a total estimate of between 330,000–390,000 Serbian victims in the NDH, 32,000 Jews, and 26,000 Gypsies, who were executed in one of those harrowing and inhuman methods cited above. To those, an unknown number of Muslims and dissident Croats has to be added. He also examines the claimed numbers of the civilian war victims in all Yugoslavia, which he estimates at over one million, some seven hundred thousand of them, or 70 percent, occurred in the Ustasha state, whose combined population made up only some 40 percent of the Yugoslavian total. That means, that aside from all the killings and war turmoil in all Yugoslavia, caused by the German occupation, by the Partisans, the *Cetniks*, the civil war, and so on, the NDH still takes the largest part, perhaps an indication of the large-scale executions in the death camps, the like of which did not exist in other parts of the country, even if we take into account the German executions of Jews and others in their directly controlled regions of the country, mainly in Serbia.[6]

Over the years Milan Bulajic has been sharing his research findings with specialized conferences on Jasenovac. During the Fourth International Conference of 2007 on Jasenovac, he rebelled against the current revisionism in the Jasenovac memorial area and the reticent role of the Vatican during the mass murder there. For him, the large number of seven hundred thousand Serbian victims of Jasenovac has been desecrated by counterclaims that minimize it down to ninety thousand, and he is bitter on this account against "certain Serbs, Jews (probably referring to Philip Cohen), and the Holocaust Memorial Museum in the United States. He mentioned that on April 6, 2006, Dragan Cavic, president of the Republic of Srpska, had spoken at the memorial area of Donja Gradina, lamented the murder of seven hundred thousand Serbian victims, and seemed to support the standard claim of Serbs that Jasenovac, to his mind "the largest killing ground of Europe," had indeed witnessed the annihilation of so many Serbs. So much so that the figure of seven hundred thousand has become like a mantra cited by the Serbs everywhere, exactly as the number of six million is cited by Jews on every occasion related to the story of the Holocaust. But numbers cannot just be thrown into the air as one wishes. They are not mere statistics; for making an inflated number so dramatic and incredible, it risks becoming iconic, like a mantra repeated, without thought or logic, and without providing any evidence. Behind the numbers there are people, who had a name; therefore those numbers have to be accounted for: the information must be painstakingly gathered and verified. For the thirty thousand or so Jews exterminated in Jasenovac, calculations were made and information collected, according to the registers of the eliminated Jewish communities under the Ustasha regime.[7] It should be possible to approximate that work of patient and long-term collection of data for the Serbs, though their numbers were much greater, and the data on the rate of their killings suppressed for many years throughout Yugoslavia.

Bulajic, a historian and member of the International Commission on the Truth about Jasenovac, disputes some of the statistics of the murdered victims, especially the Gypsies, and criticizes the removal of plaques commemorating the murders, between April 16, 2006 when he visited Jasenovac with the president of Republika Srpska, Dragan Cavic, and April 30, when he laid wreathes on the site. The old plaques had mentioned the numbers of exterminated victims; they were replaced by a marble plate that contains some details about the site, but the figures of the dead were erased. For him, that is an even graver crime than the murder itself, for part of the history of Gypsies would be thereby erased. He claims that the figure of seven hundred thousand Serbian victims is not a Serbian myth, because he had found it stated by some Croatian institutions and Croatian representatives. He recounts that the 1946 report of the National Commission for the Crimes of the Occupying Forces and their Collaborators, prepared for the International Commission of War Crimes, had concluded that it would probably never be able to tell the exact number of victims in Jasenovac, but based on the evidence and numerous witnesses, it may be said with certainty that between five hundred and six hundred thousand people were killed there. He also mentions that the *Encyclopedia of the Lexicographic Institute of Zagreb*[8] had cited exactly the same estimates.

Bulajic quotes the president of the Zagreb Jewish Community, Dr. Ognjen Kraus, as stating during the ceremony commemorating the victims of Jasenovac on April 25, 1999:

> Jasenovac is the biggest execution site for Jews in Croatia. Apart from them, the Jews from the former Kingdom of Yugoslavia and Jewish immigrants from many European countries were also killed there. Before 1941, the Jewish community in Croatia had some 25,000 members who lived in 37 communities. 21,000 perished in the Nazi and Ustasha genocide. Today, there are now around 3,000 Jews in Croatia living in 9 Jewish communities. These facts speak for themselves.[9] This place must stand as a lasting memento of the Ustasha genocide and a warning for the future of mankind. May it testify to the truth about the past. The truth cannot be erased and there is no reason to hide it. It should be admitted. Those who are guilty of genocide should be named.[10]

Bulajic also cites the Zagreb Jewish researcher, Josip Riboli, who categorically asserted that Jasenovac was a death camp, nothing less, to counter other occasional claims that it was a labor camp and that life there was not so bad after all. Despite the diverging numbers of victims cited by various quarters, he said, what is important is the nature of the crimes. Jasenovac was a criminal camp, part of a criminal system, though it was also partly a labor camp, even a prison camp, from which many prisoners were deported to work in Germany, many others were released after they served their terms, many others were granted amnesty or survived in some other way. Yet, it remains a devastating fact that many of those who entered the camp never came out of it alive.[11] Following the pattern suggested by other eyewitness survivors cited above, Dr. Josip Riboli, a Jewish survivor, said:

No one who did not have the misfortune to be in the Jasenovac camp can know what it was like. People reading accounts about it written in the newspapers today believe there is a lot of exaggeration. That is why, before we start talking about those horrors, the following fact should first be pointed out: One cannot exaggerate Jasenovac. Those things are so horrid, so abominable, that the people who had not gone through it cannot comprehend them, and those who have passed through Jasenovac, where death lurked at every step, every minute of the day and night, where every single Ustasha could kill thousands upon thousands of people and not account for any one, will wonder how they have come out of that hell alive.[12]

Bulajic, just like other writers of the Shoah, basing himself on the data of the Federation of Jewish Communities of Yugoslavia, came to the conclusion that while close to seventy thousand Jews had lived in all Yugoslavia in 1931, that number had grown to around seventy-five thousand in 1940, and to close to eighty-two thousand if we include the thousands of Jewish refugees who escaped from the Nazis in other parts of occupied Europe. Some 82 percent of them perished in the war, namely about sixty-seven thousand. Out of that totality, Ustasha sources acknowledge that close to forty thousand Jews lived in the territory of NDH, namely half of all Yugoslavian Jews, twenty thousand of whom lived in Croatia and Slavonia, twelve thousand in Bosnia and Herzegovina. In Zagreb alone there were eleven thousand Jews in 1940, most of them (some 8,700) Ashkenazi and the rest Sephardic. In addition to those victims, there were many Jews who either did not appear in their communities' registers, or were tied in mixed marriage with non-Jews, or intentionally registered as Serbs, Croats, Hungarians, and as such they were recorded as victims within those declared categories. The incomplete list of the Osijek war victims alone identified 1,628 Jews, 319 of whom were murdered in Jasenovac and 928 at Auschwitz. It can be established that some sixty transports, with fifteen thousand Jews, including men, women, and children, were dispatched to the Jasenovac camp, but since Jews were often transferred to other camps, or to various camps within the Jasenovac complex, it is hard to ascertain exact and reliable figures.

Based on the evaluation that close to forty thousand lived under the Ustasha state, and that only eight thousand survived in total, that means that some thirty-two thousand Jews vanished in or from NDH territory. From German accounts, which were precise, we learn that some 5,000 Jews were transported to Germany, mostly Auschwitz, then close to 24,000 perished in NDH lands, and some 1,500 in Italy or in the zone under Italian occupation. Of all the Jews murdered by and under the Ustashas, some fifteen thousand to seventeen thousand perished in Jasenovac. Slavko Goldstein, a leader of the Zagreb Jewish community and the father of renowned Jewish-Croat historian, Ivo Goldstein, himself reported that all members of his family had been taken to Jasenovac, but he did not know whether they ever reached that destination. Dr. Jasa Romano, who is regarded as a credible source because he also included in his estimate the undeclared Jews who were not registered in their communities, was cited by Bulajic who picked the information from Romano's *Jews of Yugoslavia 1941–1945, Victims of Genocide and Freedom Fighters*, which was published by the Jewish History Museum of the Federation of Jewish Communities of Yugoslavia. He estimated that in NDH territory, more than thirty thousand were murdered, twenty thousand of them from Croatia and some ten thousand from Bosnia and Herzegovina, excluding some Jewish refugees from other European countries. From Sarajevo alone, 7,600 Jews were murdered. Samuel Pinto, who collected the names of the victims from that city during the period of 1941–1943, found that 7,505 were killed by the Ustashas. The Museum of Genocide list compiled an "incomplete list" for the years 1941–1945, amounting to 8,296 Jews from Sarajevo, of whom 4,074 were executed at Jasenovac, and 63 were sent to Auschwitz. A list of eight hundred full names of Jewish children from Sarajevo was compiled. Pinto also collected the names of 2,900 more Jewish victims from other parts of Bosnia and Herzegovina, with harrowing detail of each of the thirty annihilated communities.[13]

And finally, to Antun Miletic, who not only worked on a precise evaluation of the Jasenovac camp's lists of victims, but he also confronted the very divergent data that were published, and tried to put some order into them and provide some explanations for them. He published his findings under the heading: *Establishing the Number of Persons Killed in the Jasenovac Concentration Camp 1941–1945.*[14] The total war casualties were officially estimated by Communist Yugoslavia at approximately 1,700,000, including military and civilian war casualties and criminal murders at camps. It was convenient for the Tito authorities to subsume the total losses under one figure without having necessarily to specify who did what to whom when and under what circumstances, in order not to kindle the interethnic enmity within the forced federation. Realizing that the varying estimates were made to serve political interests, he challenged them all, by factual findings that dug up the names, dates of birth, and dates of execution (for each individual), as well as their nationality or ethnic origin, city or village of residence, and occupation—so that colleagues, professional associations, and club members could be investigated—and all data can be verified and confirmed or refuted. Such lists were made by the federal government in 1950 and 1952, but they were never published. In 1966 the report was published by the Office of Statistics, which had been entrusted by the government to establish such a list two years earlier, in its volumes entitled: *War Victims 1941–45*, which saw the light of day in Belgrade in August of that year. Later on, the cover page of that hardback edition was stamped "Top Secret" and the lists were banned, under the excuse that "some errors had crept in," until 1992, when Yugoslavia was no more and the civil war was raging, which made the list a valuable ground for manipulation and mutual accusation.

This publication stated that close to fifty thousand victims were murdered in Jasenovac, broken down into twenty-five thousand Serbs, over ten thousand Jews, eight thousand Gypsies, five thousand Croats, and a thousand others. But Miletic considers this count extremely low. He provides as an example the village of Nabrdje near Dakovo in Slavonia, where the list speaks of 175 victims who perished in Jasenovac, while he counted in his own research the more than double figure of 388. In another village of Ustice near Novska, the list accounts for 129 victims, while he counted 152. Similarly, Zemun was claimed to have lost 166 victims, while the real death toll was 651, or four-fold; and so on for Mostar—140 versus 288, again the double; the gaps in Bosanska Dubica and Bosanska Gradiška areas are even more striking. The divergences are hard to bridge because the Ustasha destroyed the documents relating to Jasenovac more than once, and that during the fifty years that followed the war, no concerted effort was done by the government to unearth the truth. Another added difficulty emanates from the fact that the Ustashas had the habit of summarily executing all new arrivals without bothering to enter new names in their lists of the inmates. This was particularly true of transports from the urban areas of the NDH, in which cases only the number of transports and of the carriages that mass transported the victims were recorded, and only in very few of them was it mentioned that the inmates had died, let alone been murdered. Apparently the worth of human life in that death camp had reached such a low ebb that it

141

was no longer considered worthwhile to count them, and certainly not to record their names.

The Ustasha were also known for erasing the traces of their crimes, by disinterring and burning the bodies of their victims, cooking them in cauldrons, burning the living and the dead, throwing them into the Sava and its tributaries, and burying some in secluded and remote places, or in inaccessible areas like high mountains or marshland. Moreover, according to evidence collated from archivists in Zagreb, Sarajevo, and Belgrade, some archival material was destroyed to be used as raw material in papermaking. Therefore, what remained as a more credible source material were the documentation preserved by the state and provincial commissions set up for establishing the crimes of the occupier and its collaborators, combined with the numerous accounts and memories of surviving inmates and other eyewitnesses. Collections of documents and data were also published along the years in newspapers, especially in their magazine sections. All these sources were and can still be used to fill the missing pieces of the puzzle. The inmates associations, by town or province, who have access to the families of the victims and to their fellow inmates, are very valuable in filling the persisting gaps. Only if all the burial sites of over two hundred square kilometers Jasenovac complex, namely Ciglana, Gradina, Krapje, Brocice, Jablanac, Kozara, Ustice, the Dupica lime kilns, Stara Gradiška etc, are excavated and investigated, will there be enough material to reach the maximum results on the number of people murdered and buried there.

The victims in Jasenovac were mostly children (25 percent), women (25 percent), and elderly people (10 percent), who account for 60 percent of the victims murdered there. That category of victims had nothing to do with Partisans or Communists, who served as the main pretexts for arresting, incarcerating and assassinating masses of people. The author insists that we should believe the estimates stated by the Nazis and the Ustashas themselves. He quotes German generals who spoke of the numbers of murdered Serbs, though not specifically only at Jasenovac. SS general Fick was quoted as writing that the Ustashas had killed between six hundred thousand and seven hundred thousand Serbs. Herman Neubacher, the representative of the Reich's Foreign Ministry based in Belgrade wrote that Max Luburic, the Commandant of the Jasenovac camp, admitted to him that he had killed 225,000 Serbs. Colonel Edmund Glaise von Horstenau, the Nazi representative in the Ustasha state, expressed the view in February 1942 that three hundred thousand Serbs had been killed by the Ustashas, and in late 1944 he said in a report that the numbers of those with slit throats was 750,000. On September 15, 1942 Ustasha Captain Andric, the liaison officer with the Nazi Representative in Serbia, based in Belgrade, said: "Supreme Commander Massenbach attacked the bloodthirstiness of the Ustasha against the Orthodox Christians [i.e. the Serbs], claiming that to date they had killed seven hundred thousand people in Croatia." This means that the figure of seven hundred thousand was not invented in Serbia by the Serbs, as Croatian President Tudjman has claimed, but by the perpetrators themselves, at a time when they were not yet concerned about losing the war. Additionally, the Germans were well aware of what their clients were doing, and they acquiesced in, as long as it fitted their interests; and if they entertained any misgivings about their partners, the Ustasha, it was only when they considered their clients to have overstepped the boundaries set by their Nazi masters. On the other hand, if that magic number of seven hundred thousand was reached already in 1942, what about the killings that occurred in the remaining 2.5 years of the war?

From all the published estimates by various quarters, and the author gives a whole list of them,[15] he attached the highest credibility to the deposited documents of the State Commission of the Numbers of Killed in the Jasenovac Concentration Camp of Stara Gradiška, as well as to the documents of the Town Planning Bureau and the Ministry of Social Policy of Bosnia-Herzegovina in Sarajevo, which accounted for 334,114 persons killed, including 40,000 children; for 115,070 missing persons, who most probably were thrown into the pits of one of the more than a thousand execution sites across Bosnia-Herzegovina; and for 33,000 killed in urban and rural areas. In addition, Croatia had a list on which 121,000 victims of Fascist terror are registered by their full names, and of whom 51,534 perished in the camps, mostly in Jasenovac. According to the list compiled by the author himself for the camp of Stara Gradiška alone, he totaled 36,300 names of victims, including 16,300 Serbs, 14,000 Gypsies, 5,700 Jews, and 300 others. To this is added the list provided by Dragoje Lukic, which contains information on the place of execution, on full names, dates of birth, and dates of killing for almost twenty thousand children, of them twelve thousand Serbs, over five thousand Gypsies, and close to two thousand Jewish children, all murdered at the Stara Gradiška camp of Jasenovac.

The author believes that based on this evidence alone, there is no doubt that there was genocide in Jasenovac, and therefore even the numbers advanced by the minimizers do not exonerate the murderers from that crime. He also determines that the claim that Jasenovac was merely a labor camp is sharply refuted by the numbers of children murdered there, who were not brought to perform any work but because they were Serb, Jewish, or Gypsy, and in order to be exterminated for what they were, not for what they did. Moreover, since in surviving Ustasha documents those camps were called by their true name—concentration camps—it is evident that the use of the "labor" appellation was meant only to mislead outsiders, exactly as the slogan at the entrance of Auschwitz, *"Arbeit macht frei,"* did not exactly advertise the horrors that were unfolding there. One of the most senior Ustasha officials, Andrija Artukovic, wrote to Hitler in 1942 boasting of how they had dealt with the Jewish question most efficiently. It was a death camp for Jews and Gypsies, and one of the three options Serbs had to choose: death, expulsion, or conversion to Catholicism.

Notes

1. Athanasije Jevtic, *From Kosovo to Jadovno: An Account of the Journey by Protosyncellus,* translated by George B. Markovina, Belgrade, 1984.
2. See Jasenovac entry in Yad Vashem, Holocaust Records in Jerusalem.
3. Testimony by Bogdan Petkovic, in *Proceedings of the Fourth International Conference on Jasenovac,* Banja Luka, Donja Gradina, May 30–31, 2007, 397–405.
4. Sborljub Zivanovic, "Forensic Observation on the Efficiency of Catholic and Muslim Croatian Murderers' Way of Killing and Torturing Their Serbian, Jewish and Roma Victims," in *Proceedings of the Fourth International Conference on Jasenovac,* Banja Luka, Donja Gradina, May 30–31, 2007; Bulajic Milan "Jasenovac, Jewish-Serbian Holocaust (the Role of the Vatican in Nazi-Ustasha Croatia, 1941–1945; and Antun Miletic, "Establishing the Number of Persons Killed in the Jasenovac Concentration Camp 1941–1945," in *Jasernovac and the Holocaust in Yugoslavia,* The Jasenovac Research Institute, 2006.
5. Zivanovich, op. cit., 42–46.
6. Ibid., 74–77.
7. See the list of the twenty-two totally erased Jewish communities under the NDH regime, in Milan Bulajic, op. cit., 37.
8. Published in Zagreb, April 1958, Book 3, 648.
9. The communities that were wiped out under the Ustasha were: Bjelovar, Cernik, Donja Lendava, Donji Miholjac, Djakovo, Erdevik, Ilok, Karlovac, Krizevci, Kutina, Ludbreg, Nasice, Nova Gradiška, Orahovica, Pakrac, Sisak, Stara Kanjiza, Susak, Valpovo, Varazdin, Vinkovci, and Vukovar.
10. *Ha-Kol,* the organ of the Jewish community in Croatia, No. 59–60, June 1999, 4. Cited by Bulajic, 37.
11. Slavko Goldstein, "Jasenovac Was a Death Camp," in *Glas,* May 17, 2002, 6; cited by Bulajic, 38.

12. Josip Riboli, *Archives of Croatia, Territorial Commission for the Establishment of Crimes Committed by the Occupying Forces and Their Collaborators,* Central Records, May 25, 1945. Cited by Bulajic, 38.
13. See Bulajic, pp. 43–45.
14. As part of a collective book, edited by Barry Lituchy, *Jasenovac and the Holocaust in Yugoslavia,* The Jasenovac Research Institute, Belgrade, 2006.
15. See Miletic, op. cit., 8.

7

The Suppression of War Memories and Their Reemergence

The question of preserving the memory of Jadovno and Jasenovac was part and parcel of the Jadovno 1941 Conference (June 2011), regardless of the controversies and contradictions that stood out at every step of the conference, meaning that while no solutions can perhaps be ever attained to those disagreements on numbers, nothing can block the way in front of establishing a wide European consensus as to the events that constituted the genocide of Serbs, Jews, and Gypsies in those camps, and at the very least of recognizing those two death camps as part of the Holocaust. It is necessary to preserve foundational texts, such as Soskovic's *Diary From Jadovno*, then the lecture by Dr. Edo Neufeld at the Gattkon refugee camp in Switzerland in December 1943 and then published in a book: *We Survived . . . 3*, published by the Union of Jewish Communities of Serbia, as well as the book by Dr. Jasa Romano, *Jews of Yugoslavia 1941–1945*. Special attention needs to be given to the book by David Anaf, *The Crimes of Fascist Occupying Forces and Their Collaborators against the Jews of Yugoslavia*. All these efforts are necessary to research, prove, and keep records. It was emphasized at the Jadovno conference that when a society does not educate its young generation to preserve it collective patrimony, it leaves the door open for intolerance, racism, xenophobia, hatred, and anti-Semitism. By education it was meant to build social values to lend spiritual and physical strength to young people, whatever their ethnicity and religion, to oppose crimes and any evils coming from ignorance, primitive behavior, and fear from otherness. For it was felt that ultimately the young generation will find out, through their education, that human beings had thrown other men, women, and children to the pits of Velebit, where they agonized for days in a gruesome death; that they had opened the victims bellies and shoved rocks into them so that they would sink to the sea floor. And when the young people find out those horrors, are they going to regard the murderers as role models, accepting their horrible ideology, and singing songs in public squares for their honor? Are they going to trample over the most basic human values, as the Nazis did, and to become monsters and a disgrace to their nation and to human kind? No, good and righteous people need to be the role models for the young, and it's the duty of the survivors to cultivate them to become so.

Of all the occupied populations of Yugoslavia that suffered under the German and Ustasha yoke, in addition to the Serbians, Jews, and Gypsies who were systematically assembled, incarcerated, and exterminated, the Serbian Orthodox Church was particularly singled out for persecution, due to the immense ideological and religious gap that separated it from the Catholic creed of the Ustasha. In fact, the archives of the Holy Synod of Bishops of the Orthodox Church in Belgrade, as studied and interpreted by Dragan Sucur, reveal a long string of suffering in the camps of Jadovno-Gospic, to which bishops, priests, deacons, monks, and students of theological seminaries were submitted. Many of them were tortured and murdered in the cruelest ways, and some were thrown into pits alive. By murdering bishops and priests, the Ustasha tried not only to decapitate the leadership of the Serbian Orthodox Church all over the NDH, but also to destroy it completely. In the few months when the Jadovno camp was operative, two bishops, five hieromonks, fifty-six priests, two deacons, two monks, two students of theological seminaries, and one student of the Faculty of Theology were murdered. Together with them, almost forty thousand Orthodox Serbs were executed, as much for their ethnic origin as for the faith they embraced. They became the martyrs of the Church of Christ.

Milan Koljanin presented at the Jadovno Conference in 2011 an important aspect of the ideology that provided the underpinnings of the racial policy of the Ustasha. It was for him evident that it was the opportune political and military circumstances after March 27, 1941, and the Axis powers' invasion of Yugoslavia, that triggered the creation of the NDH, which fulfilled the dreams of Croatian nationalists. But though formally the new state was within the Italian sphere of interest, it was ideologically much closer to the German-Nazi model than to the Italian-Fascist one. That is the reason why there is today such a convergence of interests, similarity of feelings, yearning for more detailed knowledge, eagerness to remember and to connect with other survivors, and remind others of past horrors, underlying the commonality that links all the Jewish survivors, under the one heading of the Shoah, equally under the Nazis and the Ustasha. On the specific Ustasha front, Serbs who have also undergone the experience and horror of genocide, have linked in a very specific, intimate and concrete way with Jewish survivors, borrowing from each other themes of remembrance, modalities of memorials, and a fraternity between victims, which have produced also joint conferences and exchanges of material and genocide histories, of which the Jadovno Conference which has triggered this volume, is only one example. Something like a commonality of fate and of suffering, some of it shared in Jadovno and Jasenovac, has created a close link between the two communities.

This does not mean that by becoming a victim, the Serbs have completely whitewashed their traditional anti-Semitic attitudes or totally exonerated themselves from the Fascist and bluntly Judeophobic movements on the eve of the war. Nedic and Ljotic's coarse anti-Semitism cannot be forgotten, even when compared to the still worse Ustasha genocidal policies toward both the Jews and the Serbs (and also the Gypsies for that matter). In 1945, as Matthew Feldman relates,[1] Duro Schwartz, who survived the inferno of Jasenovac, through mere "circumstance and professional utility," wrote a memoir about his suffering under the Ustasha in that camp. He was imprisoned between fall 1941 and spring 1942 and concluded: "If all those who had gone through the camp could join their voices and the despair in their hearts into one voice and one despair, the thunder and horror of the Day of Judgment, would make itself heard." He was finally released due to his marriage to a non-Jewish woman, but still thought that "human language is not powerful enough to even approximate the reality of existence there." But he still had to face the paradox of explaining in his human language the inexplicable and inhuman deeds done to him and to others around him. So, he recorded secretly, hid his notes, and finally wrote them up to remake the unreal reality that he "lived" through. One of those fragments of recorded memory recounts:

> To break the monotony, an Ustasha walks up to us now and then and hits us with the butt of his rifle. . . . Some more naïve prisoners tried to appease him "psychologically," or as they put it, "in a nice fashion." Dr. Vlatko Donner, for example, said: "They are human beings after all. One should always be polite to human beings. Wait and see that he will be polite toward me." Lo and behold, when an

Ustasha came to him and hit him with the butt of his rifle, Donner reproached him with a plaintive voice: "Brother, do not hit me. Can't you see I am weak and ill?" But the reaction was the opposite of what he expected, as the "brother" landed a blow on his head that stunned and knocked his down. Then the "brother" gave him a few kicks for a good measure. This was the harvest of psychology and pedagogy.

Much work has been done trying to penetrate the psychology of the Ustasha and their NDH Nazi state, some of it coming to the conclusion that the Catholic Church was not only complicit in the Ustasha horrors, but even acted as the main vehicle for the development of the Croatian Catholic movement into what has been termed as "clero-fascism." Some of that scholarship even indicted Pope Pius XII for direct, or at the very least indirect, responsibility for what happened to European Jewry. Those who exonerate him of complicity, at least charge him with indifference and of closing an eye to the horrors he knew were raging around him. There are some who, without daring to write it bluntly or to state it publicly, for fear of causing damage to the improved relations between the Church and the Jews since the papacy of John Paul, even advance the argument that the stronger Jewish demands to open up the Vatican archives of World War II, and to block the Church's persistent aspiration to beatify that controversial Pope, the more pronounced the efforts of the succeeding popes will be to improve relations with Jews and Israel, so as to lessen their opposition and placate their historical bitterness against the Church establishment. Major theological issues are at stake, for example how could the infallible heads of the Church be censured today for failing to protect the Jews from genocide during the war, or for that matter from the pope-approved medieval Inquisition? For it is inescapable that condemning Tomas de Torquemada for his inhuman and cruel mass murders then, means also demeaning the popes who appointed him and approved of his deeds.

In this regard, the role of Miroslav Filipović in the murder, which was widely elaborated upon in the Jasenovac chapter above, is advanced as a proof and an illustration of the narrow complicity between the church and the Croatian state under whose auspices Jadovno and Jasenovac were possible. The same could be said about the visceral anti-Semitic trends within the Orthodox Church in Serbia, though there it did not come to the extreme genocidal expressions of the Ustashas, nor were death camps established or even envisaged, neither for Jews nor for

Croats. One would be hard-pressed to find, on the Serbian side, the equivalent of this statement, made by Dionzije Juricev, a priest and a cabinet minister of the Ustasha state, in his role as the head of the State Direction for Renewal, on October 22, 1941:

> In this country, only Croats may live from now on, because it is a Croatian country. We know precisely what we will do with the people who do not convert. I have purged the whole surrounding area, from babies to seniors. If it is necessary, I will do that here too, because today it is not a sin to kill even a 7-year old child, if it is standing on the way of our Ustasha Movement. . . . Do not believe that I could not take a machine-gun in hand just because I wear a priest's vestments. If it is necessary, I will eradicate everyone who is against the Ustasha state and its rule—right down to babies![2]

The questions of how to distill memoirs from those horrors, and how attempts to turn memoirs into ideology have hampered the efforts to preserve the memory and cultivate the patrimony of the survivors, took a central place in the Jadovno Conference, which became a code name and a symbol for the entire story of genocide of the Serbs and the Jews (and the Roma) under the Ustasha. Ivan Ceresnjes, who served as a leader of the Jewish community in Sarajevo during the Bosnian War (1992–95), shared with the conference his thoughts about memories, both based on the Ustasha lessons of the war and on his experiences of the Jewish struggle before almost final extinction after more than half-a-millennium of continued existence amidst the Muslim majority of that city. He also gave thought to the attempt of many to bridge between the history and collective memories of the Jews and the non-Jews in this regard. No easy task, he thought, due to the fundamental differences between history and memory. For, while history attempts to reconstruct the past on the basis of all the data at hand, by means of critical analysis, memory already knows the outline of the story, based on a teleological model in which past, present, and future are already designated. The memory is continuous, ritually repetitive, while history is focused on definite dates and built on chronological scaffoldings. In sacred places collective memory is perpetuated in ritual.

Since there are many more survivors of Jasenovac than of Jadovno, due to the sheer enormity of the former, and there are numbers of related relatives that were left behind to remember and raise the issue, it is evident that individuals and groups use memories of the past for present purposes and emphasize those events that fit into their own

151

image of themselves or the group. Suffice it to recollect the crowds of thousands that gathered spontaneously in Jadovno during the first memorial service, which was held as part of the conference, to comprehend the wave of renewed interest and the eagerness to see, to touch, and to exchange views; to be there, to share the grief, or to add a comment, to invoke the memory of a murdered relative, friend, or family, and to shout out loud that the horror is not and cannot be forgotten, though it had been oppressed for too long. Ljiljana Radonic, from the University of Vienna, raised the point at the conference by remarking that in the 1980s, following many years of suppression, the Holocaust became the focus of memories of World War II because the extermination of European Jews is considered the common experience from which one learned and created new structures in order to prevent recurrence of those horrors in the future. In other words, not the war's famous battles or momentous decisions, or the memories of the victims, or the extent of the misery and destruction, were worth remembering per se, but the general context of "do not forget and do not forgive," as a warning and a deterrence lest any disturbed mind might scheme and concoct similar acts of madness in the future. The Jewish Holocaust became the focus of the exercise of remembrance, all right, due to the immensity of the horror, the magnitude of the damage, and the inhumanity of what humans can do; but preemption and prevention remained the unstated subtext.

This may have worked for a while, but sixty years after the Holocaust, it is being denied, notably in Islamic and anti-Semitic circles. Worse, those Muslim circles, like Iran, the Hamas, Hezbollah, and other so-called "fanatics," who from their own point of view represent the norm of mainstream Islam, are seeking and planning to reiterate the Holocaust, paradoxically while denying it ever happened. At the same time, history has been rewritten in Eastern and Southeastern Europe, especially since the dismantling of the Soviet Bloc in 1989. In that revisionist history, the pre-Socialist period is glorified as the "Golden Era" of national freedom, while the crimes perpetrated by the collaborating regimes with their Communist oppressors are being suppressed from memory, because they are opposed to the new ethos of the national heroes. Revised history becomes identical with the nationalistic collective memory. Such a turn of events can be seen during the post-Yugoslavia wars and thereafter, as the memory of World War II and its attending horrors has been reactivated. In other words, a "war of remembrance" has been launched, in which conflicting memories and controversial narratives have come to the fore, challenging both the decency and the resilience of the other, and competing for the moral high ground, making the truth their most unfortunate victim.

In this process there is a demonization of the other party, on the one hand, and identification with war criminals, on the other; examples abound covering Slovenia, Bosnia and Herzegovina, Serbia, and Croatia. Moreover, while in the rest of Europe the preserved symbolic memory is being distanced from the historical context, and is being focused on the "innocent victims" and the Auschwitz syndrome, in Yugoslavia Jasenovac remains the symbol of the war. In the 1980s, claims Radonic, Jasenovac was still proclaimed the third largest concentration camp in Europe, but the number of victims murdered there was reduced during the Fanjo Tudjman era to thirty thousand "political opponents." A "most interesting" claim that was appended to these fabrications was that the camp continued to be operated after 1945 under the Communists, which brought the author to question whether the new exhibition at the Jasenovac Memorial area, set up in 2006, marked truly a progress, and to what extent it followed the general European trend of focusing on the individual victims without giving special attention to the specificities of Jasenovac. She claims that the plaques at Donja Gradina, on the other side of the Sava, which carry the "mythical number of seven hundred thousand" of Serbian victims, are the political backdrop for another myth: namely that pots were found in which the Ustasha allegedly made soap out of their victims. Just as in the rest of Europe, survivors of the industrialized Auschwitz death camp represent all those who survived, while from Treblinka and Sobibor, where death was individualized, there are almost no survivors to testify, so in Yugoslavia, the first Ustasha camps in Pag, Gospic and Jadovno, from which there are almost no survivors, are not part of the collective memory of the victims, while Jasenovac, which was specifically built for the Serbs, remains as the symbol of that entire blueprint of death.

The model of the Nuremberg trials after the war, and the famous cases of Nazi-hunting, and persecution in justice of infamous Nazis like Eichman and Pappon, have raised the world consciousness to the Nazi horrors, by showing in the world media the entire proceedings of the trials, with live witnesses who could detail their torments and point fingers at the accused war criminals. Efraim Zuroff, of the Simon Wiesenthal Center in Jerusalem, spoke at the conference of the significance of prosecuting Nazi war criminals and collaborators in post-Communist Europe. He particularly described the unique aspects of the collaboration with the Third Reich in the countries which were part of the Soviet Union or under Communist rule from the end of the war to 1989, emphasizing the lethal nature of such a collaboration, which unlike the situation elsewhere in Europe, included active participation in mass murder. Therefore, bringing those war criminals to justice has proven one of the most difficult Holocaust-related issues which each post-Communist country had to face in the wake of independence. The other difficult issues were: acknowledgment of guilt, commemoration of victims, documentation and history writing, education and restitution. The added complication in this case is that the prosecution of criminals is the only one of these which is time limited, adding to its difficulty and urgency.

Jovan Culibrk, who in the meantime has been consecrated as the Bishop of Ulpiana (Kosovo), dwelt in the conference, which he helped organize, on the issue of the memoirs, diaries, autobiographies and biographies by members of Allied missions in occupied Yugoslavia, as sources of research. These writings provide an enormous amount of original and firsthand source material, especially those written by Jews of Palestine who participated in various British missions, usually those organized and dispatched by M19, the Intelligence Department specialized in rescuing downed pilots. Considering the fact that their mission also included rescuing the Jews in their area of operation, they gathered information and wrote memoranda about death camps and execution sites. During the first two years of the war, very few such allied missions were dropped over Yugoslavia, but their reports of 1941 on the Gospic group of camps is invaluable. Other members of other mission groups who arrived later in Yugoslavia, collected testimonies about events and sufferings from the beginning of the war. Though these reports do not necessarily provide fundamental knowledge, they serve as excellent auxiliary material about the sufferings of 1941, less about Jadovno but more about its auxiliary camps, and later about Jasenovac and its satellites.

The Jadovno Conference provided not only testimonies about the camps and their victims, but also some input from the foreign powers that controlled much of Yugoslavian territory, notably the two major occupation powers: Germany and Italy. Raphael Israeli's contribution consisted of a wide-ranging survey of Germany's interests in the Balkans, and their direct impact on its strategic calculations in North Africa, the Middle East, and the eastern front with Russia.

The Nazi strategy shifted after the Nazi occupation of Poland and Western Europe, in the early stage of that world conflagration; and in consequence of Hitler's renouncing his ambition to vanquish Britain, as a result of America's entrance into the conflict; and in parallel with the bogged down Nazi effort on the Russian front in Stalingrad. The Nazis changed from solely relying on their allies in Central Europe and the Balkans (Italians, Romanians, Hungarians, Croats, etc.), to actual occupation of most Mediterranean shores, so as to turn those waters, and the oil resources around them, into a German lake. For that purpose, the Nazis sent their star "Desert Fox," glamorous general Erwin Rommel, to North Africa, planning to oust the British from Suez and Egypt, cementing the Italian position in Libya, ensuring the rule of Vichy France in North Africa, and defending their alliance with the Arabs of the Middle East, both via direct contact with the anti-British movements in Egypt, Iraq, and Palestine, and concocting with the Palestinian mufti, Haj Amin al-Husseini, a detailed plan for the extermination of the Jews of Palestine, as part of the final solution. Husseini, a close relative of Yasser Arafat, who was later to entertain similar ambitions, moved to Berlin during the war, met with Hitler and worked relentlessly to turn his satanic dream into reality.

In the Balkans, while some forces, like Tito's Partisans and the Greeks, resisted the Nazis through guerilla warfare, often with British backing, others, like the Ustashas, the Hungarians and Romanians, and occasionally the Serbian *Cetniks*, contributed to the German labor force, as in Vichy France and other occupied lands in Europe, and directly to the Nazi war effort, especially in the Russian front and in aiding to maintain the order in their occupied territories. Taking advantage of the Muslim demographic presence in Bosnia in the heart of Europe, a relic of Ottoman occupation, the mufti helped by recruiting an entire Bosnian SS Division to help his German masters, and he prodded the Ustasha allies of the Nazis to hasten the extermination designs against their Jewish (and Serbian) prisoners in the camps of Jasenovac. This remains as a dark chapter in Palestinian national history, when for the purpose of attaining nationhood, they aspired to physically exterminate their rivals, an ambition that has hardly changed since.

Kiril Feferman offered to the Conference a comparative study of *"Divide et Impera"* between the Nazi occupation of Yugoslavia, on the one hand, and parts of the Soviet Union, on the other. The idea was to test the respective classical colonial approach of the occupying power toward the national minorities comprising the two states. The author claims that Germany radicalized these policies markedly with regard to the non-Jewish populations of both occupied territories, emanating largely from the lifting of restrains by Nazis on their treatment of civilian populations. In both cases, the Germans suppressed the biggest national group (Russians and Serbs, respectively), but at the same time they gave favorable treatment to numerically lesser groups (Croats, Ukrainians, Bosnian Muslims, Baltic nations, etc.), with their privileges extending from autonomy to "independence." The Germans usually accorded a "free hand" to their allies in occupied Europe, as long as their designs did not collide with theirs, though they levied a price on these nations for their admission into this German-dominated "new Europe," namely total adherence to Nazi *Judenpolitik*. If, like the Ustasha, they embraced that policy enthusiastically out of their own volition, the Germans would, of course, welcome it. Two major factors stood out differentiating between the two war arenas: in the Soviet Union, Germany waged a war of extermination, in the process identifying the Soviet Jews as the Reich's mortal enemies, while in Yugoslavia, the extermination of Jews took on the form of a military operation conducted for tactical reasons, without receiving from Berlin any specific license to kill the Jews. Secondly, in Yugoslavia and the Soviet Union, other axis countries participated in the occupation and were involved in the Holocaust (Italy, Bulgaria, Hungary, in Yugoslavia; Romania and Hungary in the Soviet Union). Of particular importance was the role played by the most important German partners in the war: Italy in Yugoslavia, Romania, and in the Soviet Union. The conduct of the Italian and Romanian troops vis-à-vis the general and Jewish populations in Yugoslavia and the Soviet Union was different than their German partners and took into account their respective domestic and foreign policies, not only their war interests.

The third window into great power politics was offered to the conference by Mila Mihajlovic, who exposed the documentary history of the massacre of Serbs in Dalmatia, Lika, and Kninska Krajina by the Germans and their Ustasha allies during the years 1941–1943, in the Italian occupation zone. The entrance, deployment, and actions of the Second Italian Army in Istria and Dalmatia, carried out on April 11, 1941, came just in time to enable the elite German forces to withdraw and concentrate on the Russian front, in preparation for the eastern invasion in May (later postponed to June). Italian units were entrusted with control of a large part of the new Ustasha Croatia, with the aim of enabling Ante Pavelic to cement his authority. However, they could not have predicted that Pavelic would be mainly haunted by his "hunt for the Serbs," and therefore they were forced, under strict instructions from Rome, to become helpless observers of Ustasha violence within NDH. However, horrified, appalled, and disgusted with the barbaric Ustasha conduct, the Italian Command of the Second Army, under General Vittorio Ambrosio, wrote to the General Staff in Rome that:

> In Lika, where there is the largest number of Serbs, the political and religious battle is becoming truly horrifying, because the Ustasha commit vengeance and retaliation that was seen only in the darkest times of the Middle Ages. . . . Among the murders and slaughters of Serbian populations, the one in Glina stands out, where 650 Serbian civilians were massacred. . . . There is need to stop them, unless they want the new Croatian Kingdom [sic] to be swept with a storm of uprisings which could compromise not only its progress but its very existence. . . . The order by the [Italian] government and the General Staff to the Italian troops not to intervene should be withdrawn, as the crimes are being committed before the eyes of the command and troops of our army. . . .[3]

Such a disgust coming, after all, from the command of a military occupation force, means that the Ustasha horrors were barbaric beyond measure and tend to confirm the harrowing descriptions by Serbian victims, which are usually discarded as "Serbian propaganda." The Serbs could not have expected a more candid endorsement of their version, at least in the case of the Serbs under the Ustasha regime, where most horrors and extermination have occurred in the death camps of Jadovno and Jasenovac. The same extremism of cruelty can be assumed against the Jews, who were also rounded up, incarcerated, and annihilated systematically under the same regime in the same locations. The Italians were much more humane and sensitive about their fame as "benevolent occupiers" than the Germans who were so eager and determined to carry out the final solution as devised in the Wannsee Conference that they cared less about their reputation, although they tried to hide the human holocaust in their concentration camps under headings of *arbeit lager* (labor camps) and to plough over the mass graves where they executed hundreds of thousands of Jews and Poles in Eastern Europe. Documents indeed show that the sentiment of the occupying Italians in Croatia revolted against the passivity ordered by Rome in the face of the Ustasha criminal conduct, for fear that it "might smear the reputation and honor of Italy."[4]

Apparently, the unreasonable and revolting orders of Rome to their troops in Dalmatia and Croatia shocked not only the Italian soldiers in the field, but also the Italian civilians who became apprised of them. A Milanese citizen, a friend of Senator Salato, who spent some days in Split during the occupation, wrote:

> The occupying forces in the whole of Dalmatia and in Split maintain public order but do not interfere in other events, so there is a massacre after massacre which in some towns, like in Knin, reached horrible proportions. . . . Of course, the presence of our military in the field compromises us heavily, because they do not intervene in the defense of innocent victims.[5]

However, regardless of the orders from Rome, which were detached from the reality of the field, Italian soldiers, who were fortunately not as strictly disciplined as their German counterparts, often ignored the directives coming from above, as they did in other parts of the world that they occupied. Secretly at first, testing the reactions of their commanders, soldiers started hiding a few old men and children in their barracks. When they realized that their superiors not only refrained from punishing them when caught in the act, but also occasionally joined them in the initiative, and even helped perfecting it, they expanded their efforts to rescue and protect the Serbian population. In this fashion, shelters were erected for the Serbs in and around Italian military barracks, and when off-duty they searched for Serbs escaping Ustasha terror and hiding in caves and woods.[6] Both Italian soldiers and civilians imputed these events, relating to the ambiguity of the relations between Zagreb and Rome, to the conflicts of evaluation between the Italian military command and the Italian diplomatic mission in Croatia, trying to rationalize the seemingly contradictory reports about the enemy-friendly Serbians and the ally-enemy Croats, by the Ustasha crimes, the Serbian uprisings, the *Cetnik* and Partisan operations, and the difficult relations between Berlin and Rome. At any rate, the Italian benevolent reactions brought out the paradox that the occupying nation was much more humane to local Serbs, in trying to protect them, than their Croat compatriots who did not spare any effort to persecute and annihilate them, taking full advantage of the opportunity that Ustasha rule afforded them.

Another interesting angle of the Italian occupation is the comparative study presented at the Conference by Filippo Petrucci, on the attitudes toward Jews in Yugoslavia and Tunisia. The Vichy racial laws applied to the Jewish community of Tunisia during the Italian and Nazi occupation of the country between November 1942 and May 1943. The Jews were excluded from the public apparatus and later also hurt in the commercial domain, Tunisia being the only North African country taken over for a while by the Germans. The fact that Italians were part of those discriminatory laws, and that they were themselves influenced by their Jewish community, which had trade links with the Tunisian Jews, impacted the application of that policy altogether. In Yugoslavia, where the local Jewish community was small and had no significant link to the occupying power or to its Jewish community, its mitigating impact on its treatment by Italians was rather vague, and to the extent that it existed, it was only based on personal human compassion by the Italian administration and the military, as it was vis-à-vis the Serbs.

Readers will find interest in the presentation at the Jadovno Conference by Dani Novak, an Israeli Professor of Mathematics, presently living in the United States, and the son of survivors of Jadovno, who shared with the other participants his quest since his youth to inquire into that hitherto hidden chapter of the genocide of Yugoslavian Jewry and to investigate personally, on the ground, the secrets of that lost history. He was able to do that only the moment Yugoslavia fell apart, shed its Communism, and opened up to the world, and its boycott of Israel and Israelis was replaced by a smiling and compassionate face toward Jews in general and Israelis in particular. This reversal has been adopted apparently as a measure of rehabilitation of its horrendous image during the world war, when Yugoslavia either participated in the Holocaust via the Ustasha, or seemed to collaborate with the Germans in it. Novak, a man sixty years old, at the time of his presentation in 2011, and seventy years after the horrors that began in 1941, had lost most of his family at the hands of the Ustasha, many of them in Jadovno, including the camps of Slana and Carlobag. His parents, who lost their loved ones, had immigrated to Israel, as did many of the Holocaust survivors, but they never talked of their harrowing experiences, as has been the wont of other survivors who dread to reminisce of the hell they had left behind. So, Dani was raised as the only child in a home where a heavy atmosphere of guilt, shame, and deep sadness reigned.

Only in November 2005, did Dani Novak sense an inner calling that directed him to find out what had happened. At that time, no information was yet available on the web, and all that was known about the island Pag was that it was a popular resort area for tourists, in sharp contrast to the horrors that Dani knew took place there, though he could not find much ready detail to flesh it out. However, against all odds and obstacles, man- and nature-made, he found the cave (*jama*) of Jadovno, went all alone in the woods to explore it, and screamed from relief for long minutes when he came across it. From there he proceeded to the Slana Camp, without help or direction, so haunted was he by the obsession to reveal the hidden truth. The local folks in the small village of Metajna looked at him like a ghost from the past, hence their reluctance to share with him any shred of information, not even how to reach the site of the camp. But his obstinacy paid off, and he found the location, although there were absolutely no signs or monuments to indicate it, save a stone wall in the middle of nowhere. Dusan Bastasic from Banja Luka, also of a bereaved family, who had lost their loved ones on the same spots, but knew as little about them, discovered a year later the website that Dani had created to launch his inquiry into the matter, and since then the two of them have become sworn partners into what they regarded as the mission of their lives.

Dani's presentation does not only tell the horrendous details of what happened in the camp, how the victims were rounded up and murdered severally on in groups, stringed together by ropes or chains, and thrown into pits, the first dragging after him all the rest; the sadism, inhumanity, and cruelty of the murderers; the despair of the victims, and the sinister atmosphere around them that permitted these atrocities to go unrevealed for half a century or more; but also the efforts to explore the caves and pits, where masses of human skeletons were piled up, some of them still indicating the desperate attempts of some of the victims to climb the steep walls of the fifty meter deep pits in a vain effort to escape. Skeletons were counted and accounted for, and a database was gradually built up to try to measure the scope of the horror and the extent to which it has any credibility. All that had been skillfully and obtusely covered up for decades, with the authorities of Croatia refusing to reveal the truth, due to its explosiveness, the government of Yugoslavia trying to avoid reviving the ethnic hatred that could trigger the downfall of the Federation, and individuals either opting to toe the party line for their own safety under that regime, or suspecting that their accounts would be met with incredulousness and themselves with ridicule.

Novak's presentation, which was understandably emotional, was also characterized by his acute sense of an educational mission to bequeath that revealed history to generations to come. Hence his eagerness, together with Dusan his partner, to initiate the first ever international conference on Jadovno in Banja Luka in June 2011, and their insistence on building a memorial on the Jadovno grounds, now a pastoral site covered with lush woods, with difficult access. Inspired by *Yad Vashem* on Mount Herzl in Jerusalem, which they have visited on many occasions, they wish to establish a solid base for an indelible memory of past events, educate children about that horrible past, and ensure that those horrors should never occur again, something that is difficult to guarantee, when one is aware of the declarations of interethnic hatred in the Balkans, or takes cognizance of the genocidal outbursts that one hears about occasionally in various arenas of conflict in the world. Maybe Novak's vision of a world of "unity, hope, peace, and love" for the people of the Balkans is utopian, but his determination to educate young children, by means of books and stories, that "there is one omnipresent God, who is the father and mother of all people everywhere," and to raise a generation who brings out the cruel truth, but also learns to heal and forgive, remains a noble goal to pursue. In any case, I was privileged to be accompanied by Dani in the exploration of Jadovno, and his obsessive explanations at the threatening mouth of the open pit that had swallowed so many pitiful victims, still resonate in my ears.

In the hell of death and torture, somehow miraculously, the strength of the human spirit prevailed to such an extent that valuable works of art could be achieved and preserved, in the face of the tremendous difficulties of obtaining the necessary materials, hiding them, and performing the work of art—either as a lifesaving occupation in the death camps, or to rescue others from death by taking them in, or in the spare time that hardly existed, or by making personal sacrifices and taking grievous risks for the attainment of creative and aesthetic satisfaction. According to Dr. Mirjam Rajner, a Research Fellow at *Yad Vashem* (2005–2006),[7] within the more than 80 percent of the Yugoslavian Jewish community that perished in the camps during World War II, there were a number of talented and expressive artists. Some of them died or were killed in camps, while others lost their lives fighting with the Partisans. All of them, however, left behind a legacy of valuable artworks, which speak today about these artists' past lives and comment boldly on their tragic experiences of the Holocaust itself. During Tito's era, when the remnant of the Jewish community was coping with an identity crisis, and split between loyalty to the new Socialist Yugoslavia and to Zionism, the works of Jewish artists, showing themes of World

War II, were only occasionally exhibited. However, they were usually shown in the regional Museums of Revolution, either in single shows displaying the entire artistic opus of an individual artist, while mainly stressing their Communist and anti-Fascist background, or in group shows that celebrated the fight against Fascism and the establishment of the new, Socialist Yugoslavia.

More recently a significant change has occurred. At a time when the rise of nationalism led to the civil war of the 1990s and to the eventual collapse of Yugoslavia into separate state republics, Jews there were once again feeling the need to reexamine their identity. While many of them permanently left the country because of the war and the ensuing economic crisis, those who stayed rediscovered Judaism (being prompted by the destruction of old values during the war itself), the reappearance of anti-Semitism, and their non-Jewish neighbors' return to their own national and religious roots. *Inter alia*, the post–civil war atmosphere seems also to have sparked a need to reexamine Jewish participation in art movements, in general, and their contribution to the art of the Holocaust (a chilling oxymoron in itself) in particular. Rajner's research concentrates on a group of Jewish professional artists who were actively engaged in their craft in the concentration camp at Jasenovac and left behind valuable art works. The examination of these creations has much to tell us about life in this labor and extermination camp (another gruesome oxymoron), a subject about which not enough research had yet been done. Moreover, in cases of newly discovered art, we can learn about these imprisoned artists' prewar development, their personal lives, their attitude toward the Jewish community and their non-Jewish surroundings, and their reception in the postwar, Socialist Yugoslavia.

The Jasenovac camp, which was established in the summer of 1941, and situated on the Sava River, was actually made up of five camps. Four were near the village of Jasenovac, and the fifth was a bit further down the river, near the town of Stara Gradiška. Most of the camp was located on a confiscated estate, which included a brick factory, a chain factory, a sawmill, and an electric plant. Outside of the main camp there also was a tannery. Upon arriving at the camp, the prisoners' possessions were confiscated, and the male prisoners were sent to either work on building a dam near the river, which regularly flooded the area, or in factories. Working and living conditions were terrible, and the prisoners, who included Serbs, Jews, Gypsies, and the Croat opponents of the regime, were dying daily as the result of exhaustion, cold, hunger, diseases, and torture. They were also killed in regular mass and individual "liquidations," which were achieved mainly by slaughtering the victims, or by smashing their skulls and drowning them in the Sava River. Part of the camp near Stara Gradiška was an old fortress that was once a prison. There, the Ustasha imprisoned and murdered women and children who were mainly family members of the male prisoners held in Jasenovac. In addition to the camp for women in Stara Gradiška, there were about fifty artisans' workshops, which included ceramics, engraving, sign painting, and others. The idea to open such workshops actually came from the Jewish community in Osijek, which paid for the necessary tools, with the hope of saving some of the imprisoned Jews from the heaviest physical work in the main camp and certain death.

Daniel Ozmo (Olovo 1912–Jasenovac 1942) is the best known of these artists of Jasenovac. Because he had already became a member of the Communist party before World War II, he was for a number of years celebrated in the postwar Socialist Yugoslavia as a revolutionary hero-artist whose work was shown as an example of anti-Fascist art. Using newly found material and reexamining what was already known about Ozmo, Rajner attempted to show his less familiar side, the more vulnerable and Jewish side, hoping thus to offer an additional and different understanding of his artistic creativity in the straitjacket of a death camp. He came from a big, mainly Sephardic community. His work illustrates the destiny of many young Jews from Sarajevo who were caught in the turbulent times of World War II and the Holocaust. He was born in Olovo, a small Bosnian town, as one of nine children, and the family was very poor. Soon after Daniel's birth, the family moved to Sarajevo where he grew up. With the financial help of "La Benevolencija," the local Jewish society for culture, enlightenment, and welfare, Ozmo was able to study at the Art School in Belgrade, where he took classes in graphic art, sculpting, and watercolor. Upon finishing his studies in 1934, he returned to Sarajevo in hope of being able to financially help his family by working as an art teacher in a local high school. From that year, until the beginning of World War II, Ozmo regularly participated in the group exhibitions in Sarajevo.

Upon the return to his hometown, Ozmo became active in the Jewish leftist youth organizations such as *Matatja*, the Sarajevo-based Jewish Working Youth Society. During summers he used to attend the summer camp in Slovenia, which was organized by the Jewish Zionist Youth society *Akibah*, or he traveled throughout pre–World War II

163

Yugoslavia. In 1936 Ozmo also visited the old Sephardic community in Bitola, Macedonia, and upon his return published a linocut of its *"mahala"* (Jewish neighborhood) in *Omanut* (Art), the Jewish journal that was published in Zagreb and was dedicated to art and literature. From this time of wanderings originate also several landscapes depicting hills and woods, as well as watercolors showing little marinas, boats, and Dalmatian houses against stony hills. There were many opportunities for Ozmo to visit the seaside. In the prewar years, Jewish residents of Sarajevo used to often spend their holidays in the southern part of the Dalmatian coast. In addition, especially during the late 1930s, there were also active maritime Zionist camps, first in Sušak, near Rijeka, on the island Krk in the north, and later in Vela Luka, on the island Korčula, in the south. Prepared and run by instructors from *Eretz Israel* (Mandatory Palestine, at the time), the camps were organized to train the future *halutzim* (pioneers), Jewish youngsters who planned to immigrate to Palestine and to live by the sea, working as fishermen. At these camps then, they hoped to acquire a useful profession to apply in their future homeland, where as it was hoped, the sea would play a major role in its economic and social development.

However, already by 1937, Ozmo seemed to have turned even further left because he was expelled from his post as an art teacher, whose Communistic ideas would harm the students. His self-portrait done in the same year, was created in the linocut technique. Linocut is a relief printing process and is produced the same way as a woodcut or a wood engraving, where a flat surface of wood or lino is used as the printing surface.[8] It is extremely expressive. In 1938 he joined the newly founded Sarajevo avant-garde group *Collegium Artisticum*, which was composed mainly of young Jewish intellectuals: the musician Oskar Danon, the architect Yechiel Finci, and the dance choreographer Ana Rajs. This group published a manifesto in October 1939, stating that their main goal was to elevate the culture of their city and to actively participate in raising the consciousness of its people, regardless of their national and religious affiliation. To achieve this, *Collegium Artisticum* combined contemporary art forms in the framework of an avant-garde, socially aware, synthetic theater, which tried to unify all these forms of art with life. The group also organized theater performances, art exhibitions, and concerts, with accompanying explanations and lectures in various fields of art. In the spirit of avant-garde art and social awareness, Ozmo created his album of twenty linocuts entitled "From the Bosnian Woods" in 1939. Taking as his subjects the work of low paid woodcutters and sawmill workers in the woods surrounding his birthplace Olovo, Ozmo created a unique series of images that combined local, Bosnian scenes, German expressionist style, and social-awareness concepts. He used a similar approach in his scenes that depicted the nightlife of Sarajevo coffeehouses, simultaneously filling these pieces with local charm but also with doom and eeriness, as if prophesying what was coming. Among the works saved from that time is a drawing of an old Sephardic woman and a watercolor that showed the interior of a peasant hut, both done in 1939. Avant-garde art, Socialism, cosmopolitan ideas, those were the very ideas most threatening to any authoritarian regime, especially when led by Jews who were hated and feared in their "own right."

Ozmo's oil paintings and sculptures were almost entirely lost. At the beginning of the War in Yugoslavia, in the second half of 1941, Ozmo, who was a member of the Communist Party, decided to leave Sarajevo for the mountains, so he could join the Partisans. While leaving the city, however, he was betrayed by his contact person who turned out to be a double agent, and he was caught by the Ustasha, who transferred him to the Jasenovac concentration camp. Among about twenty of Ozmo's drawings, taken out of the camp by his Communist friend, Dr. Mladen Iveković, who was freed in September 1942, along with a group of thirty prisoners from Jasenovac, in an exchange for two high-ranking Ustashas captured the previous month by Partisans, were several portraits of his friends from a ceramics workshop, such as the one showing Slavko Brill, a Jewish sculptor from Zagreb. However, Ozmo's other works, drawings and watercolors are more unusual. Despite his knowing the harsh conditions and terrible atrocities committed daily in the camp, they seem to be calm, even pastoral depictions of surrounding landscapes. Only the title and the place where they were made recall the grim reality around him. Such renderings are not uncommon in Holocaust art, and we find them in several places. For example, the Jewish artist Otto Kaufmann painted a lush garden while in the Theresienstadt ghetto, and a Polish painter, Tadeusz Myszkowski, showed peasants working in a field even while he was a prisoner in Auschwitz. Such art is usually known as escape art because it intentionally depicts nature and normality, enabling the artist to detach himself, albeit briefly, from the abnormal reality.

Ozmo's drawings and sketches also depict the work of building a dam, one of the hardest tasks that the prisoners were forced to do in Jasenovac. According to a number of testimonies, the prisoners had to work for hours in water and mud, often under heavy rain that flooded the river. Many workers died of exhaustion, while others were killed on the spot for not working fast enough. The dead were buried nearby, or their bodies actually became part of the dam, being entombed in construction, as some other testimonies have confirmed. None of this is visible in Ozmo's work. Similarly, noncritical depictions of an orderly workshop can be seen in his drawing of the interior of the tannery. Although it does not appear that Ozmo ever worked at the tannery, his decision to draw it is interesting. The tannery was a somewhat easier (though certainly smelly) place in which to work, and it was situated outside the main grounds of the camp, near the village of Jasenovac. The tannery mainly produced boots and belts, for the Ustasha soldiers, but also fashionable articles for their women. It was run by a prisoner named Silvije Alkalaj, nicknamed Sisi. He was a Sephardic Jew from Zagreb who was a specialist in leather and fur. All the testimonies mention Sisi's courage, his good organizational skills, and his ability to create a safer place where, with the help of others, he was able to bring in a number of Jewish prisoners.

Ozmo's drawings of building the dam and of the tannery are actually more like the official photographs taken by a professional film director and photographer, Edmund Stöger, who worked for the government office and was especially sent there for that purpose. During his eight-day visit to Jasenovac, he also filmed a propaganda film entitled "Positive Work in the Jasenovac Camp." The photographs and the film were shown at the exhibition held at Zagreb's Autumn Fair between September 5 and 14, 1942. It was entitled "One Year of Work of the Concentration Camps run by Ustasha's Defence: *Their previous Work Was Politics—Our Present Politics Is Work.*" For this exhibition the Ustasha's Supervisory Service built a pavilion that resembled a camp. A barrack surrounded by barbed wire and two guard towers served as a gallery, where graphs and statistics, photographs, pictures, plaster models of many buildings in the camps, and products of various craft workshops were exhibited. Ironically, the exhibition was meant to inform the public about the usefulness and the productive work of the inmates. Because Ozmo was in the ceramics workshop, where the prisoners were forced to produce art and craft works, such as carved boxes, ashtrays, vases, figurines that sometimes were of the Ustasha leader, Ante Pavelic, or the Ustasha fighters in action, it is possible to raise a question concerning the goal of the young Jewish artist's depictions of work in the camp. The Jasenovac Memorial Museum does exhibit today some pictures and works that were exhibited in the Zagreb exhibition during the war. So far, while presented as a young prewar Communist and revolutionary, and celebrated as such during the years of Socialist Yugoslavia, these Ozmo's drawings, created in the style of idealized realism, were considered to be an act of bravery and resistance. However, it seems possible that they were actually "official" works, which the Ustasha ordered him to make, possibly in order to show them in the Zagreb exhibition. Such examples are well known among the art created during the Holocaust elsewhere in Europe.

While creating the so-called official art ordered by the perpetrators, the imprisoned artists were often also able to help the other prisoners by employing them in the workshops and offices where they worked, thus possibly saving their lives or at least delaying their death verdict. It seems that a similar situation existed in Jasenovac. Ozmo, who was the head of the ceramics workshop, seemed not to only protect the other members, but he also encouraged them by telling them that the liberation would soon come. However, he himself did not have a chance to see liberation, since he was imprisoned in a solitary cell and publicly shot on September 5, 1942, for "spreading alarming news." His art, his ideas, and his leadership were simply too much of a threat to his simple- and narrow-minded wardens. A few days before his execution, his mother, sister, and brother were also murdered. Aside from Daniel Ozmo, another four Jewish artists worked in the ceramics workshop: the sculptor from Zagreb, Slavko Brill, two painters from Bosnia, Daniel Kabiljo and Salamon Papo; and the painter and graphic artist Walter Kraus, a Jewish refugee from Vienna. Kraus, who, just before the outbreak of the war in Yugoslavia, had settled in Belgrade, where he married a local Jewish woman, was caught with his wife while trying to reach the Italian-ruled zone in Dalmatia. They were sent to the camp at Stara Gradiška. Today still very little is known about these artists and their artistic works that were created in the camp. They all died there.

Ozmo and his likes, whose extant art of the death camps has been invaluable documentation of what went on there; while in action they had saved the lives of untold numbers of other artists, who produced utilitarian art for their captors, or at least delayed their execution as long as they could satisfy their wardens. No doubt the art also gave the artist tremendous satisfaction to the artists in the midst of the doom and gloom of the camps, where they watched the daily horrors of death around them, that pushed them to continue to excel in their art, lest their turn to perish also came. But above all, watching and studying the remnants of their art today, as Dr. Rajner does, is one of the most imaginative ways to commemorate their memories and to reminisce on the death camps experience that they left behind. This is much akin to writers, poets, or other chroniclers, who either left diaries behind them, or survived to write them after the war.

Despite the diverging numbers of victims cited by various quarters, Slavko Goldstein said that what is important is the nature of the crimes, and Jasenovac was a criminal camp, part of a criminal system, though it was also partly a labor camp, even a prison camp, from which many prisoners were deported to work in Germany, many others were released after they served their terms, still others were granted amnesty or survived in some other way. Yet, it remains a devastating fact that many of those who entered the camp never came out of it alive.[9] Following the pattern suggested by other eyewitness survivors cited above, Dr. Josip Riboli, a Jewish survivor, also said:

> No one who did not have the misfortune to be in the Jasenovac camp can know what it was like. People reading accounts about it written in the newspapers today believe there is a lot of exaggeration. That is why, before we start talking about those horrors, the following fact should first be pointed out: One cannot exaggerate Jasenovac. Those things are so horrid, so abominable, that the people who had not gone through it cannot comprehend them, and those who have passed through Jasenovac, where death lurked at every step, every minute of the day and night, where every single Ustasha could kill thousands upon thousands of people and not account for anyone, will wonder how they have come out of that hell alive.[10]

On the Holocaust Day of April 13, 1999, Dr. Kraus, the head of the Jewish community of Croatia said:

> It is an insult to us when people say that such camps did not exist. It is an insult to us when they say that there was a theatre in Jasenovac and that the operetta *Little Floramy*[11] was performed there. It is an insult to us when they want to cover up the responsibility for what happened in the past and what the Ustasha regime did. Only by presenting the truth and when the crime has been condemned and punished, can we overcome the painful past. Certain individuals and groups are still reluctant to face the past or learn from it. There is need to learn from the past. Such learning would strengthen the resolve to prevent the horrors that affected the entire mankind during World War II, and that unfortunately keep affecting innocent people

in many parts of the world, and recently in our homeland as well. . . . It hurts Jews to hear that the total death toll in the Ustasha death camp of Jasenovac was 20,000 people, and to read that 9,000 Jews perished there. We wonder where those 20,000 Jews, registered in Croatia before the war, have perished, let alone what happened to the countless assimilated Jews who were also sent to Nazi or Ustasha death camps under the Nazi and Ustasha racial laws. Such manipulations with the bloody historic facts are insulting and intolerable for members of the communities that were severely affected by the genocide.[12]

Notes

1. Matthew Feldman, "Genocide Between Political Religion and Religious Politics," *Internet*, www.tandf.co.uk/journals/pdf/papers/FTMP_NDH_conclusion.pdf.
2. Cited by Feldman, op. cit., 7.
3. Citation by Mila Mihajlovic, during her presentation at the conference.
4. Ibid.
5. Ministry of the Interior in Rome, *Archives of Yugoslavia*, a document attached to the letter sent by Senator Francesco Salato to Filipo Anfuso, head of Minister's Cabinet on June 30, 1941. Cited by Mihajlovic. Ibid.
6. Italian General Staff History Archives, Envelope 523—Sassari Division Command, June 18, 1941. Cited by Mihajlovic. Ibid.
7. Mirjam Rajner was a research fellow at Yad Vashem (2005–2006) and published in its memorial writings. Her research has been published in such journals as *Jewish Art; Ars Judaica; Timorah; Nashim, A Journal of Jewish Women's Studies and Gender Issues; Studia Rosenthaliana; Jews in Russia and Eastern Europe;* and *Jewish and Christian Perspectives Series.* The following passage is based on her articles.
8. The lino block consists of a thin layer of linoleum (which can also be mounted on a wooden block) and is considerably easier to cut than wood as it is much softer. The parts of the block that are cut away surround the part that will read as the image. Then the plate in inked up by rolling the ink onto the block with a small rubber paint roller, and the image is transferred to the paper using direct pressure. The image will always appear reverse as the lino is in direct contact with the paper. The image can be drawn onto the plate with a pencil or marker before one starts cutting. A linocut can be printed by hand without a printing press.
9. Slavko Goldstein, "Jasenovac Was a Death Camp," in *Glas*, 17 May, 2002, 6; cited by Bulajic, 38.
10. Josip Riboli, *Archives of Croatia, Territorial Commission for the Establishment of Crimes Committed by the Occupying Forces and Their Collaborators,* Central Records, May 25, 1945. Cited by Bulajic, 38.
11. The best known operetta, composed by Ivo Tijardovic, and very popular at the time.
12. Bulajic, 38–39.

8

Summary and Postscript

The main issue in this volume has been the task of distilling fact and historical record from accusation and grievance. But it has become practically impossible to achieve that task, due to the many decades of smoothing over the recriminations between the various components of Yugoslavia, as long as the uniting role of Tito held sway over the federal state. Now, seventy years later, we realize that the gap in continuous research and collection of data, memoirs, oral histories, and preservation of documents and other evidence, has become irreparable. But one thing is certain: the manifestation of anti-Semitism in all parts of Yugoslavia during the war, and especially in the years leading up to the war and to German occupation, was evident, deeply rooted, and widespread, though in the Ustasha NDH extermination of the Jews (and others) was implemented as part of the state ideology, and did not need the Germans to compel them, as in other parts of the country, to act on their behalf.

The battle between primarily the Serbs and the Croats is not likely to be settled any time soon, and both seem inclined to believe that if you wash your hands clean from anti-Semitism and from collaboration with the Germans during the war, then your sense of culpability will recede. Therefore, both sides are extremely eager to accuse the other of wrong doing, a game that has been joined by Western researchers, who take sides and commit themselves totally to exonerate one party and demonize the other. They have mostly lost the power of reasoning in their heavy leaning to one party's favor, while ignoring, or even denying and refuting the other side's arguments. There is no zero-sum game here, namely that exonerating one party does not automatically demonize the other, and vice-versa. The sad reality that one comes up with, with regard to anti-Jewish policies, is that during the war, all parties were demons and villains: German Nazis, Croat Ustasha, Serbian collaborators, *Cetniks*, and Bosnian *Hanjar* recruits. The only righteous element were the many individuals, in all camps, who helped the Jews, hid them at great risks, and helped them to survive, and, to a great extent, the Communist-leaning Partisans, who absorbed the Jews in their ranks and enabled them to actively fight instead of letting them passively perish.

Germany's reconciliation with the Jewish people, and privileged relations with Israel, where most of the Jewish survivors were absorbed and rehabilitated, could not have unfolded before Germany recognized its Nazi past and repudiated it. It seems, that, in contrast, both the Serbs and the Croats, and certainly the Bosniaks, wish to make a new start by whitewashing their past, ignoring some of it, denying another part, and pretending that by splashing mud on their rivals within Yugoslavia, they can exonerate themselves from any wrong, or at least to minimize their own misdeeds in comparison with the others. But by causing the others to look worse, one does not cleanse oneself. A true new beginning starts with officially admitting the past; apologizing for it; compensating the survivors to the extent possible, where no compensation is imaginable; restituting the confiscated Jewish property that was either expropriated or destroyed; pursuing the remnants of the war criminals, as long as they are around, instituting courageous and widespread educational projects, through school textbooks, informal adult education, commemorative monuments, and the media; and founding and funding research institutes and encouraging researchers to launch government-initiated and government-funded investigations into that dark past.

It is extremely tempting not to dwell too much on the past, as the Tito regime had tried to do throughout its duration, electing to erect a blameless present of smooth relationships with all, at the expense of the rocky and dark past, that would best be ignored or dissimulated. But recent history has shown, that the past has a propensity to pop up every now and then, and no matter how hard one attempts to hide it or distort it, there will always be individuals, communities, books, documents, memories, and decent people who will keep reminding you that unsettled issues will always insist on coming up and demanding amends, until and unless they are settled. Just twenty years after the German invasion of Yugoslavia, at a time when its survivors were still around, as well as their extant tormenters and the mostly indifferent masses of bystanders, a French writer, Edmund Paris, published his study, *Genocide in Satellite Croatia*,[1] in which he passed a quite severe verdict on the Ustasha. He said that the greatest genocide during the war, in proportion to the nation's population, took place not in Nazi

Germany but in the Nazi-created puppet state of Croatia. There, in the years 1941–45, some 750,000 Serbs, 60,000 Jews, and 26,000 Gypsies—men, women, and children—perished in a gigantic holocaust.

Probably reflecting on his feeling of exaggeration regarding those figures, especially the apparently much inflated numbers of Serbs, he "apologizes" by claiming that "those are the numbers used by most foreign authors," especially the Germans, "who were in the best position to know." But Germans were not always present in Jadovno or Jasenovac, where the killing was all done by the Ustasha, and no well-ordered registers existed as in the camps of Nazi Germany. There was no way to know precisely the numbers, nor the possiblity to research them in those years of Yugoslavian smoothing over the data, in order to calm the interethnic moods domestically. Paris also recounts that Hermann Neubacher, the most important of Hitler's trouble shooters in the Balkans, had reported that the perpetrators of the crime had estimated the number of annihilated Serbs by the Ustasha at a million, but he thought that the more accurate figure would be three-quarters of a million. Another German likely to be knowledgeable, due to his presence in the area when the crime was being perpetrated, was General Lotar Rendulic, who estimated that in the first year of its existence the Ustasha state had massacred at least half a million Serbs, and many others subsequently. Other French writers have perpetuated the half a million figure, while some British authors stick, without evidence, to the seven hundred thousand figure, which is also often cited by Serbs and refuted by modern Croatia.

Whatever the precise numbers, mass murder, genocide, or holocaust there was, and even if in practice the numbers mentioned by the high estimates were not attained, due to the unexpectedly abrupt end of the war, there is no doubt that the intention of the Ustasha state was ethnocidal, but while they achieved that goal almost completely with the Jews and the Gypsies under their purview, due to their relatively small numbers, they fell short of their target, not in will but in ability, with regard to the Serbs, who were much more numerous. Judging by the statement of one of the Ustasha chiefs, Eugen Kvaternik, in 1942, there is no doubt that had the war lasted longer, and the German war fronts not collapsed, many more Serbs would have perished, and a deeper dent would have been made into their ethnic demographic pool toward their decimation. Kvaternik indeed declared: "Whatever the final outcome of the war, by the time it ends, there will be no Serbs in Croatia—and whoever wins will have to face that fact as an unchangeable determinant."[2] Thus, as Reverend Krunoslav Draganovic put it, in late 1943, when talking to British diplomats at the Vatican, "several thousand graves lie between Croats and Serbs and would be an eternal ground for a lasting vendetta," referring, of course, to the unrecognized masses of Serbs who were being massacred by the Ustasha. As he was presenting his fifty-point memorandum to the British envoys, Osborn and Montgomery, he had at the time the feeling that most Croats supported the Ustasha,[3] a claim energetically refuted today by modern Croatia. But judging from the Bosnian war of the 1990s, it is evident that the vowed vendetta did play itself out.

In the face of the attempts to efface the evidence and erase the record of the horrors of the Ustasha, which if recognized could have calmed the emotions and helped lead to reconciliation, many feel that the only way left to express the long-oppressed sentiments of the victims are explosions of violence and hatred to compensate for their denied or ignored victimhood and pain. In courthouses we often see plaintiffs, who felt that justice was denied them, exploding in wrath and violence against the judicial system that they feel denied their rights or ignored their sentiment, and especially against the accused who smile with self-contentment for their acquittal by default. They know that their relatives and loved ones were thrown live into the deep karst pits of Jadovno, or drowned handcuffed the Adriatic sea around Pag or the Sava River, or stunned with sledgehammers before they were dumped in a ditch, or had their necks slashed for the pleasure of their ruthless Ustasha wardens, or were walled up in dams, roads, or dikes. They also know that mass graves and temporary monuments were destroyed when it was clear that Hitler was losing the war, and especially later, during the Tito years of forgetting and hiding evidence, lest outbursts of emotion on the part of the victims spoil the delusions of harmony in the "Communist paradise." It is small wonder that the explosions of hatred and violence of the Bosnian War in the 1990s, on all sides of the conflict, should emerge with such a fanatic savagery.

After the passing away of most of the firsthand eyewitnesses of Jadovno and Jesenovac, new generations are rising: young Serbs who denounce the Croat denial of the Ustasha record, or of the Croat attempts to diminish it, the way Jews decry the growing trend of Holocaust denials in anti-Semitic circles in Europe and the Muslim world; or young Croats who cultivate the so-called "Serbian mythology and folklore," as their defense against the horrific crimes their ancestors are accused of. The argument that most Croats did not support the

Ustasha, and in fact were themselves their victims, is much akin to the claim much heard among young Germans and Austrians and Japanese today: most of them did not support their Fascist regimes, and had become themselves the victims thereof. They also whine against the utter destruction and death brought upon Berlin, Hamburg, and Dresden, and Tokyo, Hiroshima, and Nagasaki. They all forget that in the heyday of their regimes, they acclaimed their leaders, waged wars of death, torture, and destruction against others, unprovoked, with little or no serious attempt to unseat those mad dreamers who led them into disaster, be it Hitler, Tojo, or Pavelic. One does not want to think what would have happened if those megalomaniacs had their way, had won the war and enslaved the world. Would the do-gooders, delicate souls, and bleeding hearts of today still rise against them and claim that they were opposed to them at the time? Fortunately for humanity and civilization, there was a Churchill who stopped them, single-handedly at first, and then backed by Stalin and Roosevelt.

It is disconcerting though that in modern Croatia there are young nationalists, whose weight and influence is hard to gauge, who view some of their war criminals as patriots and national heroes; just as there are nationalist Serbs who regard some of their most atrocious leaders during the Yugoslavian civil war of the 1990s, as their admired icons; or as skinheads and Neo-Nazis in Germany and across the world, still adore Hitler, salute him and his legacy, and hope for renewal of his political mettle; or as the modern Japanese prime ministers, of the postwar new Nippon democracy still visit annually the Yasukuni shrine in Tokyo to commemorate the war heroes, including those who committed the most horrific crimes. The determining factor will hinge on the actual conduct of the governments in place, to what extent they suppress militarism and cultivate peace and democracy; how and to what extent do they combat hatred, bigotry, discrimination, and persecution in their societies, media, government activities, and judicial systems; how forthcoming they are to admit their sins and seek reconciliation with their wronged victims; how seriously do they hunt down war criminals and bring them to justice; and how open they are to restore Jewish (and Serbian, in the case of Croatia) confiscated or destroyed property and to pay some indemnity to the descendants of the victims. Only Germany seems to have made big strides on all those levels, while Japan and Croatia still have a long way to go.

Disconcerting is also a recently cited survey in Croatia, conducted in 2008, which unbelievably claims that 40 percent of Croats today justify Ustasha crimes and some 52 percent view shouting today the wartime slogan "For the Homeland, Ready!" as merely a "patriotic expression."[4] If accurate, this is very alarming indeed. A Serbian historian, Cedomir Antic, has declared in the same survey, that of all states of the Axis, Croatia remained the only one not to undergo a process of de-Nazification, that is de-Ustashization. If he meant that the process should also include admitting guilt, apologizing officially for past crimes, paying damages to the victims and their descendants, restoring property to its proprietors and educating the young generation to erase hatred and promote reconciliation, then his statement was not accurate because Japan has also been lagging behind in the same respect. But if he implied that an Ustasha-like government still rules modern Croatia, which oppresses minorities, embraces ultra-nationalist ideologies, and murders "unwanted" populations, then he is totally wrong, because contemporary Croatia, especially after the death of controversial Tudjman, has become a peaceful and harmonious society, which behaves every bit like a Western democracy, no less than new democratic Serbia after Milosevic. I believe that both the updated survey in Croatia, which revealed a revived nationalism, and the manifest Serbian loathing of it, emanate not only from the horrendous World War II war memories, but are also solidly anchored in the enmities of the Yugoslavian civil war of the 1990s, which not only is more recent and remembered by the entire new generation in both countries, but has also left a residue of an unsettled conflict despite (and perhaps because of) the imposed Dayton "agreement," which for some is the equivalent of Versailles for Hitler and his ilk, and the recipe for more conflict in the future.

More than disconcerting, however, is the mood of historical revisionism one can detect in modern Croatia, which was launched by its founder, Fanjo Tudjman, apparently in an attempt to cleanse the Ustasha past or at least to reduce its destructive effect. Denying, or diminishing the fate of Serbians and Jews under the Ustasha rule, checked against the overwhelming evidence cited above, only means an intention to escape censure and condemnation, instead of recognizing the undisputed reality of horror created by Pavelic and his followers. It is one thing for Croatians to resent their Serbian ancestral rivals and hate them, but quite another to deny history, rewrite it, pretend that unpleasant facts did not happen, and ascribe to itself events and acts of generosity that did not occur. It is all the more disturbing, when denials and historical revision concern the history of the Jews, who are well familiar with their history and have certainly done nothing to deserve Croatian hatred (quite the reverse), or to elicit the denial of the Holocaust as practiced only by anti-Semites and Israel's Arab and Muslim enemies. In Western democracies, denial of the Holocaust is punishable by law, and if Croatian deniers had lived in France or Sweden, they could easily be indicted and convicted. The Goldstein historians (Ivo and Slavko), whose integrity I have no reason to doubt, indeed recounted that the Croatian Parliamentary Commission established to investigate war crimes, stated, after laboring for 7.5 years on its report, that 331 Jews by religion and 293 Jews by nationality were "war casualties" under the Ustasha (euphemized as the Independent State of Croatia) regime, while 2,238 people of all nationalities and religions "died" (not "were murdered") in Jasenovac. This shameful, by omission and distortion, report, if quoted correctly, was officially adopted by the investigative commission on October 11, 1999.[5]

The denial and distortion cry out, even if one is not versed in this material in all its details. We have shown from an abundance of sources, that there were at least six times as many Jews murdered (not "died" or "war casualties") at the hands of the Ustasha during the war, and at least a hundred times as many Serbs and others annihilated in Jasenovac than admitted by the parliamentary commission. And the invention of "religious Jews" to distinguish from "national Jews," even before there was a Jewish state to give them nationality and citizenship, only evinces the degree of ignorance and of chutzpah of those commission members, when they undertook to minimize the figures at any price, without any regard for truth and decency. That report, if published in a liberal democracy, the like of which Croatia is aspiring to become, would have generated a lawsuit, an indictment, and a conviction, similar to what happened in Britain to David Irving who stated similar denials about a decade ago. The years it took to come to these laughable and obviously fabricated results, point not to the difficulties of finding the truth, but to the efforts to hide it in order not to enrage either the revisionist historians or Fanjo Tudjman, who led that tendency in his book, *Wastelands of Historical Reality*,[6] where the anti-Semitic passages were removed only in the English edition of 1996, before he effected his first voyage "of repentance" to Israel.

If a parliamentary commission and a president are given license in any country to revise history and rewrite it, it smacks of Communist and totalitarian historiography, where historical events veer with the winds of politics, and the past becomes much more unpredictable than

177

the future. As an ex-Tito general who should know better, Tudjman remained nonetheless a Holocaust denier, who in a decent country would have sat in prison for his atrocious words, which sound too similar to what Ahmadinejad, the President of Iran (2005–) says today in public. He wrote:

> The estimated loss of up to 6 million [Jewish] dead is founded too much on both emotional and biased testimonies and on exaggerated data in the postwar reckonings of war crimes and on the squaring of accounts with the defeated. . . . World Jewry still has the need to recall its "Holocaust" even by trying to prevent the election of Kurt Wald- heim, the former UN Secretary General, as President of Austria.[7]

On another occasion, he gave his "scientific" estimates of the total numbers of Jews who perished in the Holocaust as nine hundred thou- sand.[8] This figure was also cited by Mahmud Abbas (Abu Mazen), the present president of the Palestinian Authority, who mentioned it in his published doctorate that he completed in Moscow in the 1980s. It seems that their common source was the Moscow Communist pro- paganda of the time, which inspired both of them. He also said that many wartime Jewish deaths would not have occurred if the German armed forces had prevailed over the Soviet Union, thus allowing for a territorial solution to the Jewish question, such as a "reserve" in eastern Poland or in Madagascar.[9] His critics claim that he even justified the Ustasha state by advancing the revisionist argument that: "it was not only a collaborationist and criminal organization, but also an expres- sion of the historical desire of the Croat nation for an independent homeland." Included in the passages that were allegedly excised from the English translation to his book, was also a paragraph that called Israel to task, when he wrote that "after everything they suffered in history, particularly the hardships of World War II, the Jewish people became so brutal and conducted a genocidal policy toward the Pales- tinians, that they can rightly be defined as Judeo-Nazis." Maybe that made him feel easier, to share the title of Nazi with the Jews that his country had helped eliminate, but for his distortion of fact and his subjection of history to politics, he never apparently repented.

But that is not his greatest sin, if one takes into account the pre- posterously idiotic and childish, but vain, efforts he deployed during his lifetime to diminish the evidence of the horror and the scale of the murder in Jasenovac of the Jews and especially of the Serbs, in the vein of the parliamentary commission cited above, thus greatly freeing the Ustasha from the criminal burden of their deeds, and himself and his country from the historical weight of their inherited responsibility. He made up stories about "Jews who run Jasenovac, and were responsible for murdering Serbs and Gypsies," which he cautiously avoided in the English translation of his book, but he did not hesitate to republish them in the German version, where their reception by the Germanic readership was more likely. He repeated in his book the contention that "only" fifty thousand people "died" (not were "slaughtered") at Jasenovac, which he claimed was merely a "labor camp,"[10] a figure that would nevertheless be considered a large scale massacre in itself in other lands, and he revised that number downward when he announced in the Conference on Yugoslavia in the Hague that the number of victims was twenty thousand, when he knew that it was at least ten times larger. Conversely, he aggrandized and elevated to the degree of a cult, the numbers of Ustasha captured by the British army in Austria and surrendered to the Partisans, thus glorifying the "Croatian Holocaust," erecting monuments in their honor, and making adoring statements in their regard, at the same time that Serbian and Jewish victimhood was denied or diminished, and monuments for the real victims, Serbs and Jews, were being destroyed or desecrated.

These claims by Tudjman stand in strong contradiction to what the Goldstein historians of Zagreb Jewry have researched and published,[11] which did not escape the scrutiny of the Croatian authorities, who have elected nevertheless to ignore them. The Goldstein historians contend that the reduced numbers of murdered Jews (thirteen thousand) published by Zerjavic, did not take into account some groups of Jewish Jasenovac victims: Jews who had converted to Catholicism prior to 1941 and their descendants who were not recorded as Jews anywhere, but they were nevertheless victimized according to racial laws; the Jews who were executed in the dismantled Dakovo camp and were held in Jasenovac; and Jewish refugees from other countries, many of whom were also murdered in Jasenovac. They conclude that:

> Whatever number is taken, there is no doubt that more than half the Jewish Holocaust victims in North Croatia and Bosnia and Herzegovina were killed in the Jasenovac system of camps. Probably the number is very close to seventeen thousand, in addition to several hundred Jews from abroad and from other parts of Yugoslavia. A significant number of victims were Zagreb Jews. . . . For example, prisoner Egon Berger claims that there were about 700 Jews and about 600 Serbs in the camp on September 11, 1941,[12] but that

179

new groups kept coming. According to one list with names of 1,454 Jewish inmates in Jasenovac, obviously made at the end of 1941, 805 of them were from Zagreb. Another list of the same time had some 269 Jewish names, 53 of them from Zagreb and the majority from Sarajevo. In early November, 1941 the Jewish community in Zagreb claimed that about 4,000 Jewish men to whom they were sending aid, were imprisoned in Jasenovac. This means that there were certainly more Jews there, because a considerable number of inmates were not entered in the register of the Zagreb Jewish community. . . . Based on eyewitnesses and demographic analyses, more than 4,000 Zagreb Jews were murdered in the Jasenovac system between 1941 and 1945.[13]

The Jasenovac museum lacks the rudimentary information regarding the war crimes committed there, particularly about the victims, lumping them all together without distinction in order to dissimulate the ideology behind their racial murder. Their executioners, the Ustasha, avoided mentioning the system of racial laws implemented under that regime against non-Croatian ethnic groups, and the massive ethnic cleansing of those groups from the NDH. The atrocious perpetrators of those horrors are treated with indifference and neutrality, as if they were passive onlookers on the scene and not its organizers, instigators, and initiators. The crimes are so diminished and whitewashed as to make Jasenovac sound like a resort site, or a harmless labor camp, just one step away from denying altogether the crimes committed there. The suffering of the victims and the inhuman methods of the systematic liquidation of the inmates are totally ignored. All in all, the Jasenovac Memorial amounts to a tall concrete flower, rising up from a huge empty field covered with natural green grass. To add insult to injury, and to the anguish of those who wish to remember and to discover more details about their departed loved ones, in 2007 the Memorial of Jasenovac was awarded the international Carlo Scarpa Prize for Gardens from Treviso, Italy. The irony, anger, and shame are hard to contain because that is a prize to celebrate beauty, aesthetics, preservation of culture, and cultivating memories of civilization. That the prize should be awarded to a site that was exactly built to efface culture and humanity, to push aside humaneness, and to plaster over murder, destruction, and the most ugly attempts of genocide recorded in modern history, is no less than unbearable and unforgivable.

Under this skewed reversal of history and memory, who would remember what Jasenovac really was, if the museum does not tell its visitors that on August 23, 1941, the Ustasha newspapers made the first announcement about establishing a "labor camp" in Jasenovac, to build dams along the rivers Trebez and Lonja, tributaries of the Sava, to drain the Lonja swamps? Nor does it tell that exhausted inmates were walled up in those same dams, or that General Ivan Prpic, following the orders of his chief, Marshal Kvaternik, the commander of the Ustasha Armed Forces, informed his subordinates, in a circular of April 27, 1942, that:

> The Command of the Ustasha Surveillance Service, has informed us, in a top secret order No 139/42, that the assembly and labor camp in Jasenovac can accept an unlimited number of inmates. Therefore, please issue orders to all your subordinate command posts to send to Jasenovac all Communists who are caught during the mopping up of the areas where military operations are conducted.[14]

The harrowing implications of this guideline were double:

1. That the capacity of the camp became unlimited not only because it kept expanding, but principally because the pace of extermination was pursued in such a speed that absorption abilities for newcomers was also being increased;
2. "Communists" was only a codeword for "unwanted populations," since the number of Communist Party members was quite limited around Yugoslavia, and many of them were active in the Partisans and out of reach to the Ustasha. The untold numbers of other "Communists" who were incarcerated under the Communist scarecrow title, points to the tens of thousands of Serbs, Gypsies and Jews who were arrested and annihilated in place.

Now it is known that the Ustasha measures against their inmates, especially the Serbs, took a sharp turn for the worse after Pavelic's visit to Hitler in June 1941, when the two leaders discussed the ethnic composition of the newly established Croatian state, the issues of Muslims and Serbs, and the resettlement of Serbs and Slovenes. It was reported that Hitler said to Pavelic: "if the Croat state wants to be strong, an intolerant policy must be pursued for fifty years, because too much tolerance on such issues can only do harm."[15] It could, of course, be argued that Hitler's position and advice were not necessarily Pavelic's, but judging from what the latter later implemented in the Ustasha state, it seems that he was more zealously sold to the idea than his Nazi mentor. Indeed, according to the website of the Osteurepa—Institut in Berlin:

> The result of ethnic cleansing in the Ustasha state, which was accomplished by a wide range of forced conversions, deportations, fleeing

from the country and in executions and systematic mass-killings, was summarized by Pavelic in a conversation with German Special Envoy, Edmund Veesenmayer, at the beginning of 1943, in the statement: "at the time of the establishment of the state, we had about 30 percent Serbs, and thanks to liquidations and massacres, we have now still 12–15 percent. In this regard, excesses that occurred had somehow beneficial effects to the Croatian state."[16]

The figures given by Pavelic fit almost perfectly with the most reliable statistics we have examined above. In pre–World War II Yugoslavia, Serbs constituted 25 percent of the total population, and the inhabitants of Bosnia and Herzegovina, 40 percent. The Ustasha state included both Croatia and Bosnia, plus a part of Serbia known as Srem, and it undertook to eliminate all the Serbs, Jews, and Gypsies under its jurisdiction. That goal was achieved with the Jews and Gypsies, but due to the sudden collapse of the Nazis and their Ustashsa clients, the annihilation of the Serbs was interrupted, but now that entire enterprise is being denied or minimized. Censuses of the post war Yugoslavia had put the Serbian population in Croatia at 14–15 percent, which was maintained between 1948 and 1961. Then, a sharp drop occurred between 1971 and 1981, from more than 14 percent to 11.5 percent. In 1991 the Serbs again climbed to 12.5 percent, and today they are a mere 4.5 percent. In numbers, according to Croatia's national census, their number in Croatia was 633,000 in 1991, down to 201,000 in 2001. Of course, the latest drop in Serbian population in Croatia is not the fruit of the Ustasha policy of ethnic cleansing, but of the civil war of the 1990s; it is however certainly affected by the sad memories of the Ustasha state who impelled many of the remaining Serbs to run away.[17] As to the Jews, they numbered some twenty thousand in Croatia in 1931, but in 1948, the few individuals who survived were listed with "others," having become so insignificant as to lose their separate category. In 1953, there were still only 413 inhabitants registered as Jews, coming down to 404 in 1961, and again indicating an increase (natural and through migration under the Communist regime) to over 2,854 in 1971, and then again a decrease to 600 in 1981, and 576 in 2001. Similarly, there were 14,000 Gypsies in Croatia in 1931, but only 405 survived in 1948, soaring again to close to 9,500 in 2001.

In contemporary Serbia the situation of the Jews is not very enviable either. Of the three thousand members of the extant Jewish community, only about half are Jewish, the rest are accounted for by the non-Jewish spouses of the ethnic Jews and their children, who may be raised with some link to their or their families' Judaism. The increasing anti-Semitism in Serbia, is nothing novel to its history and culture, and it expresses itself in anti-Jewish graffiti, anti-Semitic pamphlets, and other instruments of propaganda distributed by the Californian Institute for Historical Review, which is operated by Neo-Nazis and other extremists there. However, no elected or appointed official of any significance in the Serbian state machinery has ever denied or diminished the Holocaust or dared to endorse anti-Semitic statements, as in the times of Nedic or Lijotic. Nor would any organization prevent anyone from visiting memorial sites, as it happened to the participants of the Jadovno Conference in June 2011, when they asked to visit the camps of Slana and Metaja on the Dalmatian coast but were denied.

When one reflects today about those years of hell and doom under the Ustasha, one is struck by the salient contrast between war criminals that still go free, on the one hand, and some manifestations of humanism and generosity, which are still reminisced and celebrated among the survivors. In an article of the *Los Angeles Times*,[18] based on an interview with prominent historian Ivo Goldstein, the author observes that the stone monument to the victims of World War II's early slaughters, committed by Fascists in Croatia, now stands in vandalized ruins, its central pillar has been decapitated, and someone has carefully chiseled away the plaques bearing victims' names. The entire scene is covered by a weed carpet on the entire isolated site. The journalist Tracy Wilkinson who visited the site, says that in the forest behind the monument, which refers to the Jadovno complex, down a steep path, sits another part of the memorial, in equal neglect. It is a deep, black pit tunneled into the hillside, where the bodies of hundreds of Jews and Serbs were dumped in 1941 by Croatian Ustasha, the rulers of Croatia's Nazi puppet state. As she surveyed the scene, she wrote:

> Fifty years later, these same hills around the tense, insular town of Gospic were used to dispose of more bodies, this time the Serbs and Croatian dissidents that a new generation of Croatian nationalists worked to eradicate. Such gruesome recycling of history might end there, except that it now appears that some of the same officials in charge of local government during the 1991 killings were restored to power in elections three months ago. They also are probably part of the gang that destroyed the monument to Jewish and Serbian victims. The persistent presence of people who could qualify as war criminals, contaminates most societies that emerged from the former Yugoslav federation. In Croatia, human rights activists say the government

of President Franjo Tudjman—until recently the region's closest U.S. ally—encourages impunity and cyclical violence by distorting the past and glorifying a nationalist history while overlooking the murderous side. As it attempts to build an ethnically pure state, the government has failed to purge criminals from its ranks, and in fact rewards many. "These people poison the atmosphere for everybody. If we want a better future for this country, we have to get rid of these kinds of people," said Ivo Goldstein, a history professor at Zagreb University and an opposition activist.[19]

This does not certainly sound like a people seeking reconciliation, evincing an acknowledgment of their past and acting to take a distance from what their predecessors did, and to mend their historical record. Goldstein's interest is as much personal as historical. His grandfather was among the Jews slain outside Gospic in 1941, and dumped into the deep, narrow pit. The site, known as Jadovno, in the hills about nine miles west of Gospic, which was the first death camp among twenty-six concentration camps created by Croatia's pro-Nazi World War II regime, with thousands of Jews and Serbs who were rounded up by Ustasha agents, transported in railcars to the Gospic area, forced to walk through fields, and then knifed to death—all during a three-month period in 1941. The bodies were thrown into the pit. Among the victims, according to today's tiny Croatian Jewish community, were 200 members of the Maccabee Jewish Sports Club of Zagreb. Goldstein's grandfather, also named Ivo, was a bookshop owner in the central Croatian city of Karlovac when he was taken away. His grandmother also was arrested but released before fleeing, with two young sons, to territory controlled by anti-Fascist Partisan fighters. At the better-known Jasenovac death camp in north-central Croatia, many more thousands of Serbs, as well as Jews, Gypsies, and others, were killed during World War II. Due to its size, which placed it third among the death camps of Europe, Jasenovac has been the center of international focus while Jadovno had languished ignored, until the June 2011 Jadovno Conference in Banja Luka placed it back on the gruesome map of the Holocaust.

The Jadovno monument, Goldstein and others believe, was destroyed as part of a campaign to eliminate traces of Ustasha atrocities when like-minded Fascists began to take charge of parts of Croatia after Tudjman declared the former Yugoslav republic's independence in 1991. Thousands of monuments honoring both Partisans, who defeated the Nazis, and the victims of Fascism, have been destroyed

184

all over the country in a wave of fervent nationalism that equates anti-Fascists with Communists, Serbs, and other enemies of the Croatian fatherland. Tudjman has fueled such attitudes by praising the Ustasha's stated goal of independence, even if the regime was guilty, he allowed, of certain "wrongdoings," thus attempting to lend some credibility to his statements. One of the most notorious men who rose to power in the Gospic area in 1991 was Tihomir Oreskovic, a leader of Gospic's "crisis committee," formed amid the Serbo-Croat war that raged at the time. Gospic was a frontline city, a last defense against Yugoslav-backed Serbian militia fighting against Croatian secession. Always a remote, isolated place, Gospic and its Lika Valley surroundings were under siege. In October 1991, thirteen Croats were killed there. In swift retaliation, between 120 and 200 Serbs, including judges and other civilians, were rounded up and murdered, according to human rights researchers. The bodies were concealed in the same hills that fifty years earlier had become the mass graves for other Serbian and Jewish victims. Associates of Oreskovic emerged later to describe in Croatian newspapers the slayings and general reign of terror that swept through Gospic in 1991. Officials and military police conspired to draw up lists of Serbs who were taken away and executed according to these accounts. The record of horrors kept growing, which bridged, over a hiatus of fifty years, the Ustasha of yesteryear with the horrendous savagery of the Bosnia war (1992–1995).

During the Yugoslav wars of the 1990s, both the Serbs and the Croats tried to whitewash their Holocaust and World War II track record by presenting anti-Semitism as an alien importation into their otherwise philosemitic lands. We have dwelt at length on the groups where Serbian anti-Semitism before the war was anchored, and upon their collaborators with the Nazi occupiers, who while not directly exterminating Jews, collaborated with the Nazis toward the final solution. Conversely, there were many heroic cases of Serbian human-ism and decency in which Jewish refugees were either absorbed and protected, or the lives of their Jewish neighbors were saved at the risk of their own lives. Croatia did not lag far behind the Serbs in trying to erase its own blemishes of the Ustasha years, not by pretending that no Jews were exterminated in Jadovno and Jasenovac, as part of their own genocidal effort (mainly against Serbs, but also against Jews and Gypsies), but by claiming that Serbs were even worse, something that is difficult to back up with hard evidence. On the face of it, this latter claim seems to have no leg to stand on, for the Serbs can always argue that they acted under the constraints of the Nazi occupier, who would not let up, but that Serbs themselves never initiated on their own any genocide against anyone, though some anti-Semitic outbursts are admitted among their most extreme groups. By contrast, the Ustashas excelled and even surpassed their Nazi mentors in annihilating Serbs, Jews, and others.[20] Jasenovac and Jadovno are lasting monuments to that dark history.

Contrary to the endorsement and praise showered by other quarters, Dennis Reinhartz, an American historian, said in his review of Philip Cohen's *Serbia's Secret War*, which was extensively cited above, that it belonged to the "current popular-historical and journalist literature that seeks to demonize and condemn more than to chronicle and elucidate fairly." He added that the book was in danger of degenerating itself into an irrational conspiracy history, by belonging to those histories of the Balkans that contribute little to understanding the past and its impact on the present and future.[21] Indeed, Jasa Almuly, a Belgrade Jewish author, was reported as stating, in the same vein, that he doubted whether an American physician (Cohen is a dermatologist) could write such a "political propaganda pamphlet," and he suspected that it came from Fanjo Tudjman's kitchen in Zagreb, in the form of some institute specializing in political propaganda. While this sweeping generalization sounds exaggerated and geared to demonize that writer whose work has been considered seminal and path breaking, it is nonetheless true that one does not need to be trained in history to be entrusted with writing history. Winston Churchill, who is also copiously quoted in this volume, was not trained as a historian, nor are the contemporary writers on Islamic affairs Bat Ye'or, the author of *Dhimmi* and *Eurabia*,[22] and Andrew Bostom, whose medical profession did not prevent him from publishing his two celebrated anthologies: *The Legacy of Jihad*, and *The Legacy of Anti-Semitism*.[23]

Dr. Kraus, the president of the Jewish community of Zagreb, suggested that at least the Catholic Church in Croatia should follow the example of Pope John Paul II and apologize for the past sins against the Jews. But Dr. Adalbert Rebic, one of the experts on Judaism and Christianity in Croatia, replied that the crime was not committed by the Catholic Church or on its behalf, but was committed by individuals in the name of the ideology that was subordinated to Hitler's Germany. Thus, he said "the invitation has been delivered to the wrong address, because it is the government, the Croatian president, that should apologize for those crimes, just like German Chancellor[s Adenauer and] Brandt did after the war. In addition, the Holy Father has just done that on behalf of the entire Catholic Church." Rebic put a special emphasis on the "role of the blessed Cardinal Stepinac, who in occupied Europe strongly supported the rights of the Jews, as well as the Orthodox Serbs. He said that "Cardinal Stepinac condemned the crimes, and his successors need not apologize."[24] It seems that as long as no clear cut recognition by present-day Croatia of the crimes of their predecessors, is reached, to replace the current denials and minimalization started under Tudjman, not much can be expected either from that country or from its Church, which had very clearly collaborated with the Ustasha. Even the role of Archbishop Stepinac, while recognized for the Jews he rescued, is nevertheless taken to task for the Jews he failed to save, even when he could.

This kind of attitude that attempts to diminish the harsh effects of the Ustasha policies and to dissociate today's Croatia from the horrors of its predecessors, is evident in Zagreb, not only in the complaints of Jews who precisely claim that nationalist President Fanjo Tudjman had instigated this wave of self-exoneration in his memoirs, and that many of his countrymen were happy to follow him, but also in discussions one holds with influential intellectuals and officials. The trend is clear and admitted in Zagreb that Croatia must cleanse itself from its past and mend its damaged image, to make itself ready to join Europe and to erase the horrible memoirs of Jadovno and Jasenovac. Therefore, much to one's frustration about the inability to get straight talk, open discussions of the past and bold visions of the future, all one hears in talks with officials and intellectuals is an intense endeavor to please the foreigners, to show that all is good, that the nightmares are forgotten, and the rosy future looms in the horizon. One cannot say anything that may sound controversial, contradictory, arrogant, or racist. Allah forbid. Let none of those notions be associated with today's Croatia, lest sleeping dogs awaken. Since the Serbs are posing the most immediate menace to that idyllic landscape, by constantly reminding the whole world of their concept and convictions regarding the Ustasha's horrific acts, they are understandably hated and despised, their arguments and data are rejected out of hand, and their innate "aggressive spirit" is constantly stirred up.

The Serbs, on the contrary, who are accused of the sins of the 1992–95 Bosnia War, while Croats and Bosnians who suffered at their hands deny their part in the horrors, feel they are persecuted, hunted, and victims of a Croatian onslaught that has gained impetus since

Zagreb associated with the European Union and is promised a part in it in the next round. The Serbs like to compare themselves to Israel, not only as a model of development and national strength, but mainly as a persecuted, despised, and besieged people throughout history, which redeemed itself and set itself on a new course in the forefront of nations. Questions of memory, survival, self-justification, history, and national purpose have been widely discussed, and appeals have been launched to the world to pursue justice and not let the Croats of today efface the abuses of the Ustashas of yesterday. In this endeavor, they regard themselves as a friend and companion of Israel, themselves as the Jewish people, and they let, indeed invite, other Serbs, like those of Srpska and of the Serbian diasporas across the world, to join the same state of mind, to rally around their nation the way diasporic Jews do around Israel, hoping that their association with the Jewish state, the frequent visits of their leaders, youth, cultural delegations, and *Yad Vashem* collaborators, would ultimately forge the alliance they hope could affect a renewed rapprochement with the European Union and the United States.

Notes

1. Edmund Paris, *Genocide in Satellite Croatia 1941–1945, A Record of Racial and Religious Persecutions and Massacres,* American Institute of Balkan Affairs, 1961.
2. Srdja Trifkovic, *Ustasha: Croatian Separatism and European Politics* (in Serbian), the Lord Byron Foundation for Balkan Studies, USA, 1988, 274.
3. See Tomasevic, *War and Revolution etc.,* op. cit., 578.
4. "Pola Hrvata hvali Ustashe (one half of the Croat Population praises the Ustasha)," a survey conducted by the Croatian *Vecernji List* and cited in *Press*, Belgrade, July 16, 2008.
5. Ivo and Slavko Goldstein, "Revisionism in Croatia: the Case of Franjo Tudjman, in *East European Jewish Affairs*, January 2002, 63.
6. In its Croatian form it was published in Zagreb in 1989. In English, it was published as *Horrors of War: Historical Reality and Philosophy*, (revised edition for Western readers), Evans and Company, New York, 1996. In German, it was published in Zagreb three years earlier, its version pleasing to the Germans and much closer to the original Croatian.
7. This remark, for example, appeared in the Tudjman's Croatian version of his book but was excised in the English revised translation.
8. *New York Times*, April 22, 1993, article by Diana Schemo, on the occasion of the controversy raised about the invitation of Tujman to attend the inauguration of the Holocaust Museum in Washington, DC.
9. *Journal of Historical Review,* Summer 1992, 240–3; and *The New Republic,* November 25, 1991, 16–18.
10. 312 of the original book in Croat.

11. Slavko and Ivo Goldstein, *Jews in Jasenovac*, the Jewish Community of Zagreb and Novi Liber, Zagreb, 2001, 46–47.

12. Ironically the same precise date when the 9/11 "mini-Holocaust" of the Twin Towers in New York occurred exactly sixty years later.

13. Slavko and Ivo Goldstein, *Jews in Jasenovac*, the Jewish Community of Zagreb and Novi Liber, Zagreb, 2001, 47.

14. Jozo Tomasevich, *War and Revolution*, op. cit., 400.

15. Ibid.

16. Holm Sundhausen, "Review of the German Edition of Jurcevic's, *The Emergence of the Jasenovac Myth*," published on the website of the Osteuropa-Institut in Berlin.

17. Maja Berber, Bozo Grbic, and Slavika Pavkov, *Changes in Share of Ethnic Croats and Serbs in Croatia by Town and Municipality, Based on the Results of Censuses from 1991 and 2001.*

18. *Los Angeles Times* published on July 14, 1997 by Tracy Wilkinson, under the title "*Croatia*, Alleged Criminals Thrive While Memorial Fades," and based on an interview by Ivo Goldstein, the most prominent Holocaust historian in Croatia, author of the great monograph *Holocaust in Zagreb*, among other books.

19. Ibid.

20. The very appellation Ustasha was self-appropriated by those in the Croatian nationalist movement of the prewar era who swore that the dismantling of the Yugoslavian federal state would facilitate the destruction of Serbdom and of the Orthodox Church, both of which they intensely loathed. See the *Nova Hrvatska* of May 4, 1941.

21. Dennis Reinhartz, "Serbia's Secret War: Propaganda and the Deceit of History," by Philip Cohen, in *Holocaust and Genocide Studies*, February, 2000, 302.

22. Both published by Fairleigh Dickinson University Press, London and Toronto, 1985 and 2005, respectively.

23. Both published by Prometheus Books, Amherst, N.Y, 2005 and 2008, respectively.

24. *Vecernji List*, Zagreb, April 13, 2000. Cited by Bulajic, 39.

Bibliography

Sources

Encyclopaedia of the Holocaust was published in 1990, in tandem Hebrew and English editions, by Yad Vashem (יד ושם), the Holocaust Remembrance in Jerusalem.

Protocols of the Elders of Zion was a forged document, manufactured in Czarist Russia at the turn of the twentieth century, but still claimed as authentic by anti-Semites.

A long string of scholars in Zagreb and Belgrade were gracious enough to meet with me and clarify many controversial points. I am indebted to all of them, as I am to many archive workers, museum curators, officials, eyewitnesses, journalists, community workers, and other knowledgeable people who generously shared their time, patience and wisdom with me.

I am also grateful to some of these scholars, researchers, archivists, guides, and other people of good will who either drew my attention to many books and documents, or to certain interpretations thereof, or took me around to visit sites where events had unfolded, or volunteered to translate for me from Serbo-Croatian, and more rarely, from German and Italian, the documents that would have otherwise remained inaccessible to me.

Papers and Magazines

Canadian Journal of History
(Die) Erwache
(The) Independent (London)
Nasa Borba (Belgrade)

New York Times
Obnova (Belgrade)
*(La) Revue Des Deux Monde*s (Paris)
Time Literary Supplement (Die) Zeit

Books

Anzulovic, Branimir, *Heavenly Serbia: From Myth to Genocide*, Hurst and Co., London, 1999.

Bat Ye'or, *The Decline of Eastern Christianity under Islam: From Jihad to Dhimmitude*, Fairleigh Dickinson University Press, Madison and London, 1996.

Churchill, Winston, *The Second World War: Closing the Ring, Volume V*, Houghton and Mifflin, Boston, 1951.

Cohen, Philip, *Serbia's Secret War: Propaganda and the Deceit of History*, Texas University Press, 1996.

Covic, Boze Covic (ed.), *Roots of Serbian Aggression*, Center for Foreign Languages Zagreb, 1993.

Giniewski, Paul, *Une Resistance Juive: Grenoble 1943–1945*, Cheminements. Paris, 2009.

Gitman, Esther, *When Courage Prevailed: Rescue and Survival of Jews in the Independent State of Croatia, 1941–1945*, Paragon House, St. Paul, 2011.

Goldstein, Ivo, *Croatia: A History*, McGill Press, Montreal, 2001.

Gutman, Yisrael, and Gideon Greif (eds.), *The Historiography of the Holocaust Period*, Yad Vashem, Jerusalem, 1988.

Manoschek, Walter, *Serbien ist Judenfrei: Militarische Besatzungspolitik und Judenvernichtung in Serbien, 1941–1942*, Munchen, R. Oldenburg Verlag, 1993.

Miller, William, *The Balkans: Roumania, Bulgaria, Servia and Montenegro*, Fisher Unwin, London, 1923.

Terzic, Slavenko (ed), *Islam, the Balkans and the Great Powers XIV–XX Century*, Proceedings of the conference held in Belgrade, December 11–13, 1996. Belgrade, 1997, as an edition of the Historical Institute of Serbian Academy of Sciences and Arts.

Tomasevich, Jozo, *The Chetniks—War and Revolution in Yugoslavia, 1941–1945*, Stanford University Press, 1975.

Vogel, Milan, Milan Ristovic and Milan Koljanin, *Serbia, Righteous among Nations*, JOZ, Belgrade, 2010.

Zerjavic, Vladimir, *Population Losses in Yugoslavia 1941–1945*, Zagreb, 1997.

Articles

Batakovic, Dusan, "La Bosnie-Herzegovine: le System des Alliances," in Terzic, op. cit.

Bled, Jean-Paul, "La Question de Bosnie-Hercegovine" *La Revue Des Deux Mondes*, Paris, 1876, Vol II, No 1, 237–254.

Browning, Christopher, "The Final Solution in Serbia," in *Yad Vashem Studies*, Jerusalem, 1983.

Herf, Jeffrey, Introduction to Kuntzel's book.

Jelinek, Yeshayahu, "A Historiography of Slovakian and Croatian Jewry," in Yisrael Gutman and Gideon Greif (eds.), *The Historiography of the Holocaust Period*, Yad Vashem, Jerusalem, 1988.

Keyserlingk, Robert, in his review article in the *Canadian Journal of History*, April, 1995.

Ristovic, Milan "Jews in Serbia during World War Two: Between the Final Solution to the Jewish Question, and the Righteous Among Nations," in Milan Vogel-Milan Ristovic-Milan Koljanin, *Serbia, Righteous among Nations*, JOZ, Belgrade, 2010.

Riesman, David, "Foreword," in Philip Cohen's, *Serbia's Secret War: Propaganda and the Deceit of History*, cited above.

Todorov, Vrban, "The Federalist Idea as a Means for Preserving the Integrity of the Ottoman Empire," in S. Terzic, 293–296.

Analytical Index

Mediterranean, 5-6, 85ff
Central, 94
Middle/Near East, 1ff, 4, 6ff, 85ff, 106ff
Command, 99ff
Mihailovic, Mila, 156
Mikhailovic, General Draza, xxii, 13, 16, 19, 123
Miletic, Anton, 133ff
Milosevic, President, 176
Mirkovic, Jovan, 82
Moljevic, Stefan, 8
Montenegro, xxi, 9-10, 18-19, 38
Montgomery, General, 87ff
Morocco, 6, 85, 107, 121
Moscow, 6, 178
Mossad, 34-35ff
Mosul, 96
Munich, 24
Agreement, 89, 92, 120
Muslim Brothers, 4, 7, 86, 89, 103ff
Europe Committee, 113
Far East Committee, 113
Middle East Committee, 113
Mussolini, Il-Duce, 5, 13, 47
Mustar, 105, 124
Myszkowski, Tadeusz, 165

N
Nagasaki, 175
Nasa Borba, 24-25
Nashashibi, Rageb, 90
Nazis, ix, x, xiv, xviiff, 11ff, 106ff
Neame, General, 95
Necak, Alexander, 80
Nedic, General Milan, xiv, xxiii, 2, 12ff, 16, 53-54, 183
Government, 11, 30-31
Neubacher, Hermann, 142
New Historians, xi
New York Times, 54
Nincic, Foreign Minister, 15
Niska Banja, 27
Nis, 23, 38
Normandy, 44
Norway, x, 12, 15, 16, 43
Novi Pazar, 38
Novak, Dani, 159ff
Novak, Victor, 133
Novi Sad, 27, 28, 39, 48
Nuremberg Laws/trials, 21, 57, 152
Nuri, Pasha, 89ff

O
Obnova, 22, 24
O'Connor, General, 95
Orescovic, Tihomir, 185
Oric, General Nasser, 126
Orthodox Church, xix, xx, 13-14, 19, 25, 30, 41, 49, 143, 148, 187
Holy Synod of Bishops of, 148
Osijek, 48
Ottomans, xviiff, xxii, 20-21
Tanzimat reforms, xviii
Oxford, xxii
Ozmo, Daniel, 163ff

P
Pacific, 6
Pag (island), xxii, 65-66, 68, 71, 73, 76, 77-79, 152, 159, 174
Slana Camp, 76
Pakistan, 108
Palestinians, 2, 10, 103ff
Authority, 107, 114
Revolt (see also Arab), 90
Pappon, Police Superviser, 152
Paraguay, 110
Partisans, xxii, 4, 8, 15-16, 18-20, 21, 23-24, 27-28, 33, 36, 44, 46, 48, 61-62, 122, 125, 129, 131, 136, 158, 165, 171, 180, 184
Pavelic, Ante, xiv, xxii, 3, 11, 17, 45ff, 124, 156, 175, 180
Pavle, Prince, 14, 46, 93
Regency Council, 14
Pearl Harbor, 6, 43
Peel Commission, 86, 89, 91, 116, 119
Percic, Gustav, 47
Petrovic, Bogdan, 131-132
Persian Gulf, 96
Pesic, Minister, 14
Petain, Marshal, 3, 14, 43, 46
Petar, King, 15-16, 93
Petrucci, Filippo, 158-159
Phleps, Arthur, 123
Pius XII, Pope, 159
Poland, xiv, 27, 34, 45, 61, 65
Portugal, 9
Prague, 35
Preydor, xix
Pristina, 38
Protocols of the Elders of Zion, 21, 24
Prpic, General Ivan, 180

Printed in Poland
by Amazon Fulfillment
Poland Sp. z o.o., Wrocław

24376643R00128